Killing the Messenger

100 Years of Media Criticism

REVISED EDITION

EDITED BY

Tom Goldstein

Columbia University Press

New York

Columbia University Press
Publishers Since 1893
New York   Chichester, West Sussex
Copyright © 1989, 2007 Tom Goldstein

Library of Congress Cataloging-in-Publication Data
Killing the messenger : 100 years of media criticism / edited by Tom Goldstein. — Rev. ed.
     p.   cm.
   Includes bibliographical reference and index.
   ISBN–13: 978–0–231–11832–3 (cloth : alk. paper)
   ISBN–13: 978–0–231–11833–0 (ppbk.: alk. paper)
   ISBN–10: 0–231–11832–5 (cloth : alk. paper)
   ISBN–10: 0–231–11833–3 (pbk. : alk. paper)
   1. Press—United States—History—20th century. 2. Journalism—Objectivity—United States—
History. 3. Press—United States—Influence—History 4. Privacy, Right of—United States—
History. 5. Reporters and reporting—United States—History. I. Goldstein, Tom. II. Title.
   PN4867.K45 2007
   071'.3—dc22
                                               2006029178
∞

Columbia University Press gratefully acknowledges permission to reprint the following:
Selection from *A Free and Responsible Press: Report of the Commission on Freedom of the Press*,
    ed. Robert D. Leigh, copyright © 1947 by the University of Chicago Press.
Selection from *Freedom of the Press*, copyright © 1935 by George Seldes.
    By permission of George Seldes.
"The Legend on the License," copyright © 1980 by John Hersey. First published in the *Yale Review*,
    Autumn 1980. By permission of John Hersey.
"Newspapers and the Truth," copyright © 1922 by Frederick Lewis Allen. First published in the
    January 1922 issue of the *Atlantic Monthly*. By permission of the Atlantic Monthly Company.
"Writing News and Telling Stories," *Daedalus* (Spring 1975), by Robert Darnton.
    By permission of Robert Darnton.
Prologue to A. J. Liebling, *The Press*, copyright © 1973. By permission of the estate of
    A. J. Liebling.
"The Presidency and the Press," *Commentary* (March 1971), Daniel Patrick Moynihan.
    By permission.

Killing the Messenger

For Leslie, Max, and Blaze

Supreme Court's ruling in *Times v. Sullivan* in 1964), a decade of profound social and political tumult—and a decade that led some of the best journalists to search for new forms ("new journalism" emerged) and for others to become politicized.

Once again, outsiders were often more daring and penetrating in their criticism than the press itself. Using language rarely used by journalists in appraising their own performance, Richard Nixon's vice president, Spiro Agnew, called reporters "nattering nabobs of negativism" in a memorable, if over-the-top, display of alliteration. Agnew was as unsubtle as Roosevelt was subtle, but his hyperbole became the rallying cry of the liberal media critique that continues to flourish more than a generation later. In *Commentary*, Daniel Patrick Moynihan, then in the Nixon White House, spoke derisively of reporters as "charter members of the adversary culture."

Robert Darnton, who served briefly as a reporter before pursuing a career as a French historian, studied the cultural mores of the *New York Times*, where reporters in the 1960s made up details as they needed them and wrote for one another's approval rather than for the audience.

Another take on journalists' adherence to facts is offered by John Hersey, who wrote both high-quality journalism and fiction. Hersey memorably demarcates the line between journalism and fiction. In journalism, the license must read: "None of this is made up."

The pieces included here—essays, speeches, columns, excerpts from books, and reports—reflect the period in which they were written, but, I think, they are helpful to contemporary readers. What is remarkable is the prescience of these early critics. The selection of these pieces is necessarily idiosyncratic, and space considerations and ownership rights necessarily dictated what was available. The first edition of this collection was published eighteen years ago. Since then, the volume of press criticism has grown substantially, particularly with the availability of the Internet, and this, too, inevitably affected which pieces I picked. I deleted a few selections from the first edition and added several new ones in order to elucidate issues that continue to resonate today.

Killing the Messenger

Part 1
Reporting on Public and Private Matters

The boundary between what is private and what is public is ever shifting and elusive. In the context of news gathering, a constellation of questions is raised, cutting to the bone of how journalists decide what is newsworthy.

For instance, what is important about people—their age, religion, their marital status? What if they were adopted? What if they are gay? Is any of this the public's business? Does it depend on whether the person is in public life? Are candidates for president held to stricter scrutiny than candidates for other offices? Should important figures in the private sector be held to similar standards? Is there a statute of limitations for reporting on youthful indiscretions? Are the dead entitled to privacy?

There are few hard and fast answers to these questions, which have been examined in detail for more than a century. In this section, reprinted in its entirety (but without footnotes), is probably the most famous law review article ever written, the *Harvard Law Review* article by Louis Brandeis and Samuel Warren that became the foundation for the development of privacy. The two had been law partners in Boston at a time in which proper Bostonians regarded as a disgrace the appearance of their names in print. Legal historians long thought that this article had been inspired by Warren's indignant reaction to a gossip column reporting on his daughter's wedding breakfast. But this would have been utterly impossible: she was only six or seven when the article was written. Instead, the genesis of the article most likely lay more generally in Warren's deep-seated abhorrence of invasions of social privacy.

Their influential article, doubtless more cited in legal writings than actually read, has left a permanent imprint on jurisprudence and on journalism.

Alarmed by what they viewed as the increasing depravity of the daily press—a lack of "propriety and decency"—Brandeis and Warren took the view that the individual could be protected against unwarranted intrusions and publicity without fashioning new rules of law. Over the years journalists have tilted toward disclosure and away from the protection of the private lives of those in the public eye.

Also in this section is a sampling of editorials by William Allen White, a wise country editor who became friendly with the first generation of muckrakers. But little of his exposure to the faster pace and toughness of the muckrakers rubbed off on his local coverage. He was a booster of his hometown, Emporia, Kansas, and a censor of bad news. His office had a rule, for instance, not to publish details of local divorce suits. By his example, he demonstrated that journalists could show restraint. In these editorials he sets forth his quaint but principled philosophy of what is printable and what is not.

Finally, I have included a chapter from *Freedom of the Press,* by George Seldes, probably the most durable press critic of the last century. Beginning in the late 1920s, when he was past forty and with a career as an investigative reporter and foreign correspondent behind him, Seldes dedicated himself to correct what he felt was a deeply mistaken impression of the press.

"Newspapers, like kings, pretend they can do no wrong," he wrote in 1935 in *Freedom of the Press.* Its first subtitle was *For the Millions Who Want a Free Press.* He changed it to the more biting, *An Antidote for Falsehood in the Daily Press.* In his book, he poked into the inner workings of the press and emphasized that the threats to press freedom came not only from government but from the corrupting influences of business as well. In the chapter included here he describes how the press abused four of his contemporaries—Charles A. Lindbergh Sr., who ran for governor of Minnesota and lost; Charles A. Lindbergh Jr., the aviator; Robert M. La Follette, the Progessive Party leader; and Upton Sinclair, the novelist, pamphleteer, Utopian socialist, pacifist, and press critic who wrote *The Brass Check.*

Later Seldes started a journalism review, *In fact,* with its distinctive and defiant lower case *f,* which lasted for ten years. In many ways Seldes, who died in 1995 at age 105, was the link connecting most of the press critics in the past century. In his autobiography he acknowledged his debt to Will Irwin and Upton Sinclair. So, too, he influenced those who are now the elder statesmen of the current generation of critics. Nat Hentoff once called Seldes "the father of some of us all."

The Right to Privacy

SAMUEL WARREN AND LOUIS BRANDEIS

*It could be done only on principles of private justice, moral fitness, and pub-
lic convenience, which, when applied to a new subject, make common law
without a precedent; much more when received and approved by usage.*

—I. Willis, in Millar v. Taylor

That the individual shall have full protection in person and in property is
a principle as old as the common law; but it has been found necessary
from time to time to define anew the exact nature and extent of such
protection. Political, social, and economic changes entail the recognition
of new rights, and the common law, in its eternal youth, grows to meet the
demands of society. Thus, in very early times, the law gave a remedy only for
physical interference with life and property, for trespasses *vi et armis*. Then
the "right to life" served only to protect the subject from battery in its various
forms; liberty meant freedom from actual restraint; and the right to property
secured to the individual his lands and his cattle. Later, there came a recognition of man's spiritual nature, of his feelings and his intellect. Gradually
the scope of these legal rights broadened; and now the right to life has come
to mean the right to enjoy life—the right to be let alone; the right to liberty
secures the exercise of extensive civil privileges; and the term "property" has
grown to comprise every form of possession—intangible, as well as tangible.

Thus, with the recognition of the legal value of sensations, the protection
against actual bodily injury was extended to prohibit mere attempts to do such
injury; that is, the putting another in fear of such injury. From the action of
battery grew that of assault. Much later there came a qualified protection of

From the *Harvard Law Review,* December 15, 1890

the individual against offensive noises and odors, against dust and smoke, and excessive vibration. The law of nuisance was developed. So regard for human emotions soon extended the scope of personal immunity beyond the body of the individual. His reputation, the standing among his fellow-men, was considered, and the law of slander and libel arose. Man's family relations became a part of the legal conception of his life, and the alienation of a wife's affections was held remediable. Occasionally the law halted—as in its refusal to recognize the intrusion by seduction upon the honor of the family. But even here the demands of society were met. A mean fiction, the action *per quod servitium amisit,* was resorted to, and by allowing damages for injury to the parents' feelings, an adequate remedy was ordinarily afforded. Similar to the expansion of the right to life was the growth of the legal conception of property. From corporeal property arose the incorporeal rights issuing out of it; and then there opened the wide realm of intangible property, in the products and processes of the mind, as works of literature and art, goodwill, trade secrets, and trademarks.

This development of the law was inevitable. The intense intellectual and emotional life, and the heightening of sensations which came with the advance of civilization, made it clear to men that only a part of the pain, pleasure, and profit of life lay in physical things. Thoughts, emotions, and sensations demanded legal recognition, and the beautiful capacity for growth which characterizes the common law enabled the judges to afford the requisite protection, without the interposition of the legislature.

Recent inventions and business methods call attention to the next step which must be taken for the protection of the person, and for securing to the individual what Judge Cooley calls the right "to be let alone." Instantaneous photographs and newspaper enterprise have invaded the sacred precincts of private and domestic life; and numerous mechanical devices threaten to make good the prediction that "what is whispered in the closet shall be proclaimed from the housetops." For years there has been a feeling that the law must afford some remedy for the unauthorized circulation of portraits of private persons; and the evil of the invasion of privacy by the newspapers, long keenly felt, has been but recently discussed by an able writer. The alleged facts of a somewhat notorious case brought before an inferior tribunal in New York a few months ago, directly involved the consideration of the right of circulating portraits; and the question whether our law will recognize and protect the right to privacy in this and in other respects must soon come before our courts for consideration.

Of the desirability—indeed of the necessity—of some such protection, there can, it is believed, be no doubt. The press is overstepping in every direction the obvious bounds of propriety and of decency. Gossip is no longer the resource of the idle and of the vicious, but has become a trade, which is pursued with industry as well as effrontery. To satisfy a prurient taste the details of sexual relations are spread and broadcast in the columns of the daily papers. To occupy the indolent, column upon column is filled with idle gossip, which can only be procured by intrusion upon the domestic circle. The intensity and complexity of life, attendant upon advancing civilization, have rendered necessary some retreat from the world, and man, under the refining influence of culture, has become more sensitive to publicity, so that solitude and privacy have become more essential to the individual; but modern enterprise and invention have, through invasions upon his privacy, subjected him to mental pain and distress, far greater than could be inflicted by mere bodily injury. Nor is the harm wrought by such invasions confined to the suffering of those who may be made the subjects of journalistic or other enterprise. In this, as in other branches of commerce, the supply creates the demand. Each crop of unseemly gossip, thus harvested, becomes the seed of more, and, in direct proportion to its circulation, resulting in a lowering of social standards and of morality. Even gossip apparently harmless, when widely and persistently circulated, is potent for evil. It both belittles and perverts. It belittles by inverting the relative importance of things, thus dwarfing the thoughts and aspirations of a people. When personal gossip attains the dignity of print, and crowds the space available for matters of real interest to the community, what wonder that the ignorant and thoughtless mistake its relative importance. Easy of comprehension, appealing to that weak side of human nature which is never wholly cast down by the misfortunes and frailties of our neighbors, no one can be surprised that it usurps the place of interest in brains capable of other things. Triviality destroys at once robustness of thought and delicacy of feeling. No enthusiasm can flourish, no generous impulse can survive under its blighting influence.

It is our purpose to consider whether the existing law affords a principle which can properly be invoked to protect the privacy of the individual; and, if it does, what the nature and extent of such protection is.

Owing to the nature of the instruments by which privacy is invaded, the injury inflicted bears a superficial resemblance to the wrongs dealt with by the law of slander and of libel, while a legal remedy for such injury seems to involve the treatment of mere wounded feelings, as a substantive cause of action. The principle on which the law of defamation rests, covers, however, a radically different class of effects from those for which attention is now asked. It deals only with damage to reputation, with the injury done to the individual in his external relations to the community, by lowering him in the estimation of his fellows. The matter published of him, however widely circulated, and however unsuited to publicity, must, in order to be actionable, have a direct tendency to injure him in his intercourse with others, and even if in writing or in print, must subject him to the hatred, ridicule, or contempt of his fellow-men—the effect of the publication upon his estimate of himself and upon his own feelings not forming an essential element in the cause of action. In short, the wrongs and correlative rights recognized by the law of slander and libel are in their nature material rather than spiritual. That branch of the law simply extends the protection surrounding physical property to certain of the conditions necessary or helpful to worldly prosperity. On the other hand, our law recognizes no principle upon which compensation can be granted for mere injury to the feelings. However painful the mental effects upon another of an act, though purely wanton or even malicious, yet if the act itself is otherwise lawful, the suffering inflicted is *damnum absque injuria.* Injury of feelings may indeed be taken account of in ascertaining the amount of damages when attending what is recognized as a legal injury; but our system, unlike the Roman law, does not afford a remedy even for mental suffering which results from mere contumely and insult, from an intentional and unwarranted violation of the "honor" of another.

It is not however necessary, in order to sustain the view that the common law recognizes and upholds a principle applicable to cases of invasion of privacy, to invoke the analogy, which is but superficial, to injuries sustained, either by an attack upon reputation or by what the civilians called a violation of honor; for the legal doctrines relating to infractions of what is ordinarily termed the common-law right to intellectual and artistic property are, it is believed, but instances and applications of a general right to privacy, which properly understood afford a remedy for the evils under consideration.

The common law secures to each individual the right of determining, ordinarily, to what extent his thoughts, sentiments, and emotions shall be communicated to others. Under our system of government, he can never be compelled to express them (except when upon the witness-stand); and even if he has chosen to give them expression, he generally retains the power to fix the limits of the publicity which shall be given them. The existence of this right does not depend upon the particular method of expression adopted. It is immaterial whether it be by word or by signs, in painting, by sculpture, or in music. Neither does the existence of the right depend upon the nature or value of the thought or emotion, nor upon the excellence of the means of expression. The same protection is accorded to a casual letter or an entry in a diary and to the most valuable poem or essay, to a botch or daub and to a masterpiece. In every such case the individual is entitled to decide whether that which is his shall be given to the public. No other has the right to publish his productions in any form, without his consent. This right is wholly independent of the material on which, or the means by which, the thought, sentiment, or emotion is expressed. It may exist independently of any corporeal being, as in words spoken, a song sung, a drama acted. Or if expressed on any material, as a poem in writing, the author may have parted with the paper, without forfeiting any proprietary right in the composition itself. The right is lost only when the author himself communicates his production to the public—in other words, publishes it. It is entirely independent of the copyright laws, and their extension into the domain of art. The aim of those statutes is to secure to the author, composer, or artist the entire profits arising from publication; but the common-law protection enables him to control absolutely the act of publication, and in the exercise of his own discretion, to decide whether there shall be any publication at all. The statutory right is of no value, *unless* there is a publication; the common-law right is lost *as soon as* there is a publication.

What is the nature, the basis, of this right to prevent the publication of manuscripts or works of art? It is stated to be the enforcement of a right of property; and no difficulty arises in accepting this view, so long as we have only to deal with the reproduction of literary and artistic compositions. They certainly possess many of the attributes of ordinary property: they are transferable; they have a value; and publication or reproduction is a use by which that value is realized. But where the value of the production is found not in the right to take the profits arising from publication, but in the peace of mind or the relief afforded by the ability to prevent any publication at all, it is difficult to regard the right as one of property, in the common acceptation of that term. A man records in a letter to his son, or in his diary, that he did not dine with his wife on a certain day. No one into whose hands those papers fall could publish them to the world, even if possession of the documents had been obtained rightfully; and the prohibition would not be confined to the publication of a copy of the letter itself, or of the diary entry; the restraint extends also to a publication of the contents. What is the thing which is protected? Surely, not the intellectual act of recording the fact that the husband did not dine with his wife, but that fact itself. It is not the intellectual product, but the domestic occurrence. Man writes a dozen letters to different people. No person would be permitted to publish a list of the letters written. If the letters or the contents of the diary were protected as literary compositions, the scope of the protection afforded should be the same secured to a published writing under the copyright law. But the copyright law would not prevent an enumeration of the letters, or the publication of some of the facts contained therein. The copyright of a series of paintings or etchings would prevent a reproduction of the paintings as pictures; but it would not prevent a publication of a list or even a description of them. Yet in the famous case of *Prince Albert v. Strange* (1849), the court held that the common-law rule prohibited not merely the reproduction of the etchings which the plaintiff and Queen Victoria had made for their own pleasure, but also "the publishing (at least by printing or writing), though not by copy or resemblance, a description of them, whether more or less limited or summary, whether in the form of a catalogue or otherwise." Likewise, an unpublished collection of news possessing no element of a literary nature is protected from piracy.

That this protection cannot rest upon the right to literary or artistic property in any exact sense appears the more clearly when the subject-matter for which protection is invoked is not even in the form of intellectual property, but has the attributes of ordinary tangible property. Suppose a man has a collection of gems or curiosities which he keeps private: it would hardly be contended that any person could publish a catalogue of them, and yet the articles enumerated are certainly not intellectual property in the legal sense, any more than a collection of stoves or of chairs.

The belief that the idea of property in its narrow sense was the basis of the protection of unpublished manuscripts led an able court to refuse, in several cases, injunctions against the publication of private letters, on the ground that "letters not possessing the attributes of literary compositions are not property entitled to protection"; and that it was "evident the plaintiff could not have considered the letters as of any value whatever as literary productions, for a letter cannot be considered of value to the author which he never would consent to have published." But these decisions have not been followed, and it may now be considered settled that the protection afforded by the common law to the author of any writing is entirely independent of its pecuniary value, its intrinsic merits, or of any intention to publish the same, and, of course, also, wholly independent of the material, if any, upon which, or the mode in which, the thought or sentiment was expressed.

Although the courts have asserted that they rested their decisions on the narrow grounds of protection to property, yet there are recognitions of a more liberal doctrine. Thus in the case of *Prince Albert v. Strange,* already referred to, the opinions both of the Vice Chancellor and of the Lord Chancellor, on appeal, show a more or less clearly defined perception of a principle broader than those which were mainly discussed, and on which they both placed their chief reliance. Vice-Chancellor Knight Bruce referred to publishing of a man that he had "written to particular persons or on particular subjects" as an instance of possibly injurious disclosures as to private matters, that the courts would in a proper case prevent; yet it is difficult to perceive how, in such a case, any right of property, in the narrow sense, would be drawn in question, or why, if such a publication would be restrained when it threatened to expose the victim not merely to sarcasm, but to ruin, it should not equally be enjoined, if it threatened to embitter his life. To deprive a man of the potential profits to be realized by publishing a catalogue of his gems cannot *per se* be a wrong to him. The possibility of future profits is not a right of property which the law ordinarily recognizes; it must, therefore, be an infraction of other rights which constitutes the wrongful act, and that infraction is equally wrongful, whether its results are to forestall the profits that the individual himself might secure by giving the matter a publicity obnoxious to him, or to gain an advantage at the expense of his mental pain and suffering. If the fiction of property in a narrow sense must be preserved, it is still true that the end accomplished by the gossip-monger is attained by the use of that which is another's, the facts relating to his private life, which he has seen fit to keep private. Lord Cottenham stated that a man "is entitled to be protected in the exclusive use and enjoyment of that which is exclusively his," and cited with approval the opinion of Lord Eldon, as reported in a manuscript note of the case of *Wyatt v. Wilson,* in 1820, respecting an engraving of George the Third during his illness, to the effect that "if one of the late king's physicians had kept a diary of what he heard and saw, the court would not, in the king's lifetime, have permitted him to print and publish it"; and Lord Cottenham declared, in respect to the acts of the defendants in the case before him, that "privacy is the right invaded." But if privacy is once recognized as a right entitled to legal protection, the interposition of the courts cannot depend on the particular nature of the injuries resulting.

These considerations lead to the conclusion that the protection afforded to thoughts, sentiments, and emotions, expressed through the medium of writing or of the arts, so far as it consists in preventing publication, is merely an instance of the enforcement of the more general right of the individual to be let alone. It is like the right not to be assaulted or beaten, the right not to be imprisoned, the right not to be maliciously prosecuted, the right not to be defamed. In each of these rights, as indeed in all other rights recognized by the law, there inheres the quality of being owned or possessed—and (as that is the distinguishing attribute of property) there may be some propriety in speaking of those rights of property. But, obviously, they bear little resemblance to what is ordinarily comprehended under that term. The principle which protects personal writings and all other personal productions, not against theft and physical appropriation, but against publication in any form, is in reality not the principle of private property, but that of inviolate personality.

If we are correct in this conclusion, the existing law affords a principle which may be invoked to protect the privacy of the individual from invasion either by the too enterprising press, the photographer, or the possessor of any other modem device for recording or reproducing scenes or sounds. For the protection afforded is not confined by the authorities to those cases where any particular medium or form of expression has been adopted, nor to products of the intellect. The same protection is afforded to emotions and sensations expressed in a musical composition or other work of art as to a literary composition; and words spoken, a pantomime acted, a sonata performed, is no less entitled to protection than if each had been reduced to writing. The circumstance that a thought or emotion has been recorded in a permanent form renders its identification easier, and hence may be important from the point of view of evidence, but it has no significance as a matter of substantive right. If, then, the decisions indicate a general right to privacy for thoughts, emotions, and sensations, these should receive the same protection, whether expressed in writing, or in conduct, in conversation, in attitudes, or in facial expression.

It may be urged that a distinction should be taken between the deliberate expression of thoughts and emotions in literary or artistic compositions and the casual and often involuntary expression given to them in the ordinary conduct of life. In other words, it may be contended that the protection afforded is granted to the conscious products of labor, perhaps as an encouragement to effort. This contention, however plausible, has, in fact, little to recommend it. If the amount of labor involved be adopted as the test, we might well find that the effort to conduct one's self properly in business and in domestic relations had been far greater than that involved in painting a picture or writing a book; one would find that it was far easier to express lofty sentiments in a diary than in the conduct of a noble life. If the test of deliberateness of the act be adopted, much casual correspondence which is now accorded full protection would be excluded from the beneficent operation of existing rules. After the decisions denying the distinction attempted to be made between those literary productions which it was intended to publish and those which it was not, all considerations of the amount of labor involved, the degree of deliberation, the value of the product, and the intention of publishing must be abandoned, and no basis is discerned upon which the right to restrain publication and reproduction of such so-called literary and artistic works can be rested, except the right to privacy, as a part of the more general right to the immunity of the person—the right to one's personality.

It should be stated that, in some instances where protection has been afforded against wrongful publication, the jurisdiction has been asserted, not on the ground of property, or at least not wholly on that ground, but upon the ground of an alleged breach of an implied contract or of a trust or confidence.

Thus, in *Abernethy v. Hutchinson* (1825), where the plaintiff, a distinguished surgeon, sought to restrain the publication in the *Lancet* of unpublished lectures which he had delivered at St. Bartholomew's Hospital in London, Lord Eldon doubted whether there could be property in lectures which had not been reduced to writing, but granted the injunction on the ground of breach of confidence, holding "that when persons were admitted as pupils or otherwise, to hear these lectures, although they were orally delivered, and although the parties might go to the extent, if they were able to do so, of putting down the whole by means of shorthand, yet they could do that only for the purposes of their own information, and could not publish, for profit, that which they had not obtained the right of selling."

In *Prince Albert v. Strange*, Lord Cottenham, on appeal, while recognizing a right of property in the etchings which of itself would justify the issuance of the injunction, stated, after discussing the evidence, that he was bound to assume that the possession of the etchings by the defendant had "its foundation in a breach of trust, confidence, or contract," and that upon such ground also the plaintiffs title to the injunction was fully sustained.

In *Tuck v. Priester* (1887), the plaintiffs were owners of a picture, and employed the defendant to make a certain number of copies. He did so, and made also a number of other copies for himself, and offered them for sale in England at a lower price. Subsequently, the plaintiffs registered their copyright in the picture, and then brought suit for an injunction and damages. The Lords Justices differed as to the application of the copyright acts to the case, but held unanimously that independently of those acts, the plaintiffs were entitled to an injunction and damages for breach of contract.

In *Pollard v. Photographic Co.* (1888), a photographer who had taken a lady's photograph under ordinary circumstances was restrained from exhibiting it, and also from selling copies of it, on the ground that it was a breach of an implied term in the contract, and also that it was a breach of confidence. Mr. Justice North interjected in the argument of the plaintiffs counsel the inquiry: "Do you dispute that if the negative likeness were taken on the sly, the person who took it might exhibit copies?" and counsel for the plaintiff answered: "In that case there would be no trust or consideration to support a contract." Later, the defendant's counsel argued that "a person has no property in his own features; short of doing what is libelous or otherwise illegal, there is no restriction on the photographer's using his negative." But the court, while expressly finding a breach of contract and of trust sufficient to justify its interposition, still seems to have felt the necessity of resting the decision also upon a right of property, in order to bring it within the line of those cases which were relied upon as precedents.

This process of implying a term in a contract, or of implying a trust (particularly where the contract is written, and where there is no established usage of custom), is nothing more nor less than a judicial declaration that public morality, private justice, and general convenience demand the recognition of such a rule, and that the publication under similar circumstances would be considered an intolerable abuse. So long as these circumstances happen to present a contract upon which such a term can be engrafted by the judicial mind, or to supply relations upon which a trust or confidence can be erected, there may be no objection to working out the desired protection through the doctrines of contract or of trust. But the court can hardly stop there. The narrower doctrine may have satisfied the demands of society at a time when the abuse to be guarded against could rarely have arisen without violating a contract or a special confidence; but now that modern devices afford abundant opportunities for the perpetration of such wrongs without any participation by the injured party, the protection granted by the law must be placed upon a broader foundation. While, for instance, the state of the photographic art was such that one's picture could seldom be taken without his consciously "sitting" for the purpose, the law of contract or of trust might afford the prudent man sufficient safeguards against the improper circulation of his portrait; but since the latest advances in photographic art have rendered it possible to take pictures surreptitiously, the doctrines of contract and of trust are inadequate to support the required protection, and the law of tort must be resorted to. The right of property in its widest sense, including all possession, including all rights and privileges, and hence embracing the right to an inviolate personality, affords alone that broad basis upon which the protection which the individual demands can be rested.

Thus, the courts, in searching for some principle upon which the publication of private letters could be enjoined, naturally came upon the ideas of a breach of confidence, and of an implied contract; but it required little consideration to discern that this doctrine could not afford all the protection required, since it would not support the court in granting a remedy against a stranger; and so the theory of property in the contents of letters was adopted. Indeed, it is difficult to conceive on what theory of the law the casual recipient of a letter, who proceeds to publish it, is guilty of a breach of contract, express or implied, or of any breach of trust, in the ordinary acceptation of that term. Suppose a letter has been addressed to him without his solicitation. He opens it, and reads. Surely, he has not made any contract; he has not accepted any trust. He cannot, by opening and reading the letter, have come under any obligation save what the law declares; and, however expressed, that obligation is simply to observe the legal right of the sender, whatever it may be, and whether it be called his right of property in the contents of the letter, or his right to privacy.

A similar groping for the principle upon which a wrongful publication can be enjoined is found in the law of trade secrets. There, injunctions have generally been granted on the theory of a breach of contract, or of an abuse of confidence. It would, of course, rarely happen that any one would be in the possession of a secret unless confidence had been reposed in him. But can it be supposed that the court would hesitate to grant relief against one who had obtained his knowledge by an ordinary trespass—for instance, by wrongfully looking into a book in which the secret was recorded, or by eavesdropping? Indeed, in *Yovatt v. Winyard,* where an injunction was granted against making any use of or communicating certain recipes for veterinary medicine, it appeared that the defendant, while in the plaintiffs employ, had surreptitiously got access to his book of recipes, and copied them. Lord Eldon "granted the injunction, upon the ground of there having been a breach of trust and confidence"; but it would seem to be difficult to draw any sound legal distinction between such a case and one where a mere stranger wrongfully obtained access to the book.

We must therefore conclude that the rights, so protected, whatever their exact nature, are not rights arising from contract or from special trust, but are rights as against the world; and, as above stated, the principle which has been applied to protect these rights is in reality not the principle of private property, unless that word be used in an extended and unusual sense. The principle which protects personal writings and any other productions of the intellect or of the emotions, is the right to privacy, and the law has no new principle to formulate when it extends this protection to the personal appearance, saying, acts, and to personal relations, domestic or otherwise.

If the invasion of privacy constitutes a legal *injuria,* the elements for demanding redress exist, since already the value of mental suffering, caused by an act wrongful in itself, is recognized as a basis for compensation.

The right of one who has remained a private individual, to prevent his public portraiture, presents the simplest case for such extension; the right to protect one's self from pen portraiture, from a discussion by the press of one's private affairs, would be a more important and far-reaching one. If casual and unimportant statements in a letter, if handiwork, however inartistic and valueless, if possessions of all sorts are protected not only against reproduction, but against description and enumeration, how much more should the acts and sayings of a man in his social and domestic relations be guarded from ruthless publicity. If you may not reproduce a woman's face photographically without her consent, how much less should be tolerated the reproduction of her face, her form, and her actions, by graphic descriptions colored to suit a gross and depraved imagination.

The right to privacy, limited as such right must necessarily be, has found expression in the law of France.

It remains to consider what are the limitations of this right to privacy, and what remedies may be granted for the enforcement of the right. To determine in advance of experience the exact line at which the dignity and convenience of the individual must yield to the demands of the public welfare or of private justice would be a difficult task; but the more general rules are furnished by the legal analogies already developed in the law of slander and libel, and in the law of literary and artistic property.

1. The right to privacy does not prohibit any publication of matter which is of public or general interest.

In determining the scope of this rule, aid would be afforded by the analogy, in the law of libel and slander, of cases which deal with the qualified privilege of comment and criticism on matters of public and general interest. There are of course difficulties in applying such a rule, but they are inherent in the subject matter, and are certainly no greater than those which exist in many other branches of the law—for instance, in that large class of cases in which the reasonableness or unreasonableness of an act is made the test of liability. The design of the law must be to protect those persons, with whose affairs the community has no legitimate concern, from being dragged into an undesirable and undesired publicity and to protect all persons, whatsoever; their position or station, from having matters which they may properly prefer to keep private, made public against their will. It is the unwarranted invasion of individual privacy which is reprehended, and to be, so far as possible, prevented. The distinction, however, noted in the above statement is obvious and fundamental. There are persons who may reasonably claim, as a right, protection from the notoriety entailed by being made the victims of journalistic enterprise. There are others who, in varying degrees, have renounced the right to live their lives screened from public observation. Matters which men of the first class may justly contend, concern themselves alone, may in those of the second be the subject of legitimate interest to their fellow citizens. Peculiarities of manner and person, which in the ordinary individual should be free from comment, may acquire a public importance, if found in a candidate for political office. Some further discrimination is necessary, therefore, than to class facts or deeds as public or private according to a standard to be applied to the fact or deed *per se*. To publish of a modest and retiring individual that he suffers from an impediment in his speech, or that he cannot spell correctly, is an unwarranted, if not an unexampled, infringement of his rights, while to state and comment on the same characteristics found in a would-be congressman could not be regarded as beyond the pale of propriety.

The general object in view is to protect the privacy of private life, and to whatever degree and in whatever connection a man's life has ceased to be private, before the publication under consideration has been made, to that extent the protection is to be withdrawn. Since, then, the propriety of publishing the very same facts may depend wholly upon the person concerning whom they are published, no fixed formula can be used to prohibit obnoxious publications. Any rule of liability adopted must have in it an elasticity which shall take account of the varying circumstances of each case—a necessity which unfortunately renders such a doctrine not only more difficult of application, but also to a certain extent uncertain in its operation and easily rendered abortive. Besides, it is only the more flagrant breaches of decency and propriety that could in practice be reached, and it is not perhaps desirable even to attempt to repress everything which the nicest taste and keenest sense of the respect due to private life would condemn.

In general, then, the matters of which the publication should be repressed may be described as those which concern the private life, habits, acts, and relations of an individual, and have no legitimate connection with his fitness for a public office which he seeks or for which he is suggested, or for any public or quasi-public capacity. The foregoing is not designed as a wholly accurate or exhaustive definition, since that which must ultimately in a vast number of cases become a question of individual judgment and opinion is incapable of such definition; but it is an attempt to indicate broadly the class of matters referred to. Some things all men alike are entitled to keep from popular curiosity, whether in public life or not, while others are only private because the persons concerned have not assumed a position which makes their doings legitimate matters of public investigation.

2. The right to privacy does not prohibit the communication of any matter, though in its nature private, when the publication is made under circumstances which would render it a privileged communication according to the law of slander and libel.

Under this rule, the right to privacy is not invaded by any publication made in a court of justice, in legislative bodies, or the committees of those bodies; in municipal assemblies, or the committees of such assemblies, or practically by any communication made in any other public body, municipal or parochial, or in any body quasi-public, like the large voluntary associations formed for almost every purpose of benevolence, business, or other general interest; and (at least in many jurisdictions) reports of any such proceedings would in some measure be accorded a like privilege. Nor would the rule prohibit any publication made by one in the discharge of some public or private duty, whether legal or moral, or in conduct of one's own affairs, in matters where his own interest is concerned.

3. The law would probably not grant any redress for the invasion of privacy by oral publication in the absence of special damage.

The same reasons exist for distinguishing between oral and written publications of private matters, as is afforded in the law of defamation by the restricted liability for slander as compared to the liability for libel. The injury resulting from such oral communications would ordinarily be so trifling that the law might well, in the interest of free speech, disregard it altogether.

4. The right to privacy ceases upon the publication of the facts by the individual, or with his consent.

This is but another application of the rule which has become familiar in the law of literary and artistic property. The cases there decided establish also what should be deemed a publication—the important principle in this connection being that a private communication of circulation for a restricted purpose is not a publication within the meaning of the law.

5. The truth of the matter published does not afford a defense. Obviously this branch of the law should have no concern with the truth or falsehood of the matters published. It is not for injury to the individual's character that redress or prevention is sought, but for injury to the right of privacy. For the former, the law of slander and libel provides perhaps a sufficient safeguard. The latter implies the right not merely to prevent inaccurate portrayal of private life, but to prevent its being depicted at all.

6. The absence of "malice" in the publisher does not afford a defense. Personal ill-will is not an ingredient of the offence, any more than in an ordinary case of trespass to person or to property. Such malice is never necessary to be shown in an action for libel or slander at common law, except in rebuttal of some defense, e.g., that the occasion rendered the communication privileged, or, under the statutes in this State and elsewhere, that the statement complained of was true. The invasion of the privacy that is to be protected is equally complete and equally injurious, whether the motives by which the speaker or writer was actuated are, taken by themselves, culpable or not; just as the damage to character, and to some extent the tendency to provoke a breach of the peace, is equally the result of defamation without regard to the motives leading to its publication. Viewed as a wrong to the individual, this rule is the same pervading the whole law of torts, by which one is held responsible for his intentional acts, even though they are committed with no sinister intent; and viewed as a wrong to society, it is the same principle adopted in a large category of statutory offences.

The remedies for an invasion of the right of privacy are also suggested by those administered in the law of defamation, and in the law of literary and artistic property, namely:

1. An action of tort for damages in all cases. Even in the absence of special damages, substantial compensation could be allowed for injury to feelings as in the action of slander and libel.
2. An injunction, in perhaps a very limited class of cases.

It would doubtless be desirable that the privacy of the individual should receive the added protection of the criminal law, but for this, legislation would be required. Perhaps it would be deemed proper to bring the criminal liability for such publication within narrower limits; but that the community has an interest in preventing such invasions of privacy, sufficiently strong to justify the introduction of such a remedy, cannot be doubted. Still, the protection of society must come mainly through a recognition of the rights of the individual. Each man is responsible for his own acts and omissions only. If he condones what he reprobates, with a weapon at hand equal to his defense, he is responsible for the results. If he resists, public opinion will rally to his support. Has he then such a weapon? It is believed that the common law provides him with one, forged in the slow fire of the centuries, and today fitly tempered to his hand. The common law has always recognized a man's house as his castle, impregnable, often, even to its own officers engaged in the execution of its commands. Shall the courts thus close the front entrance to constituted authority, and open wide the back door to idle or prurient curiosity?

Editorials from the *Emporia Gazette,* 1901–1921

WILLIAM ALLEN WHITE

"HONESTY PAYS," JULY 1, 1901

The valedictory of Editor Johnson of the *Peabody News* contains this statement:

> After a man has spent a score of years in a country printing office, trying to
> please the people, humoring their peccadillos, praising their good qualities and
> charitably concealing their bad ones, what has he left? Does he hold a life ten-
> ure on their goodwill? Do they appreciate him for the good he has done? No.

Well why should they appreciate such a man? Doubtless Editor Johnson is
a better man than he paints himself, but too many editors are like the one he
describes. Why should a man who "has spent a score of years trying to please
the people, humoring their peccadillos, praising their good qualities, charitably
concealing their bad ones," expect anything? He has been a panderer. He has
done the people no good. He has not helped the world. He has not added one
bit to the world's store of wisdom, to the world's store of moral courage, to the
world's store of capacity for work. If a man has been brave, if he has lambasted
the people for their folly, if he has told them their bad points as well as their
good ones, and thereby made them mend their ways, if he has put an occasional thinking cap on the people, if he has worked for their enlightenment in
spite of their ignorances—then he should expect reward and be disappointed

when he fails of it. But an editor who believes in the infallibility of the people and knuckles to them never succeeds, and he should not. A glance over the newspapers in Kansas and elsewhere in the world will prove that the editor who says what he thinks and scorns consequences is the editor who makes money. The people never respect a man who grovels to them, and they never put their money and their contempt into the same hand.

If an editor would make money he must go on the Vanderbiltian theory. It's a fine thing to love the people—but it's a poor policy to humor them. In other words, honesty is the best policy in the newspaper business as it is in the grocery and dry goods or real estate business, and an editor is not honest and does not run an honest paper, who "tries to please the people, to humor their peccadillos, to praise their good qualities and charitably conceal their bad ones." Such an editor may not know he is dishonest—but he is, and his business doesn't prosper—which is a proof of his moral poverty.

"THE SICKENING DETAILS," JUNE 2, 1911

> *The Illinois legislature has passed a bill prohibiting newspapers from publishing grue-some details. The fault is not in the newspapers, it is in the people. If the newspapers of Illinois should be prohibited from publishing such things outside newspapers would swamp the state. Newspapers are blamed for giving the people what they want. There is not a gruesome case in any town but the newspapers are besieged for information and unless they give it the public is rebellious.*
>
> *—Lawrence Journal.*

All of which is not true. The *Gazette* has printed some sickening details—as, for instance, the Thaw case—and was thoroughly ashamed of itself for so doing, and lost much more than it made. Perhaps it learned a lesson. Perhaps it did not. A famous local scandal once came upon the local court. The *Gazette* spent $25 printing a verbatim report of the evidence and didn't sell $10 worth of papers, but made both sides mad and lost money. There is an office rule not to print details of local divorce suits, statutory assaults, and other local stories in court and out involving the sex question. Excepting the big local lawsuit above mentioned, the rule has never been violated. Recently there was the nastiest kind of divorce suit in the district court. It got three lines in the *Gazette*. No one asked why we didn't insert more of it. The writer of this has been in the newspaper business steadily for twenty-six years. He has got one thing in his head: The news is what the newspapers play up. Moreover, the newspapers should be regulated. Some day the people will appoint or elect or hire town managers, and their duty, among other things, will be to go after the newspapers.

Details of murders, hangings, suicides, sex crimes, highway robberies, burglaries, and crimes of violence generally should be suppressed under the police power of the state. They are bad for public morals, and a newspaper that prints such things inveterately should be declared a nuisance.

The *Gazette* is a sinner with the rest of the craft. But it makes no claim that it is forced into it. Whenever it has fallen it has been through carelessness or natural meanness.

Newspapers could quit if they would. The community should make them quit, and some day the good sense of the people will organize and go after the newspapers just as it has gone after offenders in other walks of life. The day is coming when sickening details will be as disgusting to good people as the crimes of high finance. (*But until editors and reporters are licensed as lawyers and doctors are, this public malpractice will continue. (W.A.W.)

"SCANDAL," JUNE 22, 1913

A few months ago the town buzzed with a sad story. It did not appear in the *Gazette*. It will not appear in the *Gazette*. The sad stories of life, unless they are forced into publicity by court record, or by some crisis of a public event, are not, as a rule, good reading. Lives of men and women are not always pleasant. The good Lord, looking down on us, sees much that must make him smile and sigh at the perversity of his handiwork. For the ways of a serpent on a rock and an eagle in the air are not the only queer things in this queer world. But queer things are not important. The important things of life are its kindnesses, its nobility, its self-denials, its great renunciations.

"BUMS AND SCANDALS," MAY 23, 1921

To the Editor of the *Gazette*:

Sir: Why have you let two big divorce suits go by without a line in the *Gazette*? Are you shielding them because they are big bugs? Does the fact that a man has money keep his name out of the paper when he runs around with other women and when a poor devil gets drunk you slap his name in the paper

A Reader.

That is a fair question; the answer is this: For 26 years the *Gazette* has made an invariable rule to keep divorce scandals out of the local news. Also we have had an invariable rule to print the actual news of divorces; the names of the parties, the causes briefly stated, and the disposition of the children, if any. The community has a right to this news. But the harrowing details that mark the wreck of any home are not news; they are often salacious, sometimes debasing, and always abnormal. We have felt that the wreck of a home is bad enough; to pry among the wreckage is ghoulish. So readers of the *Gazette* who want Emporia divorce scandals elaborated should subscribe for some other paper.

Now about the drunk. The man who fills up with whisky and goes about making a fool of himself becomes a public nuisance. If permitted to continue it, he becomes a public charge. The public has an interest in him. Publicity is one of the things that keep him straight. His first offense is not recorded in the *Gazette* when he is arrested, but on his second offense and no matter how high or how low he is, his name goes in. We have printed this warning time and again; so when the drunks come around asking us to think of their wives and children, or their sick mothers or poor fathers, we always tell them to remember that they had fair warning, and if their fathers and mothers and wives and children are nothing to them before taking they are nothing to us after taking.

The bum and the divorce are treated always from the standpoint of the community interest.

The Press and the Individual

GEORGE SELDES

There is nothing covered, that shall not be revealed, and hid, that shall not be known.

The laws of most countries provide the redress when a citizen or subject is injured by the newspapers. In almost every suit, freedom of the press, its rights and privileges, are argued before judge and jury. Almost always the newspaper wins. Almost always freedom of the press is recognized, and this is as it should be, and no better fight can be waged than that for its maintenance since all other liberties depend upon it.

But freedom of the press is one thing and the invasion of the home and the privacy of the citizen is quite another, as the elder Bennett discovered (when he engaged in the so-called new journalism) and the recently departed *Graphic*—which Ring Lardner immediately called the porno-*Graphic*—later attested. The best proof of the matter is the appearance in all journalistic codes of ethics of planks respecting personal liberty and private rights.

The question is well put by a leading American journalist, William Allen White. Newspapermen, he says, are expressing deep concern nowadays over the invasion of the privacy of individuals by the press. "Is there no self-respect in our profession?" he asks. "Are we all quacks?...Have we purified our columns by refusing to accept the bribe direct only to take the bribe indirect in seeking circulation through the salacious and the pornographic? Is journalism a whited sepulchre proudly calcimined outside by our probity in the matter

From *Freedom of the Press*, 1935

of control by coarse and direct influence of advertisers while inside we are a charnel house of corruption through the circulation department? Isn't it as bad to sell a family's privacy, a man's individual rights to self-respect in order to gain circulation and so acquire higher advertising rates, isn't it as bad, I repeat, to do this as to take money directly from interested parties for perverting the news?"

In a more bitter mood Sinclair Lewis declares that recent newspaper publicity has gone mad; its "sunset wonders," he believes, are worse than honest paid advertising: "Lindbergh cannot become engaged without 110,000,000 people leeringly looking on;...that not unromantic figure Queen Marie was turned into a clown;...the judicial murder of our murderers holds daily the front page.... For this is perhaps our greatest achievement over Europe; not our electric irons nor our concrete skyscraper constructions, but our changing of the ancient right of privacy so that the most secret and perhaps agonized thoughts of any human being are the property now of any swine who cares to read them."

Another aspect of the matter, newspaper trial of accused persons, brings similar pessimism from Clarence Darrow. "Trial by jury," he believes,

is being rapidly destroyed in America by the manner in which the newspapers handle sensational cases. Of course it could not happen in England, as far as I know, or in other European countries. It is a species of mob law more insidious and dangerous than the ordinary mob law. I don't know what should be done about it. The truth is the courts and the lawyers don't like to proceed against newspapers. They are too powerful. As the law stands today, there is no important tribunal case where the newspapers are not guilty of contempt of court day after day. All lawyers know it, all judges know it, and all newspapers know it. But nothing is done about it....No new laws are necessary. The court has full jurisdiction to see that no one influences a verdict or a decision. But everyone is afraid to act!

The journalistic holiday which is being made nowadays out of a personal fortune or misfortune is thoroughly discussed by Silas Bent in *Ballyhoo,* which is required reading for those who are interested in the press generally. Louis Weitzenkorn has dramatized the tragedy of a family whose home a newspaper of the *Graphic* type has invaded. Here, as in many other instances, it is a matter not of freedom but of license of the press. In the four instances which follow in some will be told the history of men of more or less fame, who, becoming national figures, naturally had to endure a certain amount of legitimate invasion of their privacy; but at least three of these men were antagonists of the

American press, and the fourth hated a large part of it, and all have suffered abuses from it.

The four examples are Lindbergh the Bolshevik, Lindbergh the Hero, La Follette, Sr., and Upton Sinclair, the Don Quixote of our journalism. In the case of Lindbergh, Jr., and Sinclair, privacy was invaded; in all four cases the journalistic canons—Accuracy, Impartiality, Fair Play, and Decency—were violated many times.

When Charles A. Lindbergh, Sr., in 1918 was defeated for governor of Minnesota, Eva Lindbergh said: "Father had no adequate means of combating a hysterically lying press."

The newspapers of America had reason to hate Lindbergh. He was a great enemy of the bankers, he believed in the public ownership of the power companies as well as the public ownership of natural resources. He was an enemy of the Montana copper magnates and the Montana copper members of Congress, he fought the flour millers, he believed in the farmers' cooperatives, and in December 1915, he warned President Wilson that "speculations and loans in foreign fields are likely to bring us into war.... The war-for-profit group has counterfeited patriotism."

There was also a private and financial reason for national journalistic opposition. In 1911, when the packers and millers and steel and wool and other interests had got or were getting what they wanted from a businessmen's Congress, the newspapers joined in the game. The question of reciprocity with Canada had come up and suddenly the national press began a campaign to make this measure popular. It contained two important points: it freed from duty typecasting and type-setting machinery, and pulpwood and newsprint paper.

These were native industries which would be hurt, of course, and these succeeded in having the Senate Committee on Finances look into the matter. One of the disclosures was the following telegram:

New York
February 17, 1911

By request: private to editors:

It is of vital importance to newspapers that their Washington correspondents be instructed to treat favorably the Canadian reciprocity agreement, because print paper and wood pulp are made free of duty by this agreement.

HERMAN RIDDER

President,
American Newspaper Publishers' Association

The plan was for all papers to cooperate in putting through the reciprocity bill so they could get newsprint free of duty. Ridder's telegram was addressed to Democrats and Republicans, high tariff and anti-tariff advocates. In other words, at least half of the American press, which was Republican and pledged to tariff, was to run a campaign for free trade in those things which concerned their own pocketbooks.

Lindbergh opposed and voted against the bill the editors of America favored.

Practically the entire press of Minnesota opposed Lindbergh's bill to tax iron tonnage. St. Paul, Minneapolis, and Duluth newspapers were almost solid against him. In 1918 he ran for governor on the Nonpartisan or farmer's ticket. On one occasion he was arrested and jailed.

Lindbergh's platform (as given by Walter Quigley in a post-bellum introduction to *Your Country at War)* included conscription of wealth in time of war, elimination of the profiteers, price-fixing for farm produce. The campaign was vicious. Quigley arrived one day when Lindbergh was about to address ten thousand persons gathered in a grove. A sheriff and thirty sworn deputies tried to break up the meeting and the crowd wanted to fight, but Lindbergh protested it would do the party no good if blood were shed. "I suggest we adjourn a few miles south into the state of Iowa which still seems to be part of the United States," said Lindbergh. Later he was charged with conspiring to obstruct the war, but was not prosecuted. Lynn and Dora Haines, his biographers, write:

The defeat of Lindbergh again became a national affair. He was the one who must go down and every possible weapon was used against him. Never had such a campaign been waged in the state; never one more unfair. As one editor said, "this campaign is in no sense a local Minnesota affair; beneath the furious battle special privilege is waging in this state lies all the combined power of entrenched politics and wealth from Wall Street to San Francisco."

A choice sample of the journalistic campaign against Lindbergh is this editorial from a St. Cloud newspaper: "A vote for Burnquist will cheer our soldiers in France. A vote for his opponent [Lindbergh] will be sad news to them and will bring a smile to the Kaiser."

The press ruined Lindbergh. In a speech in Congress in 1916 he had said:

The public gets no information from the press about it [the money system, his favorite object of attack] for anyone who dares uncover the system and expose the schemes for deceiving the public finds that a certain part of the press will attack him and call him a radical and obstructionist, and excoriate him in every way possible. If to tell the truth about things makes him a radical, then radicals ought to be at a premium. But they have not been so far politically.

After his defeat Lindbergh wrote *Your Country at War.* Government agents raided the printing shop and destroyed the plates, also the plates of *Banking and Currency,* which attacked the big banks and the Federal Reserve Law. Lindbergh was by now known as a dangerous citizen, a Bolshevik to the Red-baiting press. The reason is obvious. Here are some of the opinions, mostly about the newspapers, he dared express from 1916 to 1918:

> It is impossible according to the big press to be a true American unless you are pro-British. If you are really for America first, last and all the time, and solely for America and for the masses primarily, then you are classed as pro-German by the big press which is supported by the speculators....
>
> "Big Business," washing the hands of their captains: In all issues of their big press and other publications, you can read about what noble patriots we have in the men who profit by the war, while it is the plain, toiling people who are really supporting the entire system, including the payment of the profits to the big fellows....
>
> It has indeed been humiliating to the American people to see how the wealth grabbers, owners of the "big press," really attempt by scurrilous editorials and specially prepared articles to drive the people as if we were a lot of cattle, to buy bonds, subscribe to the Red Cross, to register for conscription and all the other things. The people will do their duty without being hectored in advance by the "big interest" press. What right, anyway, has the "big press" to heckle the people as if we really belonged to the wealth grabbers and were their chattel property?...
>
> The attempt has been made by the press to make the farmers believe that the officers of the Nonpartisan League were selfish and later that they were not loyal Americans, also that they were Socialists, as if Socialists were criminals. Not many of those who criticize Socialists know the first principles of Socialism. Socialism and Socialists are libeled and slandered by the false and by the ignorant only, for no one who has studied Socialism can for a single moment question that it has a program whereby, if it could be followed out and put into execution, this world would be cleared of much of its misery and degradation.

Quoting parts of this book in May 1918, the *New York Times* said: "Such is the gospel which Duluth refused to hear. Such is the platform of this candidate of the Nonpartisan League. More fortunate than many of the managers and

orators of that concern, Mr. Lindbergh, so far as we know, is not under indictment for sedition."

In the *Chicago Tribune* a staff writer, Arthur M. Evans, in June 1918, wrote,
"The reader looks instinctively to see if it bears the German copyright. It
doesn't, but it contains many choice morsels of thought that might be gobbled
with relish in Potsdam." The *Tribune* Washington correspondent, according to
Margaret Ernst, telegraphed a report that in the House, Representative Miller
said that "because of the attacks he had made upon the American Government" Lindbergh should be called "a friend of the Kaiser."

In 1923 when Lindbergh went campaigning again, his son, "Slim," took him
from place to place in an airplane. They were almost killed one day when an
unidentified enemy cut a cable on the machine. The elder Lindbergh was still
known as a "red-hot Bolshevik."

Lindbergh was one of the many victims of an unfair press. The Nonpartisan
League, headed by A. C. Townley, had only its weekly magazine to answer the
attacks of its political and economic enemies. When the Lindbergh campaign
began the members of the League were called "everything under the sun—an-
archists, I.W.W.'s, pro-Germans, disloyal. They [the opposition] used the press,
the power of their money and position—every force they could muster to fight
the farmers' league."

Although Lindbergh lost, North Dakota went Nonpartisan. Said the official
League journal:

> The part the big daily press of Minnesota played in the political campaign in
> North Dakota was contemptible. For weeks before the vote, which resulted in
> the complete and sweeping victory for the Nonpartisan League, the *Pioneer
> Press* and *Dispatch* of St. Paul and the *Journal* and *Tribune* of Minneapolis
> were full of poisoned news and perverted editorial comment to the effect that
> if North Dakota votes returned Governor Frazier and the League to power it
> would be a "German victory." Every day these papers carried great headlines
> and editorials declaring that a victory for the farmers' administration would
> be a victory for disloyalty. They said that the only way North Dakota could
> "purge itself of disloyalty" would be to restore the old political gang of North
> Dakota to power and turn out the farmers' administration.
>
> This version of the North Dakota campaign was spread all over the United
> States through the activities of the poison press of Minnesota.

One of the typical stories during the campaign was that in the *St. Paul Dispatch* "to the effect that Mrs. Townley had told a woman in Detroit, Minnesota,
that she had deposited $60,000 at a Detroit bank, money that Mr. Townley had

stolen from the farmers." (I am quoting the words of the *Nonpartisan Leader.*) The Associated Press sent this by wire to all the country. It was printed in thousands of papers. Other papers copied verbatim the *Dispatch* story, which took up nearly a page.

> No deposition of this kind was ever introduced in court. No women of the name given ever existed.... It was just a hoax.... The story if true could have been verified in an hour by the Associated Press and the *Dispatch* lie nailed.... [The hoax was exposed by the Detroit banks.] So far as the *Leader* knows, no paper in American that published the original lie has yet retracted it.

During the Lindbergh campaign the organ of the League further charged that "practically every weekly and daily newspaper in Montana which is fighting the League is either a debtor to the copper trust or is owned outright by them." And again, "The newspapers do not attack the National Nonpartisan League because of any principles or convictions of their own, for they have none. They are merely the tools of those higher up, of the big business interests who are their masters. Think of the fight the organized farmers are making against war profiteering and you will see one reason for the frantic, lying articles in the poison press."

The campaign against Lindbergh, Townley, La Follette, was largely a press campaign. Wherever the progressives got a hearing they were fairly certain of making converts, but with the entire press of that section of the country against them they were terribly handicapped. As it was so much a journalistic war, the Nonpartisan League was fortunate in the midst of this campaign in gaining as a convert Walter W. Liggett who came out of the editorial office of the *St. Paul Dispatch.* He had been discharged for "disloyalty," it being alleged that he had attended a Nonpartisan League meeting and applauded. For the League Liggett wrote:

> A newspaper is a double-barreled weapon. It can suppress news entirely or distort it under misleading headlines in its news columns. If this fails to have the required result it often will continue publishing unfair attacks in its editorial columns. The editorial columns of the *St. Paul Dispatch* and *Pioneer Press* are even more unfair than their alleged news columns.
>
> The *St. Paul Dispatch* and *Pioneer Press* are notorious for their subservience to the great special interests—the railroads, the steel trust, the packers, the millers, the bankers, and the Twin City Rapid Transit Company. They have served these interests for years and done their bidding on every occa-

sion. The *Dispatch* and *Pioneer Press* can not deny that they have fought for the corporations and fought against the people every time there was a real fundamental issue involved.

Lindbergh, Sr., made no distinction between the newspapers which were fair to him and those which were unfair. He lived and died believing that the entire press was contemptible. Lindbergh, Jr.—the aviator—has always tried to distinguish between the newspapers which treated him well and those he thinks treated him badly. Moreover, on more than one occasion he issued statements in which he absolved the actions of reporters, saying they were only doing the work assigned them by the newspapers. In other words, it is the so-called rules of the so-called newspaper game which Lindbergh was challenging as much as the things done to him.

When he married privately, the tabloid press felt itself insulted. When he tried to take his honeymoon without benefit of publicity, the sensational press hounded him. One tabloid called him a "Grade A celebrity," therefore a public commodity, like gas or electric light.

The case of Lindbergh the Hero involves canon 6 of the code adopted by the American Society of Newspaper Editors: "A newspaper should not invade private rights or feelings without sure warrant of public right as distinguished from public curiosity." To Marlen Pew, Lindbergh said that several New York newspapers, five of which he named, do not respect this rule. In July 1930, Pew and Lindbergh discussed the press and privacy, and here is Pew's story of the famous interview:

Lindbergh draws the line strictly between the right of the press to report his activities as they relate to the scientific development of air travel and what he calls personal curiosity. He said in sincere terms that he valued and deeply appreciated the "remarkable liberality" of the press in support of what he terms his "work." "The constructive press has been both kind and generous to me ever since I have been flying," he said, and he mentioned newspapermen who have been helpful, intelligently critical, fair in their reports and considerate of his private rights.

Col. Lindbergh, without the slightest hesitation, but with no show of anger, also mentioned five New York newspapers which he said Mrs. Lindbergh and he had decided they could not "cooperate with and maintain our self-respect." These newspapers, he said, represent an idea of journalism to which he cannot subscribe. He called their practices "contemptible" and thought them to be "a social drag," "non-constructive," and "a waste of time." He minced no words in condemning newspapers which, in his view, cater to morbid curiosity and are concerned with private gossip to the exclusion of matters in the realm of "things, ideas, and ideals."

…Reporting their courtship, marriage, honeymoon, and recently the expectancy and arrival of their infant son, Col. Lindbergh admitted these activities had been the bane of his life, that they had been "disgusting" and "humiliating," but contended that his feeling was not against individual reporters, though he thought they might be engaged in "some more decent business." His expressed resentment was against editors and publishers who "force reporters to do these unjust and intolerable things." He said he had become fairly used to indignities from a section of the New York newspaper press and was past personal feelings in relation to them, "only I wish they would have given me time to do my work," but he felt as a citizen he had to "protest against such journalism in behalf of other persons who are similarly plagued and cannot defend themselves." He thought it weak merely to grin and bear injustice. Col. Lindbergh asserted he was "through trying to deal with them," meaning the five New York newspapers he had mentioned.

…He did not want to blame specific newspapermen. He did admit he felt outraged when some reporters followed him and Mrs. Lindbergh on their honeymoon and "for eight straight hours circled about out boat, at anchor in a New England harbor, in a noisy motorboat and occasionally called across the water to us that if we would pose for one picture they would go away." He thought that particularly mean and unworthy. He considered it absurd that he should have been forced to keep a guard constantly at duty at the gate of his wife's home, and told of an incident wherein a reporter had attempted to bribe a servant with $2,000 to "betray the secrets of the household." He also mentioned, with resentment, the publication of Mrs. Lindbergh's expectation last Spring. On no ground, in his view, could this be justified. He spoke of other disagreeable matters.

Lindbergh had forced every reporter and photographer to sign a pledge that he would use the baby's photograph only in his own paper or his own service, making sure that the following newspapers did not receive a copy: *Graphic, News, Mirror, American,* and *Journal.* When the photograph appeared in the *Daily News,* Lindbergh ascertained that it was from the copy furnished the Associated Press. *Time* reported (July 21, 1930) that several days later when an airplane belonging to a company of which Lindbergh was a technical adviser ran into a crowd, the *Daily News* headline read:

LINDBERGH *LINER* KILLS 2

At the next regular meeting of the board of directors formal protests against the Asssociated Press action in accepting a picture for distribution to clients on condition that it would not be released to certain ones were made by the editor of the *News* and the general manager of the Hearst newspapers.

On the other hand, the liberal weeklies called upon the society of editors to explain "what justification it has for existing when in the face of this monstrous persecution of Col. and Mrs. Lindbergh no voice has yet been raised by it or any of its members in any of its sessions against this degrading of their profession." Colonel Lindbergh's constitutional right to liberty and the pursuit of happiness were held infringed.

When the Lindbergh baby was kidnapped the press descended upon him again. Mitchell Dawson, Chicago lawyer, speaks of "an army of enthusiastic ghouls prying, spying and trespassing in a ruthless stampede for news," but Pew believes this report false. We do know, however, that all Colonel Lindbergh said was, "Please go away." The Lindbergh case has been summed up by Silas Bent as follows:

Charles A. Lindbergh has suffered more, probably, than any other citizen at the hands of newspapermen. They capitalized for revenue only (their revenue) a stunt flight to France, they built up about his personality a myth which he has never been quite free to dissipate, they outrageously invaded the privacy of his honeymoon, and now they have made more difficult the return by kidnappers of his son. Colonel Lindbergh has an ugly score against the daily press.

In April 1932, Colonel Lindbergh was forced to issue a statement that "the continued following of our representatives by members of the press is making it extremely difficult, if not impossible, for us to establish contact with whoever is in possession of our son...our attempts are still greatly hampered or made impossible by press activity ..." And in August, upon the birth of another son, Colonel Lindbergh issued the following statement which can leave no doubt in anyone's mind that he feels bitterly about the press:

Mrs. Lindbergh and I have made our home in New Jersey, and it is naturally our wish to continue to live there near our friends and interests. Obviously, however, it is impossible for us to subject the life of our second son to the publicity we feel was in a large measure responsible for the death of our first child.

We feel that our children have the right to grow up normally with other children. Continued publicity makes this impossible. I am appealing to the press to permit our children to lead lives of normal Americans.

Robert M. La Follette fought "invisible government." He attacked all the business interests which were supporting the Republican and Democratic parties. His financial support came largely from the Pinchots, Gifford and Amos; Charles R. Crane, William Kent, Alfred L. Baker. He had a naive belief that the Progressive Party was different from the two major parties, that it had no financial roots in the same invisible government, and he even asked Theodore Roosevelt to endorse him for the presidency in December 1911.

The Progressives, however, had decided on Roosevelt. Medill McCormick, one of the heirs of the *Chicago Tribune,* the Pinchots, and others, asked La Follette on January 19, 1912, to quit in Roosevelt's favor, but La Follette refused. He began his campaign for nomination. Twelve years later Colonel Dickinson, retired from the State Department, wrote in the *World* that Roosevelt's campaign had been underwritten "just as they would underwrite building a railroad from here to San Francisco." The underwriters were given as James Stillman, then head of the National City Bank (father of the James Stillman of divorce notoriety); E. H. Gary; E. H. Harriman; Daniel G. Reid, railroad manipulator, founder of American Can; Charles F. Brooker, vice president of the New Haven; George W. Perkins and Robert L. Bacon, Morgan partners. To fighting these very men and interests La Follette had dedicated his platform and career.

On the second of February La Follette delivered an address to the Periodical Publishers' Association, banqueting in Philadelphia. He made his usual attack on Wall Street, Morgan, the Rockefellers, the trusts, big business in general, and said that the money trust...controls the newspaper press...newspapers of course are still patronized for news. But wherever news items bear in any way upon control of government by business, the news is colored, so confidence in the newspaper as a newspaper is being undermined.... The control [of the press] comes through that community of interests, that interdependence of investments and credits which ties the publicity up to the banks, the advertisers, and the special interests. We may expect this same kind of control sooner or later to reach out for the magazines. But more than this, I warned you of a subtle new peril, the centralization of advertising that will in time seek to gag you.

La Follette was on the verge of a nervous breakdown. According to the *New York Sun* he "would recover a page, divert to explain a page discarded a half hour ago," etc. He himself said later, "I talked too long without realizing it. I went home, really ill from exhaustion." There is no doubt that he acted in a muddled manner, that his speech became a tirade, but there is absolute proof that this confirmed buttermilk drinker was not maudlin, that he had not touched a drop of alcohol, as was alleged for years afterward.

A few days later the *New York Herald* reported that La Follette "is being hustled ruthlessly inside the hearse, although he still insists that he is strong enough to occupy a seat alongside the driver." A few great papers were lenient if not impartial in their attacks upon him, but generally speaking the press of the nation smashed his career. Whether or not the publishers in Philadelphia got together and decided upon united action is not so important as the fact that the press never forgave his attack, and either by innuendo, charges of drunkenness, or by silence, for several years made it impossible for him to have a fair hearing from the reading public.

Naturally enough La Follette fought back. If he could not make himself heard in the nation, he could at least let himself go in the Senate, and he did. When the press asked for an appropriation of five million dollars to advertise the Liberty Loan in 1917, La Follette struck at the publishers' pocketbooks. He called theirs "a business that is already subsidized by the United States government to the extent of ninety million dollars a year," meaning of course the loss the post office incurs annually in carrying second-class mail. On that subject and the loan advertising he said:

> While engaged daily in impugning and questioning the loyalty and patriotism of others, the newspapers went to Congress and asked to be paid for being patriotic.
>
> The debates on the recent revenue bill throw some interesting light on the "patriotism" of newspapers—particularly when the kind of patriotism applied affects the cash register of business offices.
>
> For years and years it has been a known fact in Washington that the government has been carrying second-class mail, newspapers and magazines, at a huge deficit. Because of the tremendous influence wielded by newspapers among politicians, nothing has ever come of any efforts to reduce the deficit and place the charges on a business basis. Government estimates show that it costs 8 cents a pound for the government to carry second-class mail. The remuneration received is 1 cent a pound from the newspapers.
>
> When members of Congress began scanning about for sources of revenue to meet the huge war appropriations the second-class postage was hit upon. Members argued that at a time such as the present no business should be subsidized. It developed that the government is paying $100,000,000 for carrying second-class postage and they were receiving in return from the newspapers about $11,000,000—a subsidy of $89,000,000....
>
> The "patriotism plus profit" policy of the newspapers is most sordidly illustrated by the history of the attempt to get a $5,000,000 slice of the government money for advertising the Liberty Loan.

The Senator, however, pointed out that when the question of raising rates on second-class matter was before Congress, and when the big New York newspaper publishers adopted a resolution against any change in rates, two leading papers, the *New York Tribune* and the *Brooklyn Daily Eagle* refused to subscribe to such a move, the first named editorially calling the government loss of millions "a clear subsidy to the publishers."

Shortly after this attack on the press, Senator La Follette made a speech at St. Paul in which he favored high increases in the taxes on the war profiteers. The story which follows was compiled by Senator La Follette from the *Congressional Record* and published by him shortly before his death in 1925:

The body of Senator La Follette's address, as submitted by the official stenographer to the Committee on Privileges and Elections of the United States Senate, was a discussion of progressive policies and the necessity of organization by the farmers. In the midst of the delivery of the speech, Senator La Follette was interrupted by questions from the audience concerning the war. In response to these questions, Senator La Follette declared at one point in his speech:

For my own part I was not in favor of beginning the war. I don't mean to say that we hadn't suffered grievances; we had—at the hands of Germany. Serious grievances!

In reporting this speech to more than 1,200 newspapers in as many cities throughout the country, the Associated Press quoted Senator La Follette as follows:

I wasn't in favor of beginning the war. We had *No* grievances!

It was this false report which appeared in the *Chicago Tribune*, the *New York Times*, the *Washington Post*, and more than 1,200 other newspapers in their issues of September 21, 1917. It was reproduced by publications in every part of the country.... This speech, as reported by the Associated Press, was the immediate cause for the introduction in the Senate of a resolution to expel Senator La Follette from the body as a disloyalist.

The storm broke on Senator La Follette after the publication of the report of his St. Paul speech, quoting him as saying "We had no grievances" against Germany.

As early as October 11, 1917, Senator La Follette in an open letter to the Chairman of the Senate Committee which was investigating his right to his seat, branded the Associated Press report of his speech as "wholly false."

It was not until May 23, 1918, however—eight months after the delivery of the speech—that the Associated Press took any action on the matter. On that date, Frederick Roy Martin, Assistant General Manager of the Associated Press, wrote a letter to the Senate Committee, apologizing for the misquotation and specifically retracting the erroneous report.

Admitting that the Associated Press had "distributed inaccurately one important phrase" of the St. Paul speech, Mr. Martin concluded his letter:

> The error was regrettable and the Associated Press seizes the first opportunity to do justice to Senator La Follette.

Thus, eight months after the delivery of the speech, the Associated Press repudiated as false and untrue the statement credited to Senator La Follette and played upon the headlines of newspapers in more than 1,200 cities throughout the United States.... Why was it that Robert M. La Follette was singled out for the most savage and relentless abuse ever directed against a public man in the history of the United States? [He himself asks, and replies]: The answer is clear to every fair-minded person who will examine the official records.

Senator La Follette was pilloried and persecuted because for twenty years in Wisconsin and in the Senate he had been fighting to protect the American people from the unjust exactions of powerful corporate interests; because he had organized and led the Progressive movement; because in the midst of war he fought to lay upon organized wealth and war profiteers a fair proportion of the enormous cost of paying for the war....

"The record shows that the resolution to expel La Follette from the Senate was based on the distorted reports of the St. Paul speech, and that after an investigation of more than fourteen months, the United States Senate voted overwhelmingly to dismiss all the charges against La Follette." ...

La Follette's St. Paul speech was falsely reported to the people, and immediately made the basis of an organized demand from Chambers of Commerce, Dollar-A-Year Men, Bankers' Associations, State Councils of Defense, and other bodies, that La Follette be driven from the Senate, under the blot of treason to his country.

La Follette for years alleged that there was a conspiracy of silence against him in the press. As the official record shows, he did not obtain a retraction for eight months. That the *New York Evening Post* was ignorant of the fact that the Senator had challenged the Associated Press immediately after it made its error and that he had requested the newspapers of the country to correct it corroborates La Follette's charge. Said the *Post:*

> The Associated Press has handsomely and promptly admitted its grievous fault in misreporting Senator La Follette...but the fact remains that irreparable

injury was done to the Senator, and that a large part of the outcry against him was due to this misstatement in the one thousand newspapers which are served by the Associated Press. Senator La Follette declared at the time that the press had misquoted him, but the matter was never brought to the attention of the Associated Press until Mr. Gilbert E. Roe, his attorney, stated the fact before the Senate Committee on Inquiry on Tuesday. Why the Senator delayed so long is a mystery; but the serious wrong done by this error needs no expatiating. No amount of apology can undo it.

No, replied Senator La Follette, he did not neglect or delay.

But the newspapers neglected to make any correction but on the contrary continued for months afterward to use the false report as a text upon which to base arguments concerning the Senator and creating public sentiment against him. The Senator had no adequate opportunity to give to the public the truth of the matter. The press was not open to him. As the *Post* says, "the thought that unintentionally so extreme an injustice may be done a public man is one to sober all responsible journalism." The injustice done the public is far more serious. If public men fighting in the interest of the public may be ruined and discredited while the fight is on, the public may lose its fight and its servants become intimidated and afraid to make any real fight in its behalf.

In the 1922 campaign Senator La Follette said that the press of Wisconsin with two exceptions was opposed to him, and that inasmuch as the press of his state usually opposed him his election was an interesting proof that the press had lost political influence and that readers mistrusted their newspapers.

In 1924, however, all commentators agreed that while the smaller papers suppressed the news of the La Follette campaign, the larger city papers, notably the *New York Times,* covered it completely and objectively.

The case of Upton Sinclair has been brilliantly illuminated by President Theodore Roosevelt who said to him: "Mr. Sinclair, I have been in public life longer than you and I will give you this bit of advice: if you pay any attention to what the newspapers say about you, you will have an unhappy time."

Upton Sinclair has had an unhappy time.

The latest episode of which was his candidacy for governor of California in 1934. Then, as ever, Sinclair got a raw deal from so many newspapers that there is hardly an exaggeration in saying he got a raw deal from the press.

A newspaperman should not attempt to sit in judgment on the case of *Sinclair vs. the New York Times.* The complainant has stated his side in a pamphlet he calls *The Crimes of the Times,* and the defendant usually has chosen the role of silence.

Relations between the two began most favorably following the publication of *The Jungle*. A stockyards investigation was ordered by Theodore Roosevelt. Sinclair, who knew the contents of the report, offered a story which the Associated Press refused. It probably did not believe in its authenticity. Sinclair says that "throughout the campaign against the Beef Trust they [the A. P.] never sent out a single line injurious to the interests of the packers." But Managing Editor Van Anda, of the *Times*, not only trusted Sinclair but received him with joy and made a three-day sensation of the story. It certainly was news.

During the Colorado bloodshed Sinclair, with the cunning of an Ivy Lee, conceived the idea of breaking the silence of the newspapers by putting on a stunt in front of the Rockefeller offices in New York. It was known as "the mourning pickets." The eastern press saw it as a human-interest story and published news which counteracted the tainted stories or the silence from Colorado. Several of the reporters, says Sinclair, were men of conscience. One, Isaac Russell of the *Times*, became our friend and day after day he would tell of his struggles in the *Times* office, and how nearly every word favorable to myself or to the strikers was blue-penciled from his story. So during the Broadway demonstration…we lived, as it were, on the inside of the *Times* office, and watched the process of strangling the news.

But now the case becomes more complicated. The mourning pickets were a news item. Sinclair, however, believes that the fact that he wrote a letter to Vincent Astor chiding him about his million-dollar recreation building is equally news. And every newspaperman knows that such a letter is not news. The *Times, Herald, Press, Tribune* did not print his letter, Sinclair complains, but it is not a fair complaint, journalism being what it is and was.

On the other hand, Sinclair charges the *Times* with failure to review his *Brass Check* and with refusing money for an advertisement for that same book. Here again it seems to me he has no case. But later when James Melvin Lee of the New York University school of journalism denounced the book the *Times* published two columns of vitriol and refused to give Sinclair the equal opportunity of rebuttal. In this point I believe Sinclair is right.

He has a much better case against the Associated Press although here also it is his failure to understand the American principle of what constitutes news that leads him into error. We know that the news out of Colorado was perverted. We know that Sinclair accused the A. P. of poisoning the news there and that after a fanfare from the A. P. the cases against the *Masses* were dropped. But when Sinclair bases a test of the news on the fact that the Associated Press refused to send as news a telegram which he himself sent to President Wilson, newspapermen know that the A. P. was right, because no telegram which an individual sends is necessarily news. On the other hand, that telegram contained a serious charge of corruption which the A. P. may or may not have investigated. It certainly should have done so and published the result.

In the mourning pickets story Sinclair says, "The United Press, which is a liberal organization, sent out a perfectly truthful account of what had happened. The Associated Press, which is a reactionary organization, sent out a false account."

He enlisted the aid of John P. Gavit, managing editor of the *Post,* who wrote to Melville Stone, saying that the matter "on its face...certainly created a prima facie case of suppression of important facts regarding the situation in Denver," and Stone replied he would investigate. Nothing ever happened, so far as I can find out. The A. P. still, apparently owes Sinclair an apology.

One Chicago newspaper reviewer said of *The Jungle* that it showed Sinclair knew more about the inside of brothels than the stockyards. I do not think any large paper in America would employ a book reviewer today who reviewed in that manner.

Bennett, of the *New York Herald,* ordered a story from Sinclair, *Packingtown a Year Later,* but neither paid for it nor used it. Incidentally the *Herald* did pay him twenty-five hundred dollars for personal libel.

That Sinclair was hounded by the press and frequently libeled is an indisputable fact. He had become a public figure when he founded Helicon Home Colony which the newspapers used as a butt for jokes, just as they always use Utopian, idealistic, socialistic, "brain trust," and reform theories. The papers which cater most to the masses delight in ridiculing any action by an individual which is outside conventional mass life. It is the snobbery of the vulgar. The yellow press in its time and the tabloid press today not only cater to the *polloi* but the publishers instead of being leaders of public opinion are merely leaders of herd prejudices. A reporter from the *Sun* told Sinclair he liked Helicon Hall, its people and its idea, and "I feel like a cur to have to write as I do, but you know what the *Sun* is." The *Sun* was then still the newspaperman's newspaper. The reporter asked for an amusing story and Sinclair said his collie dog had disappeared. The *Sun* story said that even a dog refused to stay at the Sinclair Utopia.

In Los Angeles one day Sinclair unwisely remarked he could not find a barber shop because the city was so beflagged. The *Los Angeles Times* thereupon called his speech "prattlings of an anarchist."

The 1934 campaign certainly has furnished Sinclair with a grand concluding chapter to a new edition of *The Brass Check.*

No sooner had he received the nomination for governor on the Democratic ticket than the Democratic newspapers deserted him. And this is a significant fact. It brings up the whole question as to why certain newspapers are Democratic and certain newspapers are Republican, and who gets paid for being what it is, and what are the benefits, financial or otherwise, for representing a party.

Although a Democratic Party candidate, Sinclair also had a program which big business disapproved. When big business disapproves anything party lines disappear. It was so with La Follette in Wisconsin and it was so in Washington when Ridder told the Republican and Democratic press alike to support the bill making newsprint exempt from Republican tariff. "To my knowledge no daily newspaper in the state is supporting me. I believe this situation is unique in political history," sighed Sinclair.

Immediately afterward he found that "masses of falsehood" were poured over his campaign "by newspapers and radio and pamphlets." Heywood Broun's "magnificent articles exposing the California reactionaries were appearing in the *New York World-Telegram,* but were not wanted in California." There is no law requiring subscribers to Broun's column to print them, but there is an agreement that the column must not be cut or distorted and Broun himself has complained against certain papers for doing so.

Sinclair had another unhappy experience with the *San Francisco News.* He claims that he told one of the editors a story in confidence and that that confidence, which journalists respect fanatically throughout the world, was broken when the story appeared in the paper under the signature of another staff member.

Summing up the reports in the eastern press regarding his campaign, Sinclair says:

The great newspapers of the country also reported the battle, mostly according to their prejudices. The *New York Times* gets its California stories from George P. West of the *San Francisco News* and Chapin Hall of the *Los Angeles Times.*

West, who used to be a civil liberties man, has become a tired liberal, and talked to me sadly about his lack of faith, and the inevitability of Fascism in America. In his writings he did his best to equal the *Los Angeles Times* in depreciation of our movement; but Chapin Hall ran clean away from him in the last couple of weeks when he sent to the *New York Times* a story about the Communists supporting us in California. What do you think was his sole bit of evidence? That fake Communist circular which had been got out by Creel headquarters two months back, and was now reproduced on the front page of "Ham" Cotton's newspaper! Not merely had this wretched piece of trickery been exposed in the EPIC News, but a facsimile of it had been reproduced in *Today* of October 6, with a statement of its fraudulent nature. "All the News That's Fit to Print," says the majestic *New York Times.*

It is not necessary to go to the liberal weeklies for proof that Sinclair got a raw deal. After the *Nation* called it "one of the nastiest campaigns on record" and the *New Republic* said that the press lied about Sinclair, the *New York Daily News* reported the tricks of the Hollywood movie producers; Broun in the *World-Telegram* mentioned the "dirty tactics" and "willful fraud"; the Scripps-Howard papers printed the statement from Los Angeles that

> local newspapers have struck a new low in political reporting. The big dailies make little pretense of printing both sides of the conflict and most of them have passed the sentence of silence on the big Sinclair meetings. The *Los Angeles Times* displays daily a box quoting from Mr. Sinclair's earlier writings on marriage, the church, the Legion, other American establishments. The series has proved damaging to Mr. Sinclair.

Early in the campaign the *New York Times* had reported that a West Coast newspaper had headlined it, "This is not politics. This is war." When the battle was over Sinclair had polled more than eight hundred and seventy-five thousand votes, which every fair-minded man admitted was a remarkable showing when the money the Republicans had spent and their control of the press is considered. Many eastern newspapers thought it quite a victory for Sinclair. But the *New York Times* began its editorial the next morning with these remarkable words: "The total failure of the Sinclair campaign" and concluded with "the people of California...attacked the entire Sinclair plan and repudiated it emphatically." Several days later the *Times* reported in its news columns that the governor-elect was using Sinclair platform planks.

The hysterical Red-baiting *Los Angeles Times* naturally enough called Merriam's victory a "retreat from Moscow." It said that the state had "served notice on the world yesterday that she has not gone crazy. There was nothing uncertain or equivocal about her answer to Upton Sinclair's invitation to forsake her proven paths for the red route of radicalism....It has given the nation-wide radical movement a set-back from which it will not soon recover. The retreat from Moscow has started."

But the unfairest document, in my estimation, was the front-page interview of the *New York Times* of September 2, 1934, in which William Randolph Hearst denounced Sinclair, Communism, Socialism, and Bolshevism. The cable contained the statement that the *Times* "invited" Mr. Hearst to interrupt his vacation in Bad Nauheim to comment on developments at home. It seems to me that the *Times* has gone very far afield when it chooses, of all men in the world, the rival publisher Hearst as a stick with which to beat Sinclair. This is a continuation of the feud with an amazing weapon. It is reminiscent of the James

Melvin Lee attack on *The Brass Check*. The *Times*, refusing to review the book, published Lee, and then refused Sinclair space to reply. Now it called upon the man the *Times* regards as holding the lowest place in American journalism to join in a common attack upon the enemy. It parallels the interview other papers had with Al Capone in which the gangster denounced Bolshevik methods.

And yet "Fair Play" stands high in the code of the American Society of Newspaper Editors.

Part 2

The Power of the Press and How to Curb It

In the past century dissatisfaction with the press has manifested itself in various forms. A common thread runs through the following excerpts, namely, that the the the press makes money at the expense of sound journalism.

In fourteen installments in *Collier's* in 1911, Will Irwin, a former newspaper reporter and editor of *McClure's* magazine, dealt exhaustively with what he called "the most powerful extrajudicial force in society, except religion." He also called journalism "the most romantic calling of modern times." In the first comprehensive contemporary look at press practices, he grappled with the definition of news, examined the ethics of his colleagues, decried sensationalism (a newspaper, he said, should behave like a "gentleman"), championed reporter power, and took on cowardly publishers who were wedded to wealth. In a quixotic request, he admonished publishers to avoid close association with businesses.

In his 1919 book *The Brass Check* (named after the token given to a man who had paid for the services of a prostitute) Upton Sinclair, in raw, staccato prose, painted a picture of a false, cowardly press dominated by its business offices and advertisers. He could not find a publisher for the book, so he published it himself; it became a bestseller as had his earlier novel, *The Jungle*, an unremitting attack on the meatpacking industry. In *The Brass Check*, he called the press a slave to capitalism, engaged in suppressing truth and spreading falsehoods. As an alternative to control by the media barons, he proposed public ownership.

In his 1962 memoirs Sinclair recalled how much difficulty he had in coming up with a title of his volume. He toyed with such possibilities as *Typhoid Mary, The Gas Attack, The Daily Lie, Give Us This Day Our Daily Lie*, and

The Madame Kept. Then, he wrote in his memoirs, "it struck me that *The Brass Check* was a fine title for a book about the prostitution of the press."

The mainstream press shunned him. The *New York Times* did not review his book but did carry an article about a speech given by a professor on the fallacies of the book. When Sinclair asked to reply to this attack, the *Times* editorialized that such a "pestiferous and defiling insect" should not be given space.

In 1942 a systematic inquiry into the press was suggested by Henry R. Luce, a founder of Time, Inc., which along with the *Encyclopedia Britannica* financed the grandly titled Commission on the Freedom of the Press, chaired by Robert Maynard Hutchins, a product of New England Calvinist stock and then chancellor of the University of Chicago. The commission, the epitome of the Eastern academic elite, consisted mostly of outstanding academics, primarily from the Ivy League. Among its luminaries were Zechariah Chafee Jr., a Harvard law professor; Archibald MacLeish, the poet and former assistant secretary of state; Reinhold Niebuhr, the theologian; Beardsley Ruml, the chair of the Federal Reserve Bank of New York; and Arthur M. Schlesinger, the historian. Notably no working journalists or publishers were included.

The commission complained that the press rejected any kind of examination of its performance. In a theme sounded before and since, it deplored the concentration of power in the media. It warned that the power of the press giants was growing and warned the press to reform itself. Otherwise intrusive regulation would be inevitable. From the report emerged what became known as the "social responsibility theory" of the press—that it is the media's duty to act responsibly and to serve society. In recent years the report has been greatly influential in shaping the public's views toward the press. It provided the intellectual underpinning out of which has grown the campaign to upgrade the ethical standards of journalists. At the time it was published, most journalists ignored it. Luce himself criticized the report for what he called its "appalling lack of even high school logic."

Very few newspapers bothered to report on the commission's findings. The leading press critic of the day, A. J. Liebling, found the report to be soft.

From 1945 to 1963 Liebling wrote nearly a hundred columns for the *New Yorker* called "The Wayward Press." Like Will Irwin and Upton Sinclair before him, he decried the anti-labor tendencies of the press. Just before he died in 1963, he collected articles in a book called *The Wayward Pressman.* In the introduction to his collection, which is included here, Liebling complained bitterly, and with humor, about greedy media barons and the precariousness of relying on advertising ("the country's present supply of foreign news, therefore, depends largely on how best a number of dry goods merchants in New York think they can sell underwear").

The American Newspaper

WILL IRWIN

A STUDY OF JOURNALISM IN RELATION TO THE PUBLIC

THE POWER OF THE PRESS

When the investigator looks for some formulation of the larger principles of journalism in relation to its times, he finds nothing. Try all the books listed under "Journalism" in the Astor Library in New York or the Congressional Library in Washington. You will discover only a few treaties on the making of newspapers, a few volumes of pleasant reminiscences, one interesting but incomplete and shallow history. Dig further; the great social philosophers, who have worked out the relations of law, religion, commerce, of all the other permanent human forces, to the modern organization of society, mention journalism only in passing or not at all. Of the subtler modern philosophers, Robert Louis Stevenson presents a type. Democratic as he was in sentiment and practise, he touched journalism only to revile it as the worthless imitator of his own higher art.

Now, religion, law, science, art infused the ancient world as well as the modern; we had recognized them, had worked out their principles and their relation to society, before the great flowering of the human spirit in the nineteenth century. Their maturity goes back always to a formative youth. But this alone of our intellectual forces is new. Two centuries ago there was no such thing. A century ago we had newspapers so-called, but they were only infant second cousins to

From *Collier's*, 1911

the modern newspaper. A generation still lives which saw the birth of journalism in its present form. It has burst into the world with a flare of trumpets, but it has not even crept into the slow consciousness of the philosophers....

POWER THROUGH THE NEWS

In this series, and in later articles by other hands, *Collier's* set about to explore the uncharted country. That we shall say any final word upon journalism, we are not so egregious as to believe. But it is perhaps the first attempt, in the United States at least, to study the subject fully and candidly. Mainly, it will be a piece of reporting; on the lamp of civilization, itself hidden behind the brilliance of its own rays, we are about to turn our flashlight. Others, we hope, will follow with larger philosophies of the subject, with the creation of laws, the formulation of public sentiment, which shall turn this new intellectual force, at present so wasteful and uncontrolled, into its proper relation toward progressive civilization. We are looking only for the truth, so far as our point of view permits us to perceive the truth. The work will be limited by our capacities; it will not be limited by any passion other than the passion for truth, by any desire other than the desire to know.

We shall arrive at few conclusions; but one I would better state in the beginning, that we may have done with it. The "power of the press" is greater than ever before. They who deny this are looking back to the old age when all party lines were definite, when men first swallowed a formula and then bent their intellectual powers to prove it. That was the golden age of the editorial; and these panegyrists of older times assume that the editorial page still swings all the power of the press. The world runs differently now since Darwin. The power of the press has shifted.... Indeed, line for line, it is greater, if for no other reason than that in the last generation not every one was a newspaper reader, while now the audience of the daily press includes all human beings with two eyes and an elementary education.

This has come to be the age of the reporter. In even its simplest form, news is the nerves of the modern world. Because of the press in its news function, San Diego, Seattle, and Boston, days apart by the swiftest trains, know as soon as New York and Washington that the insurance companies are under fire, that the Government has been swindled on glove contracts. So, and only so, is democracy possible in this immense country. Stated otherwise, the newspaper, in this simplest activity, furnishes the raw material for public opinion. If you want a concrete comparison, put our own small cities beside the Stratford of Shakespeare's time. Four or five days from London by existing means of travel, the intelligent burgher of Stratford had only the dimmest notion of events at the capital or on the far borders. His news came by inaccurate word of mouth from late visitors to London, or by an occasional royal proclamation tainted with the Government point of view. His mind was the prey of rumors and extravagant reports. From his very ignorance about the larger world, he would have been an impossible unit in a democracy. Perhaps I only state the obvious here; but I do it that we may keep fairly before us the newspaper's most important public function.

So much for colorless news; but, as we shall see when we come to considered reporting, colorless news is an impossible ideal. When Pilate asked: "What is truth?" he expressed the eternal quandary of the news editor. Truth, absolute truth, is a hypothesis. No man, from a cub reporter writing a dog-fight to a star writing a political convention, but puts into his work a point of view. Yielding to that tendency, newspapers, good and bad, honest and venal, have come more and more to put their views into their news columns, to relate events from a basis of opinion. The *Chicago Tribune,* in its late exposé of Senator Lorimer, went far beyond a simple statement of the facts—that popular Representatives had taken money to vote for a United States Senator. Every paragraph in that story, as told by the *Tribune,* was infused with moral indignation. When the Insurgents forced Speaker Cannon from the Committee on Rules, but did not pass the resolution calling for his resignation, the *San Francisco Bulletin,* Insurgent in opinion, announced in its news headlines: "Corrupt Wealth Loses Control of the House of Representatives—Cannon Is At Last Repudiated—Great Demonstration Follows the Victory." In neighboring Los Angeles is the *Times,* firm for the Republican organization. "Speaker Cannon Triumphant in Defeat," announced its headlines—"Insurgents Lose Nerve in the Heat of Battle—Mercerized Republicans Dare Not Support an Attempt to Dislodge Uncle Joe." In fact, there is no colorless newspaper, though a few approximate it; every news report has some point of view, expresses some mission of God or of the Devil....

WHAT IS NEWS?

News is the main thing, the vital consideration to the American newspaper; it is both an intellectual craving and a commercial need to the modem world. In popular psychology, it has come to be a crying primal want of the mind, like hunger of the body. Tramp windjammers, taking on the pilot after a Song cruise, ask for the papers before they ask, as formerly, for fresh fruit and vegetables. Whenever, in our later Western advance, we Americans set up a new mining camp, an editor, his type slung on burro-back, comes in with the missionaries, evangel himself of civilization. Most dramatically the San Francisco disaster illuminated this point. On the morning of April 20, 1906, the city's population huddled in parks and squares, their houses gone, death of famine or thirst a rumor and a possibility. The editors of the three morning newspapers, expressing the true soldier spirit which inspires this most devoted profession, had moved their staffs to the suburb of Oakland, and there, on the presses of the *Tribune,* they had issued a combined *Call-Chronicle-Examiner.* When, at dawn, the paper was printed, an editor and a reporter loaded the edition into an automobile and drove it through the parks of the disordered city, giving copies away. They were fairly mobbed; they had to drive at top speed, casting out the sheets as they went, to make any progress at all. No bread wagon, no supply of blankets, caused half so much stir as did the arrival of the news.

We need it, we crave it; this nerve of the modern world transmits thought and impulse from the brain of humanity to its muscles; the complex organism of modern society could no more move without it than a man could move without filaments and ganglia. On the commercial and practical side, the man of even small affairs must read news in the newspapers every day to keep informed on the thousand and one activities in the social structure which affect his business. On the intellectual and spiritual side, it is—save for the Church alone—our principal outlook on the higher intelligence. The thought of legislature, university, study, and pulpit comes to the common man first—and usually last—in the form of news. The tedious business of teaching reading in public schools has become chiefly a training to consume newspapers. We must go far up in the scale of culture before we find an intellectual equipment more a debtor to the formal education of school and college than to the haphazard education of news.

Axiomatically, then, the quality of news, its freedom from undue bias and taint, is supremely important. Could one slant or taint all news at its source, he would vitiate all public intelligence. Could one raise the standard of all news at its source, he would correspondingly elevate public intelligence. And since it is so vital, we must stop here to consider what news is, before we consider what, in the ideal, should be the attitude of writer and editor toward his product.

It looks simple at first sight. News is a report of just what occurs in the world, or rather what has just occurred. But a million billion things occur hourly in the world, from the movement of the finger by which I write this line to the surging of the crowd which is at this minute harrying strike-breakers along the Canadian border. The movement of this finger is not news, while the surge of that crowd is; and something more than importance divides them. My neighbor, John Smith, a virtuous man of well-conducted life, is just going to his office. He will do business honorably all day, come home, eat his dinner, enjoy the evening with his family, and go to bed. That, again, is not news. The world is working hard today on a million mighty labors. Tomorrow will be Sunday; most of the million on million human units in it will listen to sermon or mass, and rest and be virtuous and reasonably happy. And that is not news, while the raging of a thousand men along our border is—decidedly. Tell the former fact to a man, and he is bored; tell the latter, and he stops to listen.

Here lies the distinction, and it is also a definition: The beating of strike-breakers is news because it is a departure from the established order....

With our education in established order we get the knowledge that mankind in bulk obeys its ideals of that order only imperfectly. When something brings to our attention an exceptional adhesion to religion, virtue, and truth, then that becomes in itself a departure from regularity, and therefore news. The knowledge that most servants do their work conscientiously and many stay long in the same employ is not news. But when a committee of housewives presents a medal to a servant who has worked faithfully in one employ for fifty years, then that becomes news, because it calls our attention to a case of exceptional fidelity to the ideals of established order. The fact that mankind will consume an undue amount of news about crime and disorder is only a proof that the average human being is optimistic, that he believes the world to be true, sound, and working upward. Crimes and scandals interest him most because they most disturb his picture of the established order.

That, then, is the basis of news. The mysterious news sense which is necessary to all good reporters rests on no other foundation than acquired or instinctive perception of this principle, together with a feeling for what the greatest number of people will regard as a departure from the established order. In Jesse Lynch Williams's newspaper play, "The Stolen Story," this passage occurs:

(Enter Very Young Reporter; comes down to city desk with air of excitement.)

VERY YOUNG REPORTER *(considerably impressed)*: Big story. Three dagoes killed by that boiler explosion!

THE CITY EDITOR *(reading copy, doesn't look up)*: Ten lines.

(Continues reading copy.)

VERY YOUNG REPORTER *(looks surprised and hurt. Crosses over toward reporters' tables. Then turns back to city desk. Casual conversational tone)*: By the way. Funny thing. There was a baby in a baby carriage within fifty feet of the explosion, but it wasn't upset.

THE CITY EDITOR *(looks up with professional interest)*: That's worth a dozen dead dagoes. Write a half column.

(Very Young Reporter looks still more surprised, perplexed. Suddenly the idea dawns upon him. He crosses over to table, sits down, writes.)

Both saw news; but the editor went further than the reporter. For cases of Italians killed by a boiler explosion are so common as to approach the commonplace; but a freak explosive chemistry which annihilates a strong man and does not disturb a baby departs from it widely.

Last year Porter Charlton, rich and well connected, murdered his wife, a woman who had given up "society" to go on the stage, crammed the body into a trunk which he sunk in Lake Como, and fled to America. In the same week several other men in humble circumstances murdered their wives. Why did the Charlton case get so much more attention and interest from writers and readers? Mainly because it departed further from the customs of the established order. The "upper class," having a better opportunity, is supposed to be less given to the greater crimes than the "lower." Women in "society" do not generally go on the stage. Wife murderers are not generally so hardened as to cram the body into a trunk and sink it in a lake. Of course, since mankind is complex, other factors entered into the case, such as that basic instinct of snobbery which makes us like to contemplate beings greater and more esteemed than ourselves. But the deepest reason for interest in the Charlton case was the wide departure which it presented from the normal.

This interest is in itself a progressive force; it lies close to the noblest practical activities of the human spirit. Invention, moral heroism, and genius in art are nothing but the discovery of something useful or fine apart from the established order.

The subject-matter of which it treats greatly modifies news interest in the masses and in the individual. First of all: We prefer to read about the things we like.

The chief business of a true yellow journalist is to find the class of news which will interest the greatest number of people; and to this end yellow journalism has made a formula: "Sport for the men, love and scandal for the women," says an executive of the Scripps papers. "Power for the men, the affections for the women," expresses it better. Power is a man's business, his chief intellectual liking; politics, wealth, and sport are all different manifestations of it. Affection is a woman's business; love is affection at its height; scandal, affection gone wrong. Every trained journalist understands that no minor news succeeds better than a story about an animal—such as the dog who rescued his master from fire or drowning. Aside from the basic news interest which they represent, their departure from the accepted order, these stories "go" because most people like animals; else we should have no cats but mousers and no dogs but hunters. The rule holds with stories about little children and, especially, those about beautiful women. Herein the yellow editor, who sprinkles his pages with the phrase "pretty girl," lays hold on the universal, since both sexes, from different causes, glory in the beauty of woman. As I have hinted before, interest in the doings of high society, which get so much space in our sensational publications, and so much more in the English press, proceeds from that instinct of snobbery which democracy cannot cure. The under stratum yearns to those brighter beings and would like to resemble them. Even when it envies, it pays tribute to the principle, since envy is only liking and disappointment mixed in bad chemical combination.

Theatrical managers are still citing, for amusement and instruction, the great interest which New York took in the third act of Denman Thompson's *Old Homestead.* The scene was the thing; it represented the exterior of Grace Church at night. Every New Yorker had seen the real Grace Church, yet people crowded the theater to witness its canvas counterfeit. Their motive introduces the second factor which intensifies news interest in the individual:

Our interest in news increases in direct ratio to our familiarity with its subject, its setting, and its dramatis personae.

Nor is this an outgrowth of the first principle, that liking governs news interest. While by nature we characteristically like our relatives, and by association and man's free choice our friends and environment, this principle goes deeper. For example, we do not love our enemies, in spite of Christianity's two thousand years; and yet a piece of news which relates either the good fortune or the disaster of an enemy is most important to any normal man.

The interest in familiar things, people, and places—publications have waxed greater on no other policy. Tomorrow you may open your newspaper and discover that your next door neighbor has been arrested for speeding his automobile or has fallen from a scaffold and broken his leg. Though the item occupy only an inch in the column, it will probably cause more discussion at the breakfast table than two columns about an earthquake in Peru, a famine in Russia, or a rebellion in the Sudan. Of course, with increase of intelligence and education, with mental broadening, the circle of familiarity widens; the man of culture may care as much to read of the Russian famine as of his neighbor's arrest; but that is because he has read of Russia or studied the wheat supply....

THE SELFISH INTEREST

News is a commercial necessity as well as an intellectual satisfaction, part of our business as well as part of our thought. And so:

Our interest in news is in direct ratio to its effect on our personal concerns.

The fact that Reading common stock has dropped two points is hardly news at all in the absolute, so slight a variation from the regular and accepted does it proclaim. To the man who holds ten thousand shares of Reading common, it may be the most important news in any paper. The *Leadville Herald-Democrat* and the *Butte Miner* publish daily columns of "notes from the mines," just as the *New York Sun* publishes a Wall Street edition. Not once a week does anything happen in the mines which rises to news in the absolute by presenting a striking departure from routine and custom. Unilluminated by personality or color, these notes make little appeal to that interest in familiar things which the *Boston Globe*'s suburban notes satisfy. The people of Leadville and Butte want them because mining, their only industry, affects the fortunes of all, and the slightest change in the policy or conduct of a mine may take away the individual's employment or increase the receipts of his grocery.

THE SENSE OF PROPORTION

Finally comes the most obvious factor of all, but by no means the least influential.

Our interest in news increases in direct ratio to the general importance of the persons or activities which it affects.

This principle is hardly worth examples. News about President Taft is more interesting than news about John Smith, because Taft is more important in the world than Smith. So Taft's sore throat is "worth" a paragraph to every newspaper in the United States, while Smith's broken leg draws scarcely a line in his country weekly. A dramatic change in the fortunes of the Standard Oil Company is supremely interesting; the unexpected foreclosure on Baccigalupi's corner grocery gets rightly no space in the newspapers. This is merely the working of man's sense of proportion.

THE FEELING FOR THE DRAMATIC

These are not the only factors that intensify news interest, but they are the chief ones. Sense for the clash and adjustment of character and incident which we call drama is a factor. That a woman finds her long-lost child after ten years' search is mild news; that she finds him in the next hospital cot, fellow victim of a train wreck, is great news. So with the sense of humor. Such newspapers as the *Kansas City Star,* the *New York Sun,* and the *Chicago Tribune* daily print stories which have only slight interest through departure from the accepted order, through popular liking for their subject matter, through self-interest, or through the importance of the persons and interests involved. But they fall naturally into such form, or the skillful reporter casts them in such form that they amuse....

THE EDITOR AND THE NEWS

Every night there happen in New York, Philadelphia, and Chicago a thousand events which fit the definition of news; and information on most of them reaches the newspaper offices. Not one-tenth of them, however, get into print. The editor's work, therefore, is always selective. According to his point of view as transmitted through the trained men under him, he prints certain things and omits certain things, uses one item as a "front-page feature" and another as a "filler." If you live in the radius of four or five big city newspapers, compare, tomorrow, the right-hand or "outside" column of their front pages. This column, by the immemorial custom of American journalism, holds the day's most important piece of news, as the editor sees news. Unless there is something exceptionally important afoot, you will find one printing in that column a social scandal or an episode which drags in society by the heels; another political story; another movement in high finance. A Scripps newspaper, with the Scripps outlook on economic and social questions, has in that preferred position an account of a working man's strike in Sweden, a Hearst newspaper a breach of promise suit, an Ochs newspaper a railway merger.

THE QUANDARY OF THE EDITOR

Now, in making this selection, two lights guide the honest editor. In the first place, he must sell his newspaper. He, like anyone else not wholly an artist who ministers to the intellectual needs of the populace, must consider not only what he would give the public, but what the public will take. He himself may be scholarly in his tastes; the discovery of a Sapphic ode in a Greek excavation, or the fact that Professor Wallace has found another document concerning the life of Shakespeare, may be to him the most highly important news of the day. He knows, however, that a hundred potential readers will be far more interested in the latest picturesque murder. Editors exist who have naturally the popular point of view, whose interests are those of the man in the street. They are the born commercial successes of the craft; of such, for example, are many of the best Hearst editors—like Andrew Lawrence.

The other light to his feet is his conception of what the public should want; and there are men in the profession who are guided by this light alone. They will make no concessions to popularity for revenue's sake. Such men, if they manage to remain in the business, never achieve heavy financial success, although they may, through their limited circulations among highly intelligent people, have great personal and professional influence....

FACT OR GOSSIP?

"Most news," says Tiffany Blake, "is not fact, anyway. It is gossip about facts." In this, I think, he has said a wise and final word. News, as it works out in newspaper practice, amounts to gossip, the impressionist picture of truth. It is gossip organized to our uses, subdued to our hand, and raised to both a science and an art. For before journalism was, the town or tribal gossip discharged, in irregular and primitive fashion, most of the lower functions of a newspaper and some higher ones. He "mixed," he found by force of his prying curiosity the things which were his business as a member of the tribe, and the things which were no one's business. After that, he circulated through town or settlement, telling. And I conceive of one gossip, expressing most closely the bad sense we have come to feel in that word, whose tongue wagged on the hinges of malice and vanity, who spread no good thing about his enemies, and who made a mountain of rumor from a molehill of fact for the satisfaction of attracting attention. To him tribe or town listened, though they despised. He was a curse to his world. Foolish rumor and baseless report play a large part in the history of all ages down to the one which brought accurate journalism, and the springs of destructive rumor were such tribal gossips.

Another kind of gossip there must have been. I imagine a man of ready speech, rolling and curious eye and attractive manner, an ornament to any fireside, who came with his mouth full of greater and better things. The chiefs and the council had decided to change the spring planting from the east field to the west; that was a good thing; he had dug into the land and found it rich. Rab had wounded Ush and stolen away his wife; that was a pity, and Rab had his hands full with her, which served him right. A sickness was on the cattle in the northern fold; let those in other parts of the village keep their cows away lest the devil get them also. The chief's counselor had been caught stealing. Many thought that the tribe should exercise its immemorial right of deposing the unfit leader. I imagine him telling these tales of the day with the narrative gift, but also with a ripe philosophy and a point of view as high and progressive as the age knew. I think of him as ignoring the trivial things, the mere surmises, the facts which, spread abroad, would have injured individuals without benefiting the tribe. Such as he helped the upward march from tool to machinery, tribe to nation.

THE POINT OF VIEW

Each of these gossips had the eager curiosity and the burning desire to communicate its results which mark the real journalist. The difference between them consisted partly in moral intention, but mainly in point of view. And that necessity for approaching truth from a point of view rules us of the twentieth century A.D. as it did them of the twentieth century B.C., though they spoke simple things by word of mouth to one full fireside, and we complex things by word of pen and type and lightning press to a hundred thousand firesides. Nothing above a market report, or a tabulation of stock fluctuations, but shows the point of view of him who wrote.

Picking at random, as a Scotch soothsayer pricks his Bible for a sign, I lay my finger on a piece of news in this morning's *Boston Post.* It is an item, a "stick" long, from Lynn; it relates to a young girl who went to sleep with a revolver under her pillow. The revolver exploded in the night, wounding her in the shoulder. As you read it, you find the reporter's point of view. It was a "regrettable accident." "Restlessness in sleep" was the probable cause. A reader sympathizes with the young woman. I imagine its treatment from other points of view. First, the flippant and jocular—the girl who went "heeled" for that old fetish of humor, the man under the bed, and shot only herself. Then the sensational, hinting, by a twist here and a turn of phrase there, that there was more in the case than the girl told. Then the heavy monitory, implying—if only by inserting the adverb "carelessly"—that girls should not keep revolvers under their pillows. Be a journalist anything more than a clod, anything less than an archangel, he must have a human point of view; be his work any warm expression of himself, anything beyond a dry, unreadable lump, he must throw on it that light which is an expression of character and belief.

The old editor, feeling about for proper use of the news-force, either overemphasized this factor or ignored it. The blatant old party organ published, if Democratic, only the Democratic rallies and speeches, ignoring the Republican or sneering at their meetings in little ten-line reports. The point of view was there, but bigoted, narrow, and unfair. Another kind of editor, who left no descendants to this generation, held, as the fettered English do, that news should be colorless, that all expression should come in the editorial columns. So he killed art in reporting, reducing it to a mechanical formula, thereby dulling the minds of his readers and forfeiting some of his hold on his public....

THE REPORTER AND THE NEWS

Truth, fogged by the imperfections of human sight, hidden under the wrappings of lies, stands the final aim of a reporter when he goes out on a news tip. It is the working hypothesis of a reporter, "Why don't our newspapers tell the truth?" ask politicians and excellent ladies of women's clubs. Could they only know the difficulty of reaching an approximation to the hidden fact! Accurate perception of the event which has just happened before the eyes of flesh is so exceptional as to be almost unknown. Hugo Munsterberg tried an experiment once before his Harvard class in psychology. As the students settled themselves to the lecture, two men rose from the front seat and started to fight. Others joined in to separate or to assist them. A minute of lively action followed. "Gentlemen," said Dr. Munsterberg, when the disturbance was quelled, "we have only been acting for your benefit, a little drama, rehearsed beforehand. We know, for we followed our lines, just what happened. Please write down all you saw." The resultant papers differed ridiculously from each other; and all differed materially from fact. Later, Munsterberg produced another such drama, this time warning the class, asking them in advance to observe, and to write out their observations. The results were only a little less inaccurate. A professor at a Kansas university, imitating the Munsterberg experiment, staged a pretended "shooting scrape." One of the actors sprang into the melee flourishing a monkey wrench. Not a member of the class but saw it as a pistol. The steamer *Rio de Janeiro* struck the reef off Fort Point in the Golden Gate, ran out toward the sea in the darkness and ebb tide, and sank, blowing her whistle until the water drowned her steam. In the subsequent inquiry the duration of her whistle blasts became important. A company of soldiers was quartered just above Fort Point; most of them heard the blasts. Part of their drill in soldiering had consisted in counting off seconds. Yet some said that the blasts were ten seconds long, some two minutes, and some that there was just one continuous blast.

Now the reporter really approaches accuracy of perception. Daily training has made him so. Had Professor Munsterberg produced his drama before a body of journalists, I venture that their reports would have varied but little in statement of fact; I venture that certain individuals among a body of reporters watching the Kansas experiment would have detected the monkey wrench, and that had there been a trained journalist in the barracks over Fort Point we should know more than the Government ever learned about the means the *Rio* took to save herself.

But the reporter sees few of his comedies, tragedies, dramas, and little novels of the street firsthand. He is not there when the trains collide, the maniac shoots, or the thief escapes. He must take his information secondhand from witnesses with untrained and imperfect eyes. The courts, when they come to adjudicate these matters, will have trouble enough and to spare in getting at the probable truth; yet lawyers and detectives have weeks to weigh, sift, and correct by that circumstantial evidence which is often the best evidence, where reporters have but minutes.

This would be difficult enough were all the witnesses of the events which he sets about to chronicle disingenuous and truthful. But no one is so beset by the falsity of man as this same reporter. "Half the population," someone says, "is trying to keep out of the newspapers and half trying to get in." And both these classes lie consistently, or employ press-agents to do the lying for them. In unraveling these tangled things, in arriving at his results—marvel of accuracy in view of his difficulties—the reporter's feet, like Patrick Henry's, are guided by the one lamp of experience. Roughly acquainted with all classes of men, all kinds of human institutions—for each day brings him in contact with a fresh aspect of life—he develops an intuition, which is only crystallized experience, for the probable fact hidden under human contradictions and lies. You, reader, as a consumer of newspapers, do not often see a newspaper story about a little girl lured away from home and imprisoned in a dark cellar by a villain. Yet cases of that kind are commonly reported to the police. Now experience has shown that a certain kind of hysterical girl who has played truant from home for a day or so usually falls back on her Laura Jean Libbey and invents such an excuse to her family. The girl's assertion is uncontradicted; but the reporter, remembering previous cases, does not accept the story unless it has strong circumstantial corroboration. Here we have an obvious case of experience in action.

In this elemental function of finding just what happened, reporters and those editors in most immediate touch with them are, by and large, about as sincere as we may expect imperfect humanity to be. The untruth in our journalism resides elsewhere. William Jennings Bryan once raised the question: "Have we an honest press?" Were news investigation all of journalism, the answer would need to be a strong affirmative. Excepting for the very "yellow" reporter, who has lost his sense of truth and proportion, these men are after the facts and nothing else. Indeed, reporting is an unsurpassed training in sincerity. And where news results seem untruthful, the fault lies often with the reporter's judgment, not his intentions. He may accept, in the first excitement following disaster, the statement of some hysterical official that twenty people are dead, may telephone in this estimate for an extra, and may find later that the victims number only two or three. Here the public is partly to blame, since it demands immediate information. News editors, in throwing out extras while the event is still fresh, generally make allowances for this tendency and cut down the first figures. "Halve 'em," is the rule of a great press bureau. And in late years the roster of victims grows rather than diminishes with succeeding extras....

ALL THE NEWS THAT'S FIT TO PRINT: THE CODE OF ETHICS

Now, strangely, these men at the bottom of the profession—if we measure standing by salary and public esteem—have come the nearest of all American journalists to forming a professional spirit and formulating an ethical code. Not all reporters hold that code, of course, but the best, the directing journalists of tomorrow, do. These are its main articles:

First—Never, without special permission, print information which you learn at your friend's house, or in your club. In short, draw a strict line between your social and professional life. The journalist must keep such a line if he is to be anything but a pariah. The layman generally does not understand this. The remark, thrown at him across a dinner table, "Of course, this is not for publication," offends the very young reporter; later, iteration breeds indifference.

Second—Except in the case of criminals, publish nothing without full permission of your informant. The caution, "But this is not for publication," stands between every experienced reporter and a world of live, sensational matter. As a rule, reporters and their directing editors abide by this article of the code to the last item. It is a question not so much of morals as of convenience. In news-gathering, acquaintance is half the battle.

A man once betrayed goes forever off your calling list; continue the process, and you lose all acquaintance. Politicians, popular clergymen, police officials, and others who have daily contact with reporters understand this working agreement. The Washington corps has called Theodore Roosevelt "the greatest journalist of us all." He showed this in his confidences to the newspapermen. Again and again he told the reporters, at his daily interviews, the whole secret of a blind event. "This is for your own information. Don't print it until I tell you," he would say. And wo to the wight who did it! Seldom was Roosevelt betrayed, and then only on minor points.

Not only convenience holds good reporters to this article of faith, but also a real sense of morals. I know a reporter who was ostracized for years by his fellows because he published matter after the admonition of secrecy from his informants. The breaking-point came when seven men from as many newspapers went to interview a politician under fire. He gave them the formal news, and later the story of his private relation to the event. "But you won't print *that*, of course," he added. "Oh, no!" responded all the reporters except this one. He published it; the story was a fine beat. "You didn't notice that I didn't say 'No,'" he said in extenuation. This read him out of the craft.

Third—Never sail under false colors. State who you are, what newspaper you represent, and whether or not your informant is talking for publication. If there is keyhole work to be done, leave that to the detectives, who work inside the law.

Fourth (and to Henry Watterson, the cardinal article in the code)—Keep this side of the home boundary. Remember that when the suicide lies dead in the chamber there are wretched hearts in the hall, that when the son is newly in jail intrusion is torment to the mother. Nearly all reporters who expect to remain in the business respect articles one and two. Articles three and four most of them would like to respect. They cannot do so, however, without permission of their directing editors and of the publisher, a court of last resort. Half the reporting staffs are forced to do distasteful things because the publisher needs the news and does not care how the mere agent gets it. Yet with the passing of yellow journalism, and the contemporaneous passing of the craze for beats, publishers begin to see that enlightened self-interest may demand observance of even these articles. The reporter is, to the plain citizen, the visible representative of his newspaper. A violated home becomes a hostile home; and certain journals owe their special facilities for news getting to the decency and acceptability of their reporters. There are city editors as scrupulous about the methods of their men as any reporter could wish. On the *New York Sun* and *Post,* the *Kansas City Star,* the *Chicago Post,* the *Boston Transcript,* and the *Washington Star,* the reporter who presented information plucked from a wastebasket, or bullied from a woman at the back door, would be presenting an application for discharge. Most of these newspapers have their shortcomings; in some, the vices may be more harmful to the body politic and social than any lapse in manners. But they do insist on decent relations between the reporter and his public.

THE LIMITS OF GENTILITY

The newspaper should be a gentleman—such is the whole formula. However, some arbiter of manners has said: "It is never gentlemanly to knock a man down, but sometimes a gentleman must do it, nevertheless." When the law is not the regulator of society but its disturber, not the protector of the weak but the bulwark of the brutal strong, then the newspaper, chief expression of public opinion, becomes agent of a justice higher than formal law. Justice is grim business; its processes from arrest to execution are not pretty. And in such a fight as that with the Quy gang in Philadelphia or Tammany in New York, a few breaches of mere manners count for little beside the ultimate object. When Watterson made his criticism of our press, several American editors expressed themselves in approval or opposition. Ernest S. Simpson, editor of the *San Francisco Call,* stated the other side. He said:

> It is a well-recognized function of American journalism to play the part of an electric light in a dark alley. The light exposes ugliness, and until it is exposed ugliness will not be cleaned up. The people who most fear publicity talk most of sensational journalism. Let Colonel Watterson take care that he is not charged hereafter with trying to turn off the electric light in the dark alley.

THE VOICE OF A GENERATION

Logically, I should close this series with a view of the present state of American journalism. It is impossible, however, to do that with fairness and certitude. No one can state his own period in terms of time and eternity. His eyes are too near the object. Then, too, there is a special difficulty. This is a transition period. In American journalism, as in American statecraft, we are sloughing off dead skin and the new is not yet hardened to use. In spite of the evils and excesses in our journalism, the curve of progress appears to run upward....

In the profession itself lies our greatest hope. In spite of all commercial tendencies, its personnel and intelligence are improving year by year. Visiting from newspaper shop to newspaper shop last year, I was struck with the general and noble dissatisfaction of the men over the present condition in their craft. It was not the whine of the half-baked old-time newspaperman—"this is a rotten business!" They are coming to realize the importance of their profession, its usefulness, its potential standing. Their dissatisfaction is only disgust for a control which forces the reporter to drop a "good story" because it leads to the iniquity of some "friend" of the paper, which forces the editorial writer to write against all his opinions because the source of income is involved. The sentiment is young, but growing; it has not yet crystallized in results. In ten years of journalism, I have not known five writers for the daily press who left their employment over a matter of opinion....

Most of the faults which I have enumerated in showing the darker side of our wonderfully able, wonderfully efficient, and wonderfully powerful daily journalism might all be gathered under the cover of this one generic fault— take it by and large, *it does not speak to its generation*. It is the mouthpiece of an older stock; it lags behind the thought of its times.

For in the uninterrupted flow of the coming and going of men, time somehow arranges generations like the generations of a family. We had one such after the Civil War. The men of that day broke ground. They performed miraculous labors; they tamed a continent. In the dust and scuffle of their war with unharnessed nature, they took little time to analyze the nicer moral questions, or to consider the ends to which their warfare led. They worshiped success and its rewards; the stories which made their hearts glow were stories of poor boys grown rich and great—they never inquired how. John D. Rockefeller was long, to his own generation, the pattern for youth that he is to himself.

"WE OF THE THIRTIES"

Then, after that little Spanish War, so poor in action, so rich in consequences, a new earth held up its smoky hands to the same old heaven. We in our thirties and forties, who are now doing and directing that work of America, are not nearly so respectful toward immediate success. We found the continent broken and tamed; we are considering the new forces loosed by the work of the nineteenth century, and wondering how we may reduce them to the power of law before they overwhelm us. It may be a less able generation; it is surely a more moral one. And our chief concern with such a phenomenon as John D. Rockefeller is to see that no one ever repeats his kind of success.

To us of this younger generation our daily press is speaking, for the most part, with a dead voice, because the supreme power resides in men of that older generation. Could the working journalists of our own age tell us as frankly as they wished what they think and see and feel about the times, we should have only minor points to criticize in American journalism.

Selection from *The Brass Check*

UPTON SINCLAIR

Once upon a time there was a little boy; a nice little boy, whom you would have liked if you had known him—at least, so his mother says. He had been brought up in the traditions of the old South, to which the two most important things in the world were good cooking and good manners. He obeyed his mother and father, and ate his peas with a fork, and never buttered the whole slice of his bread. On Sunday mornings he carefully shined his shoes and brushed his clothes at the window, and got into a pair of tight kid gloves and under a tight little brown derby hat, and walked with his parents to a church on Fifth Avenue. On week-days he studied hard and obeyed his teachers, and in every field of thought and activity he believed what was told him by those in authority. He learned the catechism and thought it was the direct word of God. When he fell sick and the doctor came, he put himself in the doctor's hands with a sense of perfect trust and content; the doctor knew what to do, and would do it, and the little boy would get well.

The boy's grandfather had been a Confederate naval officer, drowned at sea. The boy's father had spent his youth in Virginia during the agonies of the Civil War, thus missing most of his education. After the war the family was ruined, and the father had to enter into competition with Yankee "hustle," handicapped by a Southern gentleman's quaint notions of dignity, and also by a Southern

The Brass Check was published in 1919.

gentleman's weakness for mint-juleps. So the last week's board bill was generally a matter of anxiety to the family. But always, no matter how poor the family
might be, the little boy had a clean white collar, and a copy of the *New York
Sun* every morning. This paper was beautifully printed, smooth and neat; the
little boy knew all its peculiarities of type, and he and his father and his mother
accepted every word they read in it, both the news-columns and the editorial
page, precisely as they accepted the doctor's pills and the clergyman's sermons,
the Bible and the multiplication table and Marian Harland's cookbook.

The *New York Sun* was edited by one of the bitterest cynics that ever lived in
America. He had been something of a radical in his early days, and had turned
like a fierce wolf upon his young ideals. He had one fixed opinion, which was
that everything new in the world should be mocked at and denounced. He had
a diabolical wit, and had taught a tradition to his staff, and had infected a good
part of American journalism with the poison of his militant cynicism. Once
every twenty-four hours the little boy absorbed this poison, he took it for truth,
and made all his ideas of it.

For example, there were women who were trying to be different from what
women had always been. There was a thing called "Sorosis." The boy never knew
what "Sorosis" was; from the *Sun* he gathered that it was a collection of women
who wanted to have brains, and to take part in public affairs—whereas the *Sun*
acidly considered that woman's place was the home. And the boy found it easy
to agree with this. Did not the boy's grandmother make the best ginger-cakes of
any grandmother in the whole city of Baltimore? Did not his mother make the
best chocolate cake and the best "hot short-cake"—that is, whenever the family
could escape from boarding houses and have a little kitchen of its own. The boy
was enormously fond of chocolate cake and short-cake, and of course he didn't
want women neglecting their duties for fool things such as "Sorosis."

Also there were the Populists. The little boy had never seen a Populist, he
had never been given an opportunity to read a Populist platform, but he knew
all about the Populists from the funny editorials of Charles A. Dana. The Populists were long-haired and wild-eyed animals whose habit was the corn-fields
of Kansas. The boy knew the names of a lot of them, or rather the nicknames
which Dana gave them; he had a whole portrait-gallery of them in his mind.
Once upon a time the *Sun* gave some statistics from Kansas, suggesting that the
Populists were going insane; so the boy took his pen in hand and wrote a letter
to the editor of the *Sun,* gravely rebuking him. He had never expected to read
in the columns of the *Sun* a suggestion that Populists might go insane. And the
Sun published this feeble product of its own "smartness."

Later on the boy discovered the *New York Evening Post,* the beau ideal of a
gentleman's newspaper, and this became for years his main source of culture.

The *Evening Post* was edited by E. L. Godkin, a scholar and a lover of righteousness, but narrow, and with an abusive tongue. From him the boy learned that American politics was rotten, and he learned the cause of the rottenness: First, there was an ignorant mob, composed mainly of foreigners; and second, there were venal politicians who pandered to this mob. Efforts were continually being made by gentlemen of decency and culture to take the government away from these venal politicians, but the mob was too ignorant, and could not be persuaded to support a clean government. Yet the fight must be kept up, because conditions were going from bad to worse. The boy witnessed several "reform campaigns," conducted mainly by the *Evening Post* and other newspapers. These campaigns consisted in the publication of full-page exposures of civic rottenness, with denunciations of the politicians in office. The boy believed every word of the exposures, and it never occurred to him that the newspapers might be selling more copies by means of them; still less did it occur to him that anybody might be finding in these excitements a means of diverting the mind of the public from larger and more respectable forms of "graft."

There was a candidate for district attorney, William Travers Jerome by name, a man with a typical *Evening Post* mind, making an ideal *Evening Post* candidate. He conducted a "whirlwind" campaign, speaking at half a dozen meetings every evening, and stirring his audience to frenzy by his accounts of the corruption of the city's police-force. Men would stand up and shout with indignation, women would faint or weep. The boy would sit with his fingernails dug into the palms of his hands, while the orator tore away the veils from subjects which were generally kept hidden from little boys.

The orator described the system of prostitution, which was paying its millions every year to the police of the city. He pictured a room in which women displayed their persons, and men walked up and down and inspected them, selecting one as they would select an animal at a fair. The man paid his three dollars, or his five dollars, to a cashier at the window, and received a brass check; then he went upstairs, and paid this check to the woman upon receipt of her favors. And suddenly the orator put his hand into his pocket and drew forth the bit of metal. "Behold!" he cried. "The price of a woman's shame!"

To the lad in the audience this BRASS CHECK was the symbol of the most monstrous wickedness in the world. Night after night he would attend these meetings, and the next day he would read about them in the papers. He was a student at college, living in a lodging-house room on four dollars a week, which he earned himself; yet he pitched in to help this orator's campaign, and raised something over a hundred dollars, and took it to the *Evening Post* candidate at his club, interrupting him at dinner, and no doubt putting a strain on his patience. The candidate was swept into office in a tornado of excitement, and did what all *Evening Post* candidates did and always do—that is, nothing. For four long years the lad waited, in bewilderment and disgust, ending in rage. So he learned the grim lesson that there is more than one kind of parasite feeding on human weakness, there is more than one kind of prostitution which may be symbolized by the BRASS CHECK.

THE STORY OF A POET

The boy, now become a youth, obtained a letter of introduction from his clergyman to the editor of his beloved *Evening Post,* and at the age of sixteen was given a trial as reporter. He worked for a week collecting odd scraps of news, and when the week was over he had earned the generous sum of two dollars and sixty-seven cents. This was his first and last experience as newspaper reporter, and it confirmed his boyish impression of the integrity of the journalistic profession. His work had consisted of compiling obituary notices about leading citizens who had died. "John T. McGurk, senior partner of McGurk and Isaacson, commission-merchants of 679 Desbrosses Street, died yesterday of cirrhosis of the liver at his home, 4321 George Washington Avenue, Hoboken. Mr. McGurk was 69 years of age, and leaves a widow and eleven children. He was a member of the Elks, and president of the North Hoboken Bowling Association." And these facts the *Evening Post* printed exactly as he had written them. In a book which will not have much to say in favor of American journalism, let this fidelity to truth, and to the memory of the blameless McGurk, have its due need of praise.

The youth took to writing jokes and jingles, at which he earned twice as much as the *Evening Post* had paid him. Later he took to writing dime novels, at which he made truly fabulous sums. He found it puzzling that this cheap and silly writing should be the kind that brought the money. The editors told him it was because the public wanted that kind; but the youth wondered—might not at least part of the blame lie with the editors, who never tried giving anything better? It was the old problem—which comes first, the hen or the egg?

We have spoken jestingly of the traditions of the old South, in which the youth was brought up; but the reader should not get a false impression of them—in many ways they were excellent traditions. For one thing, they taught the youth to despise a lie; also to hate injustice, so that wherever in his life he encountered it, his whole being became a blaze of excitement. Always he was striving in his mind to discover the source of lies and injustice—why should there be so much of them in the world? The newspapers revealed the existence of them, but never seemed to know the causes of them, nor what to do about them, further than to support a reform candidate who did nothing but get elected. This futility in the face of the world's misery and corruption was maddening to the youth.

He had rich relatives who were fond of him, so that he was free to escape from poverty into luxury; he had the opportunity to rise quickly in the world, if he would go into business, and devote his attention thereto. But would he find in business the ideals which he craved? He talked with businessmen, also he got the flavor of business from the advertisements in the newspapers—and he knew that this was not what he was seeking. He cultivated the friendship of Jesus, Hamlet, and Shelley, and fell in love with the young Milton and the young Goethe; in them he found his own craving for truth and beauty. Here, through the medium of art, life might be ennobled, and lifted from the muck of graft and greed.

So the youth ran away and buried himself in a hut in the wilds of Canada, and wrote what he thought was the great American novel. It was a painfully crude performance, but it had a new moral impulse in it, and the youth really believed that it was to convert the world to ways of love and justice. He took it to the publishers, and one after another they rejected it. They admitted that it had merit, but it would not sell. Incredible as it seemed to the youth, the test by which the publishers judged an embryo book and its right to be born, was not whether it had a vision and beauty and a new moral impulse; they judged it as the newspapers judged what they published—would it sell? The youth earned some money and published the book himself, and wrote a preface to tell the world what a wonderful book it was, and how the cruel publishers had rejected it. This preface, together with the book, he sent to the leading newspapers; and thus began the second stage of his journalistic experiences!

Two newspapers paid attention to his communication—the New York Times, a respectable paper, and the New York American, a "yellow" paper. The American sent a woman reporter, an agreeable and friendly young lady, to whom the author poured out his soul. She asked for his picture, saying that this would enable her to get much more space for the story; so the author gave his picture. She asked for his wife's picture; but here the author was obdurate. He had old-fashioned Southern notions about "newspaper notoriety" for ladies; he did not want his wife's picture in the papers. There stood a little picture of his wife on the table where the interview took place, and after the reporter had left, it was noticed that this picture was missing. Next day the picture was published in the New York American, and has been published in the New York American every year or. two since. The author, meantime, has divorced his first wife and married a second wife—a fact of which the newspapers are fully aware; yet they publish this picture of the first wife indifferently as a picture of the first wife and of the second wife. When one of these ladies says or does a certain thing, the other lady may open her paper in the morning and receive a shock!

Both the *New York Times* and the *New York American* published interviews with the young author. It had been his fond hope to interest people in his book and to cause them to read his book, but in this he failed; what both the interviews told about was his personality. The editors had been amused by the naive assumption of a young poet that he might have something of importance to say to the world; they had made a "human interest" story out of it, a journalistic tidbit to tickle the appetites of the jaded and worldly-wise. They said scarcely anything about the contents of the book, and as a result of the two interviews, the hungry young author sold precisely two copies!

Meantime he was existing by hack-work, and exploring the world in which ideas are bought and sold. He was having jokes and plots of stories stolen; he was having agreements broken and promises repudiated; he was trying to write worthwhile material, and being told that it would not sell; he was trying to become a book reviewer, and finding that the only way to succeed was to be a cheat. The editor of the *Independent* or the *Literary Digest* would give him half a dozen books to read, and he would read them, and write an honest review, saying that there was very little merit in any of them: whereupon, the editor would decide that it was not worthwhile to review the books, and the author would get nothing for his work. If, on the other hand, he wrote an article about a book, taking it seriously, and describing it as vital and important, the editor would conclude that the book was worth reviewing, and would publish the review, and pay the author three or four dollars for it.

This, you understand, was the "literary world," in which ideas, the most priceless possession of mankind, were made the subject of barter and sale. In every branch of it there were such petty dishonesties, such tricks of the trade. There were always ten times as many people trying to get a living as the trade would support. They were clutching at chances, elbowing each other out of the way; and their efforts were not rewarded according to their love of truth and beauty, but according to quite other factors. They were dressing themselves up and using the "social game," they were exposing and pretending; the women were using the sex lure. And everywhere, when they pretended to care about literature and ideas, they were really caring about money and "success" because it would bring money. Everywhere, above all things else, they hated and feared the very idea of genius, which put them to shame, and threatened with annihilation their petty gains and securities.

From these things the youth fled into the wilderness again, living in a tent with his young wife, and writing a story in which he poured out his contempt upon the great Metropolis of Mammon. This was "Prince Hagen," and he sent it to the *Atlantic Monthly,* and there came a letter from the editor, Professor Bliss Perry, saying that it was a work of merit and that he would publish it. So for weeks the young author walked on the top of the clouds. But then came another letter, saying that the other members of the *Atlantic* staff had read the story, and that Professor Perry had been unable to persuade them to see it as he saw it. "We have," said he, "a very conservative, fastidious and sophisticated constituency."

The young author went back to his "pot-boiling." He spent another winter in New York, wrestling with disillusionments and humiliations, and then, fleeing to that wilderness for a third summer, he put his experience into "The Journal of Arthur Stirling," the story of a young poet who is driven to suicide by neglect and despair. The book was given to the world as a genuine document, and relieved the tedium of a literary season. Its genuineness was accepted almost everywhere, and the author sat behind the scenes, feeling quite devilish. When the secret came out, some critics were cross, and one or two of them have not yet forgiven the writer. The *New York Evening Post* is accustomed to mention the matter every once in a while, declaring that the person who played that trick can never receive anyone's confidence. I will not waste space discussing this question, save to point out that the newspaper reviewers had set the rules of the game—that love and beauty in art were heeded only in connection with personalities and sensation; so, in order to project love and beauty upon the world, the young author had provided the personalities and sensation. As for the *Evening Post* and its self-righteousness, before I finish this book I shall tell of things done by that organ of Wall Street which qualify decidedly its right to sit in judgment upon questions of honor.

THE MENTAL MUNITION-FACTORY

A solution that comes at once to mind is state-owned or municipal-owned newspapers. This is the orthodox Socialist solution, and is also being advocated by William Jennings Bryan. Fortunately, we do not have to take his theories, or anyone's theories; we have facts—the experience of Los Angeles with its public paper, the *Municipal News,* which was an entire success. I inquire of the editor of the paper, Frank E. Wolfe, and he writes:

> The *Municipal News?* There's a rich story buried there. It was established by an initiative ordinance, and had an ample appropriation. It was launched in the stream with engines going full steam ahead. Its success was instantaneous. Free distribution; immense circulation; choked with high-class, high rate advertising; well edited, and it was clean and immensely popular.

Otis said: "Every dollar that damned Socialistic thing gets is a dollar out of the *Times* till." Every publisher in the city reechoed, and the fight was on. The chief thing that rankled, however, was the outgrowth of a clause in the ordinance which gave to each political party polling a three per cent vote a column in each issue for whatsoever purpose it might be used. The Socialist Labor Party nosed out the Prohibitionists by a fluke. The Socialists had a bit of a margin in the preceding elections, so the Reds had two columns, and they were quick to seize the opportunity for propaganda. The Googoos, who had always stoutly denied they were a political party, came forward and claimed space, and the merry war was on. Those two columns for Socialist propaganda were the real cause for the daily onslaught of the painted ladies of Broadway (newspaper district of Los Angeles). There were three morning and three evening papers. Six times a day they whined, barked, yelped, and snapped at the heels of the *Municipal News.* Never were more lies poured out from the mouths of these mothers of falsehood. The little, weakly whelps of the pornographic press took up the hue and cry, and Blanche, Sweetheart, and Tray were on the trail. Advertisers were cajoled, browbeaten, and blackmailed, until nearly all left the paper. The *News* was manned by a picked staff of the best newspapermen on the coast. It was clean, well edited, and gave both sides to all controversies—using the parallel column system. It covered the news of the municipality better than any paper had ever covered it. It was weak and ineffective editorially, for the policy was to print a newspaper. We did not indulge in a clothes-line quarrel—did not fight back.

The *News* died under the axe one year from its birth. They used the initiative to kill it. The rabble rallied to the cry, and we foresaw the end.

The paper had attracted attention all over the English-reading world. Everywhere I have gone I have been asked about it, by people who never dreamed I had been an editor of the paper. Its death was a triumph for reaction, but its effect will not die. Some day the idea will prevail. Then I might want to go back into the "game."

City-owned newspapers are part of the solution, but not the whole part, As a Socialist, I advocate public ownership of the instruments and means of production; but I do not rely entirely upon that method where intellectual matters are concerned. I would have the state make all the steel and coal and oil, the shoes and matches and sugar; I would have it do the distributing of newspapers, and perhaps even the printing; but for the editing of the newspapers I cast about for a method of control that allows free play to the development of initiative and the expression of personality.

In a free society the solution will be simple; there will be many groups and associations, publishing their own papers, and if you do not like the papers which these groups give you, you can form a group of your own. Being in receipt of the full product of your labor, you will have plenty of money, and will be surrounded by other free and independent individuals, also receiving the full product of their labor, and accustomed to combining for the expression of their ideas. The difference is that today the world's resources are in the hands of a class, and this class has a monopoly of self-expression. The problem of transferring such power to the people must be studied as the whole social problem, and not merely as the problem of the press.

Fortunately there are parts of America in which the people have kept at least a part of their economic independence, and have gone ahead to solve the problem of the "kept" press in true American fashion—that is, by organizing and starting honest newspapers for themselves. The editor of the *Nonpartisan Leader,* Oliver S. Morris, has kindly written for me an account of the experiences of the Nonpartisan League, which I summarize as follows:

The League commenced organization work early in 1915 in North Dakota. By the summer of the next year it had forty thousand members, yet no newspaper in the state had given, even as news, a fair account of the League's purposes. Every daily paper in the state was filled with "gross misinformation and absurd lies." So the League started a little weekly paper of its own. With this single weekly, against the entire daily press of the state, it swept the primaries in June 1916.

Then the League decided to have a daily paper. The *Courier-News* of Fargo had been for sale, but the owners would not sell to the League. The League went ahead to start a new paper, actually buying machinery and taking subscriptions; then the *Courier-News* decided to sell, and its circulation under League ownership now exceeds the total population of Fargo.

The League at present has weekly papers in seven states, with a total circulation of two hundred thousand, and another weekly, the *Non-partisan Leader,* published in St. Paul, with a circulation of two hundred and fifty thousand. It is starting co-operative country weekly papers, supervising their editorial policy and furnishing them news and editorial service; over one hundred of these weekly papers are already going. There is another League daily in Grand Forks, North Dakota, and one at Nampa, Idaho. Finally, the League is going ahead on its biggest venture, the establishment of a daily in Minneapolis. This paper is to be capitalized at a million dollars, and the stock is being sold to farmer and labor organizations throughout the state. Says Mr. Morris: "Many wealthy professional and businessmen, disgusted with the controlled press, have purchased stock, and are warm boosters for the League publications." Also he says:

One of the chief results of the establishment of a League press is a different attitude on the part of many existing papers. With competition in the field, many publishers who have hitherto been biased and unfair have been forced to change their tactics. Few of these papers have gone over to the League side of political and economic questions, but they have been forced at least to print fair news reports on both sides of the question in their news columns, reserving their opposition to the movement for their editorial columns. That, of course, is fair enough. The menace of the controlled press in America is due to the fact that as a rule this press does not confine its arguments and opposition to the editorial columns, but uses the news columns for propaganda, and, failing to print the news, printing only a part of it, distorting it or actually lying, sways opinion through the news columns.

Such is the procedure in places where Americans are free. But what about our crowded cities, with their slum populations, speaking forty different languages, illiterate, unorganized, and dumb? Even in these cities there have been efforts made to start newspapers in the interest of the people. I know few more heroic stories than the twenty-year struggle to establish and maintain the *New York Call*. It began as a weekly, *The Worker*. Even that took endless campaigns of begging, and night labor of devoted men and women who earned their livings by day-time labor under the cruel capitalist grind. At last they managed to raise funds to start a daily, and then for ten years it was an endless struggle with debt and starvation. It was a lucky week when the *New York Call* had money enough to pay its printing force; the reporters and editors would sometimes have to wait for months. A good part of the space in the paper had to be devoted to ingenious begging.

The same attempt was made in Chicago, and there bad management and factional quarrels brought a disastrous failure. At the time of writing, there are Socialist dailies in Butte, in Seattle, and in Milwaukee, also a few foreign-language Socialist dailies. There are numerous weeklies and monthlies; but these, of course, do not take the place of newspapers, they are merely a way of pamphleteering. The people read falsehoods all week or all month, and then at last they get what portion of the truth the *Appeal to Reason* or the *Nation* or the *Liberator* or *Pearson's* can find room for. In the meantime the average newspaper reader has had his whole psychology made of lies, so that he cannot believe the truth when he sees it.

There are a few millionaires in America who have liberal tendencies. They have been willing to finance reform campaigns, and in great emergencies to give the facts to the people; they have been willing now and then to back radical magazines, and even to publish them. But—I state the fact, without trying to explain it—there has not yet appeared in America a millionaire willing to found and maintain a fighting daily paper for the abolition of exploitation. I have myself put the proposition before several rich men. I have even known of cases where promises were made, and plans drawn up. My friend Gaylord Wilshire intended to do it with the proceeds of his gold-mine, but the gold-mine has taken long to develop. I had hopes that Henry Ford would do it, when I read of his purchase of the *Dearborn Independent*. I urged the matter upon him with all the eloquence I could muster; he said he meant to do it, but I have my fears. The trouble is his ignorance; he really does not know about the world in which he finds himself, and so far the intellectual value of the *Dearborn Independent* has been close to zero.

So our slum proletariat is left to feed upon the garbage of yellow journalism. Year by year the cost of living increases, and wages, if they move at all, move laggingly, and after desperate and embittered strife. In the midst of this strife the proletariat learns its lessons; it learns to know the clubs of policemen and the bayonets and machine-guns of soldiers; it learns to know capitalist politicians and capitalist judges; also it learns to know Capitalist Journalism! Wherever in America the workers organize and strike for a small portion of their rights, they come out of the experience with a bitter and abiding hatred of the press. I have shown you what happened in Colorado; in West Virginia; in Paterson, New Jersey; in Calumet, Michigan; in Bisbee, Arizona; in Seattle, Washington. I could show you the same thing happening in every industrial center in America.

The workers have come to realize the part which the newspapers play; they have come to know the newspapers as the crux of the argument, the key to the treasure-chamber. A modern newspaper, seen from the point of view of the workers, is a gigantic munition-factory, in which the propertied class manufactures mental bombs and gas-shells for the annihilation of its enemies. And just as in war sometimes the strategy is determined by the location of great munition-factories and depots, so the class-struggle comes to center about newspaper offices. In every great city of Europe where the revolution took place, the first move of the rebels was to seize these offices, and the first move of the reactionaries was to get them back. We saw machine-guns mounted in the windows of newspaper offices, sharpshooters firing from the roofs, soldiers in the streets replying with shrapnel. It is worth noting that wherever the revolutionists were able to take and hold the newspapers, they maintained their revolution; where the newspapers were retaken by the reactionaries, the revolution failed.

In Petrograd the *Little Gazette*, organ of the "Black Hundreds," became the *Red Gazette*, and has remained the *Red Gazette*. The official military organ, the *Army Fleet*, became the *Red Army and Fleet*. The *Will of Russia*, organ of

Protopopov, last premier of the Tsar, became the *Pravda,* which means "Truth." In Berlin, on the other hand, the *Kreuz-Zeitung,* organ of black magic and reaction, became for a few days *Die Rothe Fahne,* the "Red Flag"; but, alas, it went back to *Kreuz-Zeitung* again!

Will it come this way in America? Shall we see mobs storming the offices of the *New York Times* and *World,* and *Chicago Tribune,* the *Los Angeles Times?* It depends entirely upon the extent to which these capitalist newspapers continue to infuriate the workers, and to suppress working-class propaganda with the help of subservient government officials. I personally am not calling for violent revolution; I still hope for the survival of the American system of government. But I point out to the owners and managers of our great capitalist news-organs the peril in which they place themselves, by their system of organized lying about the radical movement. It is not only the fury of resentment they awaken in the hearts of class-conscious workingmen and women; it is the condition of unstable equilibrium which they set up in society, by the mass of truth they suppress. Today every class-conscious workingman carries about with him as his leading thought, that if only he and his fellows could take the printing-offices and hold them for ten days, they could end forever the power of Capitalism, they could make safe the Co-operative Commonwealth of America.

I say ten days, and I do not speak loosely. Just imagine if the newspapers of America were to print the truth for ten days! The truth about poverty, and the causes of poverty; the truth about corruption in politics and in all branches of government, in journalism, and throughout the business world; the truth about profiteering and exploitation, about the banking graft, the plundering of the railroads, the colossal gains of the Beef Trust and the Steel Trust and the Oil Trust and their hundreds of subsidiary organizations; the truth about conditions in industry, the suppression of labor-revolts and the corrupting of labor movements; above all, the truth about the possibilities of production by modern machinery, the fact that, by abolishing production for profit and substituting production for use, it would be possible to provide abundance....

THE PROBLEM OF THE REPORTER

... Must a reporter be a cringing wretch, or else a man of honor in search of a job? Might not a reporter be a member of an honored profession, having its own standards, its sense of duty to the public? Obviously, the first trouble is that in his economic status the reporter is a sweated wage slave. If reporting is to become a profession, the reporters must organize, and have power to fix, not merely their wage-scale, but also their ethical code. I wrote an article calling for a "reporters' union," and [Isaac] Russell [a reporter for the *New York Times*] began to agitate among New York newspapermen for this idea, which has now spread all over the country.

What would be the effect upon news writing of a reporters' union? What assurances have we that reporters would be better than owners? Well, in the first place, reporters are young men, and owners are nearly always old men; so in the newspaper world you have what you have in the world of finance, of diplomacy, of politics and government—a "league of the old men," giving orders to the young men, holding the young men down. The old men own most of the property, the young men own little of the property; so control by old men is property control, while control by young men would be control by human beings.

I have met some newspaper reporters who were drunken scoundrels. I have met some who were as cruel and unscrupulous as the interests they served. But the majority of newspaper reporters are decent men, who hate the work they do, and would gladly do better if it were possible....

THE PRESS SET FREE

Some years ago Allan Benson told me of his troubles as an honest journalist; I asked him to repeat them for this book, and he answered:

> I doubt if my experiences as a daily newspaper editor would serve your purpose. When I was a daily editor I edited. I printed what I pleased. If I could not do so, I resigned. I didn't resign with a bank account to fall back upon—I resigned broke.

I am sorry that I struck my friend Benson in an uncommunicative mood. It doesn't in the least interfere with my thesis to learn that some editors resign; it's plain enough to the dullest mind that it doesn't help the public when an honest man resigns, and a rogue or a lickspittle takes his place....

Here, as everywhere, the salvation of the world rests upon you, the workers of hand and brain. I took up half this book telling how the capitalist press lied about one man; you said, perhaps, that I liked to be in the "limelight"; anyhow, I was only one writer-fellow, and it didn't matter to you what the newspaper did to a writer-fellow. But now I make my appeal for yourself, for your wives and your children. I have shown you how this knavish press turns the world against you; I have shown how it turns you against yourself—how it seduces you, poisons your mind, breaks your heart. You go on strike, and it plays upon your fears, it uses your hunger and want as weapons against you; it saps your strength, it eats out your soul, it smothers your thinking under mountain-loads of lies. You fall, and the chariot of Big Business rolls over you.

These men who own the world in which you struggle for life—what is it that they want? They want power, power to rule you. And what is it that you want? You want power to rule yourself. Between those two wants there is eternal and unending and irreconcilable war—such is the class struggle, and whether you will or not, you take your part in it, and I take mine, I, a writer-fellow who wants to write the truth, appeal to you, the laboring fellows of hand and brain, who want to read the truth, who *must* read the truth, if civilization is not to perish. I cry to you: "Help! Help against the lying, kept press!"

I cry to you for the integrity of your calling, for the honor and dignity of Journalism. I cry to you that Journalism shall no longer be the thing described by Charles A. Dana, master-cynic of the *New York Sun*, "buying white paper at two cents a pound and selling it at ten cents a pound." I cry to you that Journalism shall be a public ministry, and that you who labor in it shall be, not wage-slaves and henchmen of privilege, but servants of the general welfare, helping your fellow-men to understand life, and to conquer the evils in nature outside them, and in their own hearts. Why cannot the men and women of this great profession form a society with a common mind and a common interest and a common conscience, based upon the fact that they are all necessary, they have each, down to the humblest office-boy, their essential part in a great social service?

By the blindness and greed of ruling classes the people have been plunged into infinite misery; but that misery has its purpose in the scheme of nature. Something more than a century ago we saw the people driven by just such misery to grope their way into a new order of society; they threw off the chains of hereditary monarchy, and made themselves citizens of free republics. And now again we face such a crisis; only this time it is in the world of industry that we have to abolish hereditary rule, and to build an industrial commonwealth in which the equal rights of all men are recognized by law. Such is the task before us; go to it with joy and certainty, playing your part in the making of the new world, in which there shall be neither slavery nor poverty, in which the natural sources of wealth belong to all men alike, and not one lives in idleness upon the labor of his fellows. That world lies just before you and the gates to it are barred only by ignorance and prejudice, deliberately created and maintained by prostitute journalism.

A FRAME-UP THAT FELL DOWN

When I first talked over this book with my wife, she gave me a bit of advice: "Give your facts first, and then call your names." So throughout this book I have not laid much stress on the book's title. Perhaps you are wondering just where the title comes in!

What is the Brass Check? The Brass Check is found in your pay-envelope every week—you who write and print and distribute our newspapers and magazines. The Brass Check is the price of your shame—you who take the fair body of truth and sell it in the market-place, who betray the virgin hopes of mankind into the loathsome brothel of Big Business. And down in the counting-room below sits the "madame" who profits by your shame; unless, perchance, she is off at Palm Beach or Newport, flaunting her jewels and her feathers.

Please do not think that I am just slinging ugly words. Off and on for years I have thought about this book, and figured over the title, and what it means; I assert that the Brass Check which serves in the house of ill-fame as "the price of a woman's shame" is, both in its moral implications and in its social effect, precisely and identically the same as the gold and silver coins and pieces of written paper that are found every week in the pay-envelopes of those who write and print and distribute capitalist publications.

The prostitution of the body is a fearful thing. The young girl, trembling with a strange emotion of which she does not know the meaning, innocent, confiding and tender, is torn from her home and started on a road to ruin and despair. The lad, seeking his mate and the fulfillment of his destiny, sees the woman of his dreams turn into a foul harpy, bearer of pestilence and death. Nature, sumptuous, magnificent, loving life, cries: "Give me children!" And the answer comes: "We give you running sores and bursting glands, rotting lips and festering noses, swollen heads and crooked joints, idiot gabblings and maniac shrieks, pistols to blow out your brains and poisons to still your agonies." Such is the prostitution of the body.

But what of the mind? The mind is master of the body, and commands what the body shall do and what it shall become; therefore, always, the prostitution of the mind precedes and causes the prostitution of the body. Youth cries: "Life is beautiful, joyous! Give me light, that I may keep my path!" The answer comes: "Here is darkness, that you may stumble, and beat your face upon the stones!" Youth cries: "Give me Hope." The answer comes: "Here is Cynicism." Youth cries: "Give me understanding, that I may live in harmony with my fellow-men." The answer comes: "Here are lies about your fellow-men, that you may hate them, that you may cheat them, that you may live among them as a wolf among wolves!" Such is the prostitution of the mind.

When I planned this book I had in mind a sub-title: *A Study of the Whore of Journalism.* A shocking subtitle; but then, I was quoting the Bible, and the Bible is the inspired word of God. It was surely one of God's prophets who wrote this invitation to the reading of *The Brass Check:*

Come hither; I will shew unto thee the judgment of the great whore that sitteth upon many waters;

With whom the kings of the earth have committed fornication, and the inhabitants of the earth have been made drunk with the wine of her fornication.

For eighteen hundred years men have sought to probe the vision of that aged seer of the lonely isle of Patmos. Listen to his strange words:

So he carried me away in the spirit into the wilderness: and I saw a woman sit upon a scarlet colored beast, full of names of blasphemy, having seven heads and ten horns. And the woman was arrayed in purple and scarlet color, and decked with gold and precious stones and pearls, having a golden cup in her hands full of abominations and filthiness of her fornication:

And upon her forehead was a name written, MYSTERY, BABYLON THE GREAT, THE MOTHER OF HARLOTS AND ABOMINATIONS OF THE EARTH.

Now, surely, this mystery is a mystery no longer! Now we know what the seer of Patmos was foreseeing—Capitalist Journalism! And when I call upon you, class-conscious workers of hand and brain, to organize and destroy this mother of all iniquities, I do not have to depart from the language of the ancient scriptures. I say to you in the words of the prophet Ezekiel:

So the spirit took me up, and brought me into the inner court; and behold, the glory of the Lord filled the house.

And I heard him speaking unto me out of the house:

Now let them put away their whoredom, and the carcasses of their kings, far from me, and I will dwell in the midst of them forever.

As I am about to send this book to press, I take one last look at the world around me. Half a million coal-miners have struck, a court injunction has forced the leaders to call off the strike, the miners are refusing to obey their leaders—and the newspapers of the entire United States are concealing the facts. For a week it has been impossible for me to learn, except from vague hints, what is happening in the coal-strike. And at the same time, because of false newspaper stories from Centralia, Washington, a "white terror" reigns in the entire West, and thousands of radicals are beaten, jailed, and shot.

I have pleaded and labored long to avoid a violent revolution in America; I intend to go on pleading and laboring to the last hour. I know that thousands of my readers will, like myself, be desperately anxious for something they can do. I decided to work out a plan of action; something definite, practical, and immediate.

I propose that we shall found and endow a weekly publication of truth-telling, to be known as "The National News." This publication will carry no advertisements and no editorials. It will not be a journal of opinion, but a record of events pure and simple. It will be published on ordinary newsprint paper, and in the cheapest possible form. It will have one purpose and one only, to give to the American people once every week the truth about the world's events. It will be strictly and absolutely nonpartisan, and never the propaganda organ of any cause. It will watch the country, and see where lies are being circulated and truth suppressed; its job will be to nail the lies, and bring the truth into the light of day. I believe that a sufficient number of Americans are awake to the dishonesty of our press to build up for such a paper a circulation of a million inside of a year....

Our editor will not give much space to the news that all other papers publish. The big story for him will be what the other papers let alone. He will employ trained investigators, and set them to work for a week, or maybe for several months, getting the facts about the lobby of the Beef Trust in Washington, the control of our public schools in the interest of militarism, the problem of who is paying the expenses of the American railway mission in Siberia. Needless to say, the capitalist press will provide the "National News" with a complete monopoly of this sort of work. Also it will provide the paper with many deliberate falsehoods to be nailed. When this is done, groups of truth-loving people will buy these papers by the thousands, and blue-pencil and distribute them. So the "National News" will grow, and the "kept" press will be moved by the only force it recognizes—loss of money.

There are in America millions of people who could not be persuaded to read a Socialist paper, or a labor paper, or a single tax paper; but there are very few who could not be persuaded to read a paper that gives the news and proves by continuous open discussion that it really does believe in "the truth, the whole truth, and nothing but the truth." I do not think I'm too optimistic when I say that such a publication, with a million in circulation, would change the whole tone of American public life.

Selection from the "Report of the Commission
on Freedom of the Press"

ROBERT MAYNARD HUTCHINS

WHAT CAN BE DONE?

The thirteen recommendations made in this chapter reflect the conviction, stated at the beginning of this report, that there are no simple solutions to the problem of freeing the press from the influences which now prevent it from supplying the communication of news and ideas needed by the kind of society we have and the kind of society we desire.

These recommendations have been grouped according to the source from which action must come—government (including the courts), the press itself, and the public. We consider it particularly important to lay before the press and the public the measures which each of them may take in order that the press may give the service which the country requires and which newspapers, magazines, books, motion pictures, and radio, as now technically equipped, are capable of furnishing. The more the press and the public are willing to do, the less will be left for the state; but we place our recommendations as to legal action first because freedom of the press is most commonly thought of in relation to the activities of government.

We do not believe that the fundamental problems of the press will be solved by more laws or by governmental action. The Commission places its main reli-

This report was issued in 1947.

ance on the mobilization of the elements of society acting directly on the press and not through governmental channels.

No democracy, however, certainly not the American democracy, will indefinitely tolerate concentrations of private power irresponsible and strong enough to thwart the aspirations of the people. Eventually governmental power will be used to break up private power, or governmental power will be used to regulate private power—if private power is at once great and irresponsible.

Our society requires agencies of mass communication. They are great concentrations of private power. If they are irresponsible, not even the First Amendment will protect their freedom from governmental control. The amendment will be amended.

In the judgment of the Commission everyone concerned with the freedom of the press and with the future of democracy should put forth every effort to make the press accountable, for, if it does not become so of its own motion, the power of government will be used, as a last resort, to force it to be so.

The American people recognize that there are some things the government should do. For example, Americans place their trust in private enterprise, but they do not object to having the government run the post office. They believe in individual initiative, but they do not carry the doctrine of self-help so far as to dispense with courts of law. Though we may like to think of government merely as a policeman, we know that it does play a positive role at many points in our society and that in any highly industrialized society it must do so.

Under our system the legislature may pass no law abridging the freedom of the press. But this has never been thought to mean that the general laws of the country were inapplicable to the press. The First Amendment was intended to guarantee free expression, not to create a privileged industry. Nor has the First Amendment been interpreted to prevent the adoption of special laws governing certain types of utterance. Nor is there anything in the First Amendment or in our political tradition to prevent the government from participating in mass communications: to state its own case, to supplement private sources of information, and to propose standards for private emulation. Such participation by government is not dangerous to the freedom of the press.

The principal aim of this section of our report is not to recommend more governmental action but to clarify the role of government in relation to mass communication.

1. We recommend that the constitutional guarantees of the freedom of the press be recognized as including the radio and motion pictures.

In view of the approaching advent of the broadcast facsimile newspaper and the development of the newsreel and the documentary film, constitutional safeguards for the radio and the motion picture are needed more than ever. We believe that such regulation of these media as is desirable can and should be conducted within the limitations which the federal and state constitutions now place upon the regulation of newspapers and books....

In the case of radio this recommendation would give constitutional support to the prohibition against censorship in the Communications Act. It would not prevent the Federal Communications Commission from denying a license on the ground that the applicant was unprepared to serve the public interest, convenience, and necessity. Nor would it prevent the Commission from considering, in connection with an application for renewal, whether the applicant had kept the promises he made when the license was granted and had actually served the public interest, convenience, and necessity. This recommendation is intended to strengthen the prohibition against censorship, not to guarantee licensees a perpetual franchise regardless of their performance. The air belongs to the public, not to the radio industry.

2. We recommend that government facilitate new ventures in the communications industry, that it foster the introduction of new techniques, that it maintain competition among large units through the antitrust laws, but that those laws be sparingly used to break up such units, and that, where concentration is necessary in communications, the government endeavor to see to it that the public gets the benefit of such concentration.

We accept the fact that some concentration must exist in the communications industry if the country is to have the service it needs. People need variety and diversity in mass communication; they must also have service, a quantity and quality of information and discussion which can often be supplied only by large units.

The possibilities of evil inherent in concentration can be minimized by seeing to it that no artificial obstructions impede the creation and development of new units. In the communications industry it is difficult to start new units because of the large investment required and because of the control of the existing units over the means of distribution.

Little can be done by government or any other agency to reduce the cost of entering the industry except to adjust governmental charges, such as tax laws and postal rates, to facilitate new enterprises, and to prevent established interests from obstructing the introduction of new techniques. Tax laws and postal rates should be restudied with a view to discovering whether they do not discriminate against new, small businesses and in favor of large, well-established ones.

As for new techniques, an invention like FM radio offers the possibility of greatly increasing quantity and diversity in broadcasting. The cost of the equipment is low, and the number of frequencies large. We believe that the Federal Communications Commission should fully exploit the opportunity now before it and should prevent any greater concentration in FM radio than the service requires.

Government can stop the attempt by existing units of the press to monopolize distribution outlets. The types of governmental action called for range from police protection and city ordinances which would make it possible for new newspapers and magazines to get on the newsstands to antitrust suits against motion picture companies which monopolize theaters.

The main function of government in relation to the communications industry is to keep the channels open, and this means, in part, facilitating in every way short of subsidy the creation of new units in the industry.

The Commission believes that there should be active competition in the communications industry. It inclines to the view that the issue of the size of the units competing is not one which can best be dealt with by law. The antitrust laws can be invoked to maintain competition among large units and to prevent the exclusion of any unit from facilities which ought to be open to all; their use to force the breaking-up of large units seems to us undesirable.

Though there can be no question that the antitrust laws apply to the communications industry, we would point out that these laws are extremely vague. They can be very dangerous to the freedom and the effectiveness of the press. They can be used to limit voices in opposition and to hinder the processes of public education.

Since the Commission looks principally to the units of the press itself to take joint action to provide the diversity, quantity, and quality of information and discussion which a free society requires, it would not care to see such action blocked by the mistaken application of the antitrust laws. Honest efforts to raise standards, such as we suggest elsewhere in this chapter, would not be thwarted, even though they result in higher costs.

Since the need for service is the justification for concentration, the government should see to it that, where concentration exists, the service is rendered; it should see to it that the public gets the benefit of the concentration. For example, the Federal Communications Commission should explore the possibilities of requiring the radio networks to increase the number of their affiliated stations and of using clear-channel licenses as a means of serving all the less populous regions of the country. The extension of radio service of the quality supplied by the networks and the maintenance and multiplication of local stations are of the first importance. There are only two ways of obtaining these results: they can be achieved by the acceptance of responsibility by the industry, or they can be achieved by government ownership. We prefer the former.

3. As an alternative to the present remedy for libel, we recommend legislation by which the injured party might obtain a retraction or a restatement of the facts by the offender or an opportunity to reply.

The only legal method by which a person injured by false statements in the press may vindicate his reputation is a civil action for damages. The remedy is expensive, difficult, and encumbered with technicalities. Many injured persons hesitate to sue because of the "shadow of racketeering and blackmail which hangs over libel plaintiffs."

The proposed remedy should operate quickly while the issue is before the public. It should lead to an increase in the practice, now common among the responsible members of the press, of voluntarily correcting misstatements. It ought to diminish lying in the press.

We are opposed to the group libel laws now under discussion in several states. We believe that an action for libel should be a civil suit brought by a person who can show that he, as an individual, was damaged by a false statement about him. We fear that, if an individual may sue or initiate a criminal prosecution, because a group he belongs to has been criticized falsely, the law might be used to suppress legitimate public controversy. The Commission has given extensive consideration to numerous suggested methods of reducing lying in the press by law. We insist that, morally considered, the freedom of the press is a conditional right—conditional on the honesty and responsibility of writer, broadcaster, or publisher. A man who lies, intentionally or carelessly, is not morally entitled to claim the protection of the First Amendment. The remedy for press lying, however, must go deeper than the law can go. We are reluctant to suggest governmental interference with the freedom of the press; we see many difficulties of enforcement; we do not find in the present situation justification for stronger legislation than that which we here propose.

4. We recommend the repeal of legislation prohibiting expressions in favor of revolutionary changes in our institutions where there is no clear and present danger that violence will result from the expressions.

The Supreme Court has held that expressions urging the overthrow of the government by force are within the protection of the First Amendment unless there is a clear and present danger that these expressions will lead to violence. We believe that this sound principle is violated by the peacetime sedition clauses of the Alien Registration Act of 1940 and by the various state syndicalism acts which make it a crime to advocate the overthrow of the government by force, irrespective of the probable effect of the statements. The really dangerous persons within the scope of these laws can be reached by the conspiracy statutes and the general criminal law. As applied to other persons, which is most likely to be the case, these laws are of dubious constitutionality and unwise. Yet only a few of the agitators who are prosecuted can succeed in getting before the Supreme Court. Consequently, so long as this legislation remains on the statute books, its intimidating effect is capable of stifling political and economic discussion. These acts ought to be repealed.

5. We recommend that the government, through the media of mass communication, inform the public of the facts with respect to its policies and of the purposes underlying those policies and that, to the extent that private agencies of mass communication are unable or unwilling to supply such media to the government, the government itself may employ media of its own.

We also recommend that, where the private agencies of mass communication are unable or unwilling to supply information about this country to a particular foreign country or countries, the government employ mass communication media of its own to supplement this deficiency.

We should not think it worthwhile to make the recommendations if it were not for the fact that in recent years there have been increasingly strident charges that the government is exceeding its proper functions and wasting the taxpayers' money when it undertakes to inform the people in regard to its program or to supplement and correct the picture of this country which the press has projected to other parts of the world or which results from misinformation or lack of information.

Doubtless some governmental officers have used their publicity departments for personal or partisan aggrandizement. But this evil is subject to correction by normal democratic processes and does not compare with the danger that the people of this country and other countries may, in the absence of official information and discussion, remain unenlightened on vital issues.

In addition to supplying information at home and abroad, the government has special obligations in international communications, which are elaborated in *Peoples Speaking to Peoples:* to use its influence to reduce press rates all over the world; to obtain equal access to the news for all; to break down barriers to the free flow of information; and to collaborate with the United Nations in promoting the widest dissemination of news and discussion by all the techniques which become available.

WHAT CAN BE DONE BY THE PRESS?

The recommendations we have made for action by government, though they are minimal, could be reduced still further in the domestic field, at least, by the action of the press itself. Existing units of the press could abstain from attempts to monopolize distribution outlets; they could insist that new techniques be made available and freely used; the press could of its own motion make it a rule that a person injured by a false statement should have an opportunity to reply. We believe that these changes are bound to come through legislation if they do not come through the action of the press and that it would be the part of wisdom for the press to take these measures on its own initiative.

The communications industry in the United States is and, in the opinion of the Commission, should remain a private business. But it is a business affected with a public interest. The Commission does not believe that it should be regulated by government like other businesses affected with a public interest, such as railroads and telephone companies. The Commission hopes that the press itself will recognize its public responsibility and obviate governmental action to enforce it.

It may be argued that the variety, quantity, and quality of information and discussion which we expect from the press cannot be purveyed at a profit and that a business which cannot operate at a profit cannot last under a system of private enterprise. It has been said that, if the press is to continue as a private business, it can succeed only as other retailers succeed, that is, by giving the customers what they want. On this theory the test of public service is financial success. On this theory, too, the press is bound by what it believes to be the interests and tastes of the mass audience; these interests and tastes are discovered by finding out what the mass audience will buy. On this theory, if the press tries to rise higher than the interests and tastes of the mass audience as they are revealed at the newsstands or at the box office, it will be driven into bankruptcy, and its existence as a private business will be at an end.

We have weighed the evidence carefully and do not accept this theory. As the example of many ventures in the communications industry shows, good practice in the interest of public enlightenment is good business as well. The agencies of mass communication are not serving static wants. Year by year they are building and transforming the interests of the public. They have an obligation to elevate rather than to degrade them.

The gist of the recommendations in this section of our report is that the press itself should assume the responsibility of providing the variety, quantity, and quality of information and discussion which the country needs. This seems to us largely a question of the way in which the press looks at itself. We suggest that the press look upon itself as performing a public service of a professional kind. Whatever may be thought of the conduct of individual members of the older, established professions, like law and medicine, each of these professions as a whole accepts a responsibility for the service rendered by the profession as a whole, and there are some things which a truly professional man will not do for money.

1. We recommend that the agencies of mass communication accept the responsibilities of common carriers of information and discussion.

Those agencies of mass communication which have achieved a dominant position in their areas can exert an influence over the minds of their audience too powerful to be disregarded. We do not wish to break up these agencies, because to do so would break up the service they can render. We do not wish to have them owned or controlled by government. They must therefore themselves be hospitable to ideas and attitudes different from their own, and they must present them to the public as meriting its attention. In no other way can the danger to the mind of democracy which is inherent in the present concentration be avoided.

2. We recommend that the agencies of mass communication assume the responsibility of financing new, experimental activities in their fields.

Here we have in mind activities of high literary, artistic, or intellectual quality which do not give promise of immediate financial return but which may offer long-term rewards. Only in a few metropolitan areas can the citizen easily gain access to a wide variety of motion pictures and radio programs. Elsewhere discriminating, serious minorities are prisoners of the estimate of mass taste made by the industry. Motion pictures, radio programs, newspapers, and magazines aimed at these minorities may not make money at the beginning. They require a considerable investment. They do not attract capital seeking quick profits. Nonprofit institutions can do something in this field, but they should not be expected to do the whole job. The responsibility of the industry for diversity and quality means that it should finance ventures of this kind from the profits of its other business.

3. We recommend that the members of the press engage in vigorous mutual criticism.

Professional standards are not likely to be achieved as long as the mistakes and errors, the frauds and crimes, committed by units of the press are passed over in silence by other members of the profession. As we indicated in Chapter 5, the formal organization of the press into a profession, with power in the organization to deprive an erring member of his livelihood, is unlikely and perhaps undesirable. We have repeatedly evidenced our desire that the power of government should not be invoked to punish the aberrations of the press. If the press is to be accountable—and it must be if it is to remain free—its members must discipline one another by the only means they have available, namely, public criticism.

4. We recommend that the press use every means that can be devised to increase the competence, independence, and effectiveness of its staff.

The quality of the press depends in large part upon the capacity and independence of the working members in the lower ranks. At the present time their wages and prestige are low and their tenure precarious. Adequate compensation, adequate recognition, and adequate contracts seem to us an indispensable prerequisite to the development of professional personnel.

Elsewhere in this chapter we shall refer to education for journalism. Here we would merely indicate that the press can do a good deal to improve the quality of its staff by promoting an intelligent educational program, both for young people and for men and women who are already at work in the field. The type of educational experience provided for working journalists by the Nieman fellowships at Harvard seems to deserve extension, if not through private philanthropy, then with the financial assistance of the press itself.

5. We recommend that the radio industry take control of its programs and that it treat advertising as it is treated by the best newspapers.

Radio cannot become a responsible agency of communication as long as its programming is controlled by the advertisers. No newspaper would call itself respectable if its editorial columns were dominated by its advertisers and if it published advertising, information, and discussion so mixed together that the reader could not tell them apart. The importance and validity of this recommendation seem to us so obvious as not to require argument. Radio is one of the most powerful means of communication known to man. With the advent of facsimile and television, it will become more powerful still. The public should not be forced to continue to take its radio fare from the manufacturers of soap, cosmetics, cigarettes, soft drinks, and packaged foods.

WHAT CAN BE DONE BY THE PUBLIC?

The people of this country are the purchasers of the products of the press. The effectiveness of buyers' boycotts, even of very little ones, has been amply demonstrated. Many of these boycotts are the wrong kind for the wrong purposes; they are the work of pressure groups seeking to protect themselves from justifiable criticism or to gain some special advantage. The success of their efforts indicates what a revolt of the American people against the service given them by the press might accomplish.

We are not in favor of a revolt and hope that less drastic means of improving the press may be employed. We cannot tell what direction a revolt might take; it might lead to government control or to the emasculation of the First Amendment. We want the press to be free, and a revolt against the press conducted for the purpose of giving the country a truly free press might end in less freedom than we have today.

What is needed, first of all, is recognition by the American people of the vital importance of the press in the present world crisis. We have the impression that the American people do not realize what has happened to them. They are not aware that the communications revolution has occurred. They do not appreciate the tremendous power which the new instruments and the new organizations of the press place in the hands of a few men. They have not yet understood how far the performance of the press falls short of the requirements of a free society in the world today. The principal object of our report is to make these points clear.

If these points are clear, what can the people do about them? They have, or they can create, agencies which can be used to supplement the press, to propose standards for its emulation, and to hold it to its accountability.

1. We recommend that nonprofit institutions help supply the variety, quantity, and quality of press service required by the American people.

We have indicated our belief that the agencies of mass communication have a responsibility to the public like that of educational institutions. We now wish to add that educational institutions have a responsibility to the public to use the instruments employed by the agencies of mass communications. The radio, the motion picture, television, and facsimile broadcasting are the most powerful means of molding the minds of men. That is why we worry about their exclusive appropriation by agencies engaged in the pursuit of profit. Not that educational institutions are free from financial problems and the pressures associated with them. But the nonprofit corporation does not exist for the purpose of making profits. It is peculiarly able to enlist the cooperation of all who are interested in the cultural development of the country. Hence it can render those services which commercial enterprise cannot offer on a profit-making basis.

It can restore an element of diversity to the information and discussion reaching the public by organizing the demand for good things and by putting out good things itself. A chain of libraries, schools, colleges, and universities, together with the various religious organizations, could establish the documentary film in mass communication. A chain of educational FM stations could put before the public the best thought of America and could make many present radio programs look as silly as they are.

The business of organizing demand requires nothing but realization of the importance of the opportunity and cooperation, to which educational institutions are notoriously averse. The business of putting out good things requires in addition a determined effort to acquire the professional skill that is needed if the efforts of nonprofit corporations are not to be scorned as the work of second-rate amateurs.

We cannot believe that nonprofit institutions will continue to fail to grasp the opportunity they have before them. It has always been clear that education is a process which goes on through the whole of life. It has always been clear that, as working hours diminished and leisure increased, a responsibility devolved upon educators to help people make wise use of their leisure. Now a new urgency is added to this duty. The world seems on the brink of suicide, and the ultimate catastrophe can be avoided only if the adult citizens of today can learn how to live together in peace. It will not be enough to educate the rising generation; the time is too short. The educators have the enormous task of trying to make the peoples of the earth intelligent now. It is fortunate that, as their task has grown greater and more pressing, technology has given them new instruments of incredible range and power.

2. We recommend the creation of academic-professional centers of advanced study, research, and publication in the field of communications. We recommend further that existing schools of journalism exploit the total resources of their universities to the end that their students may obtain the broadest and most liberal training.

The importance of the field of communications does not seem to us to have been adequately recognized by the educational institutions of the country. We doubt that new professional or technical training schools should be established in this area. We do see, however, a need for centers of investigation, graduate study, and critical publication. These are, in fact, so important that without them it is unlikely that the professional practices and attitudes which we recommend to the press can ever become characteristic of the communications industry.

Preparation for work in the press seems to us to require the best possible general education. It is important that students who enter schools of journalism should not be deprived of liberal education because they have made up their minds that they want to work in the press. Few schools of journalism can develop a liberal curriculum within their own faculties. It is therefore imperative that they associate themselves as closely as possible with other departments and schools of their universities.

3. We recommend the establishment of a new and independent agency to appraise and report annually upon the performance of the press.

The public makes itself felt by the press at the present time chiefly through pressure groups. These groups are quite as likely to have bad influence as good. In this field we cannot turn to government as the representative of the people as a whole, and we would not do so if we could. Yet it seems to us clear that some agency which reflects the ambitions of the American people for its press should exist for the purpose of comparing the accomplishments of the press with the aspirations which the people have for it. Such an agency would also educate the people as to the aspirations which they ought to have for the press.

The Commission suggests that such a body be independent of government and of the press; that it be created by gifts; and that it be given a ten-year trial, at the end of which an audit of its achievement could determine anew the institutional form best adapted to its purposes.

The activities of such an agency would include:

1. Continuing efforts, through conference with practitioners and analysis by its staff, to help the press define workable standards of performance, a task on which our Commission has attempted a beginning.
2. Pointing out the inadequacy of press service in certain areas and the trend toward concentration in others, to the end that local communities and the press itself may organize to supply service where it is lacking or to provide alternative service where the drift toward monopoly seems dangerous.
3. Inquiries in areas where minority groups are excluded from reasonable access to the channels of communication.
4. Inquiries abroad regarding the picture of American life presented by the American press; and cooperation with agencies in other countries and with international agencies engaged in analysis of communication across national borders.
5. Investigation of instances of press lying, with particular reference to persistent misrepresentation of the data required for judging public issues.
6. Periodic appraisal of the tendencies and characteristics of the various branches of the communications industry.
7. Continuous appraisal of governmental action affecting communications.
8. Encouragement of the establishment of centers of advanced study, research, and criticism in the field of communications at universities.
9. Encouragement of projects which give hope of meeting the needs of special audiences.
10. The widest possible publicity and public discussion on all the foregoing.

The above recommendations taken together give some indication of methods by which the press may become accountable and hence remain free. We believe that if they are carried out, press performance will be brought much closer to the five ideal demands of society for the communication of news and ideas which were set forth in the second chapter: (1) a truthful, comprehensive, and intelligent account of the day's events in a context which gives them meaning; (2) a forum for the exchange of comment and criticism; (3) the projection of a representative picture of the constituent groups in the society; (4) the presentation and clarification of the goals and values of the society; (5) full access to the day's intelligence.

Plainly, each of these five ideals will be served by more than one of our recommendations. Instead of stating those relationships in detail, we think that it will be more helpful to point out how the various recommendations will supplement each other in remedying some aspects of the press as it now exists which have constantly disturbed the members of the Commission during our investigation.

The failure of radio to reach all citizens adequately can be relieved through the licensing policy of the F.C.C., while the international coverage of American news and opinions can be extended by various measures proposed in *Peoples Speaking to Peoples.*

Deliberate falsifications and reckless misstatements of fact will be lessened by a new legal remedy compelling the publication of a retraction or reply and, even more, by the assumption of a greater responsibility for accuracy on the part of the press, by the readiness of newspapers and other agencies of communication to criticize one another for gross departures from truthfulness, and by periodic appraisals of press accuracy issuing from a body of citizens.

The inclination of the press to adapt most of its output to the supposed desires of the largest possible number of consumers and the resulting trends toward sensationalism and meaninglessness can be reduced by similar periodical appraisals from citizens and by the initiation of new activities for the benefit of specialized audiences on the part of the press itself as well as nonprofit institutions. In the case of radio, the quality of output can be improved through organizations of listeners in the communities and through the determination of the industry to take control of its programs out of the hands of the advertisers and their agents.

The greatest difficulty in preserving free communications in a technical society arises from the concentration of power within the instruments of communication. The most conspicuous example of this is in the ownership of instrumentalities, but the concentration also exists in the power of advertisers, of labor organizations, of organized pressure groups—all capable of impairing the free interchange of news and ideas. The danger is that the entire function of communications will fall under the control of fewer and fewer persons.

Among the consequences of this concentration, the output of the press reflects the bias of owners and denies adequate expression to important elements in communities.

In order to counteract the evil effects of concentration, we have urged that newspapers and other agencies of mass communication regard themselves as common carriers of information and discussion, that the entry of new units into the field be facilitated, and that the government prevent monopolistic control of outlets by the sources of production.

Finally, members of the Commission were disturbed by finding that many able reporters and editorial writers displayed frustration—the feeling that they were not allowed to do the kind of work which their professional ideals demanded, that they were unable to give the service which the community needs from the press. A continuation of this disturbing situation will prevent the press from discharging its responsibilities toward society. As remedies we have urged the press to use every means that can be devised to increase the competence and independence of the staff, and we have urged universities and schools of journalism to train existing or potential members of the press in the exercise of judgment on public affairs. In many different ways the rank and file of the press can be developed into a genuine profession.

The outside forces of law and public opinion can in various ways check bad aspects of press performance, but good press performance can come only from the human beings who operate the instrumentalities of communication.

We believe that our recommendations, taken together, give some indication of methods by which the press may become accountable and, hence, remain free. The urgent and perplexing issues which confront our country, the new dangers which encompass our free society, the new fatefulness attaching to every step in foreign policy and to what the press publishes about it mean that the preservation of democracy and perhaps of civilization may now depend upon a free and responsible press. Such a press we must have if we would have progress and peace.

Robert M. Hutchins	Charles E. Merriam
Zechariah Chafee, Jr.	Reinhold Niebuhr
John M. Clark	Robert Redfield
John Dickinson	Beardsley Ruml
William E. Hocking	Arthur M. Schlesinger
Harold D. Lasswell	George N. Shuster
Archibald MacLeish	

The End of Free Lunch

A. J. LIEBLING

I n Great Britain, the government, whether of Right or Left, considers the state of the press a matter of public concern. When, early this past winter, Lord Rothermere, owner of the morning *Daily Mail* and the *Evening News* in London, bought the *News-Chronicle* (morning) and the *Star* (evening) and scuttled them, thus making life easier for his own papers, there were questions in Parliament. When, a month or two later, Cecil King and Roy Thomson, each the proprietor of a press empire, made rival bids for Odhams Press, which publishes the *Daily Herald* and the Sunday newspaper *People,* a storm broke that compelled the Prime Minister to appoint a Royal Commission to investigate the state of the press. Doing so, he said, in part: "The recent developments are widely taken to suggest that conditions…are such as to lead inevitably toward concentration of ownership and a reduction in—to quote the words of the Royal Commission of 1949—the number and variety of the voices speaking to the public through the press." The 1949 Royal Commission was appointed by a labor government. Here the Tory Prime Minister, like his predecessors, acknowledged that the more voices, and the more various they that spoke, the better for the public.

In the United States, the American Newspaper Publishers' Association would treat such a pronouncement as heresy and interference in their own

This piece was written in 1963.

damned business, not to mention an infringement of the freedom of the press and a partisan pronouncement—since the press being almost exclusively Republican, any criticism is implicitly Democratic.

Yet the United States is much further advanced toward a monovocal, monopolistic, monocular press than Britain. With the decline in the "number and variety" of voices there is a decline in the number and variety of reporting eyes, which is at least as malign. *Editor & Publisher,* a trade publication, recently stated that of 1,461 American cities with daily newspapers, all but 61 were one-ownership towns—that is, monopolies. In Great Britain, where the London papers circulate everywhere, the regional journals cannot dent the London hold on news and opinion. The typical American monopoly is local rather than national. The big-city papers, since they do not arrive, cannot deny the *local* monopoly. Sixty or seventy years ago, the founders of great newspaper chains, like E. W. Scripps and William (the Real Article) Randolph Hearst, would fight for 20 cities simultaneously with 20 newspapers, taking on three or four enemy newspapers in each city. They would win in one place, lose in another, and struggle on without profit for anybody in a third. It was a costly and wasteful process.

The industry's ideal now is absolute control in a moderate number of cities, or even one. These become one-ownership towns, and as the publisher turns monopolist, his troubles end. He is in the position of a feudal lord after the period of wars in the Middle Ages ended. He has his goods, but he need no longer fight for it. He is a *rentier.*

Such properties fall into only three classes: good, better, and bestest. There are no poor ones, since the proprietor can impose his own terms; he gets all the advertising, all the circulation, and he can give, in return, exactly as much or little newspaper as his heart tells him. Newspaper proprietors are not distinguished as a class for large or talkative hearts.

As the number of cities in the United States with only a single newspaper ownership increases, news becomes increasingly nonessential to the newspaper. In the mind of the average publisher, it is a costly and uneconomic frill, like the free lunch that saloons used to furnish to induce customers to buy beer. If the quality of the free lunch fell off, the customers would go next door.

When New York State created its Alcohol Board of Control after the repeal of the prohibition amendment, the A.B.C. abolished the handout. With no free lunch to be had anywhere, the customers continued to buy beer, and the saloonkeepers raised the price and pocketed the difference. In a monopoly situation, the paper can cut out news as the saloons cut out free lunch. There is no longer a place next door for the customers to go to. They will continue to buy the paper to read the advertisements. The advertisers will continue to buy space in order that they be read.

Under present conditions, frightened still by old superstitions about what newspapers are for, the publisher, out of force of habit and because he does not wish to be called a piker, usually provides for the customer a smattering of press association scraps and syndicated features. The saloonkeeper, in the same moral position, puts out a few stale pretzels and moldy salted peanuts.

Each publicly blames his own soft heart for his display of generosity. It comes under the head of public service, and the newspaper owner probably will make a speech about it at the next convention of the American Newspaper Publishers' Association. He will then suggest that the Associated Press, a burden on all of them, ought to cut down on excessive foreign coverage; he often sees a dispatch almost a hundred words long. But such vestigia offer little to rely on for the future. Like the immigrant orthodox Jew, who learns to dispense first with his side curls, then his beard, and at length his skullcap, the publisher will progressively shed his scruples.

With the years, the quantity of news in newspapers is bound to diminish from its present low. The proprietor, as Chairman of the Board, will increasingly often say that he would *like* to spend 75 cents now and then on news coverage but that he must be fair to his shareholders.

This, of course, is the current excuse for every instance of ignobility. A drug company, controlling 95 percent of its own shares, says it would *like* to hold the profit on its pet pill down to 1,500 percent, but it has to protect the minority shareholders, all widows of F.B.I. men strangled by juvenile delinquents. The president of a motor company says he would *like* to build cars that would last at least a year, but he could do it only at the expense of his shareowners, who are entitled to maximum profit and are without exception paraplegics. He then whips around backstage and exercises his option on the three shares that he has let his uncle hold during the annual meeting. And so it goes, even in novels. The popular hero-victim is the thief-in-spite-of-himself, the fundamentally decent corporation executive who has to steal for the stockholders. He is a Robin Hood misunderstood, since the stockholders are a cross-section of the American Public, and the American Public is not rich. There will, almost inevitably, be proxy fights within newspaper corporations, as there are within railroads, in which potty widows with two shares will arise to denounce management for extravagance. They will say that a telephone-answering service for murderers who want to turn themselves in and a subscription to *Time* should be enough of a news side.

Many proprietors, moreover, have a prejudice against news—they never feel at home with it. In this they resemble racing owners who are nervous around horses.

The corrective for the deterioration of a newspaper is provided, in nineteenth-century theory, by competition, which is governed equally by nature's abhorrence of a vacuum and Heaven will protect the working girl. Theoretically, a newspaper that does not give news, or is corrupt, or fails to stand up for the underdog attracts the attention of a virtuous newspaper looking for a home, just as the tarantula, in the Caribbees, attracts the blue hornet. Good and bad paper will wrestle, to continue our insect parallel. Virtue will triumph, and the good paper will place its sting in the bad paper's belly and yell, "*Sic semper* Newhouse management!" or something of the sort. Then it will eat the advertising content of the bad paper's breadbasket.

This no longer occurs. Money is not made by competition among newspapers, but by avoiding it. The wars are over, and newspaper owners are content to buy their enemies off, or just to buy them. The object of diplomacy is to obtain an unassailable local position, like a robber-castle, in New Orleans or Elizabeth or Des Moines, and then levy tribute on the helpless peasantry, who will have no other means of discovering what is playing at the Nugget

To cite an example of the new strategy of noncombat: the Hearst people, who have a paper in Albany, buy the second paper and thus make a monopoly. They sell the Detroit *Times* and skedaddle from that city, leaving the purchaser, the Detroit *News,* with an evening monopoly there. This substitutes two monopolies for two competitive situations. All the respective owners need by way of a staff is a cash register.

The old system was abandoned even before the historically recent deaths of the last specimens of the Giant Primordial Gobblers. William (the Genuine) Randolph Hearst, Joseph Medill Patterson, and Col. Robert Rutherford McCormick, when they went into a city, tried to make its inhabitants obey them as well as pay tribute. Their personalities howled, and they displayed their photographs constantly on their meal tickets. The men of the new order do not meddle with the locals as long as they come up with the tithe. They are, for the public, faceless, and their coups are often inside jobs. Hearst tried to take cities by storm, but the new men prefer a rendezvous at the back gate.

Mr. Samuel I. Newhouse, the archetype, specializes in disgruntling heritors or profiting by their disgruntlement. A family feud is grist to his mill, but if he can't get a paper that way he will talk beautifully of the satisfactions of cash, rapidly quoting sections of the capital-gains law as he accepts his hat. If the owner shows him the door, he exhibits no resentment.

"I regret that you do not feel you can sell me the overcoat now, Madame," he says as he backs down the porch steps, "but if your husband dies and you should reconsider, I do hope you'll give me the first chance to make you an offer." (Mr. Roy Thomson, the Canadian who has taken to buying newspapers in Britain, is the same sort.) Newhouse and Thomson, quizzed about their politics, are evasive. They have no political ideas; just economic convictions.

The function of the press in society is to inform, but its role is to make money. The monopoly publisher's reaction, on being told that he ought to spend money on reporting distant events, is therefore exactly that of the proprietor of a large, fat cow, who is told that he ought to enter her in a horse race.

To concretize the dichotomy, as I might write if I were a popular sociologist, last summer I made a talk before a small group of fellowship winners that got reported in *Newsweek*. In it I said that the Washington *Star*, a disgustingly rich newspaper with an unassailable position, spent millions on promotional activities while it maintained only one foreign correspondent. In the *Star's* opinion this ill-merited a reproach, because there are even richer, if that is remotely conceivable, papers that have no foreign correspondents at all. I got an indignant letter, day and date with the magazine, from a Mr. Newbold Noyes, Jr., vice president of the *Star*, saying it spent only $375,000 a year on promotion. This, of course, would run into millions pretty fast, but I accept the correction, if it is one. He did not say that the *Star* had more than one foreign correspondent, though, so I assume it hasn't. They may, indeed, have fired that one.

Newspapers were not the first to discover the superiority of noncompetition. Corporations, instead of exhorting their executives to get out there and fight for dear old Westinghouse, or for dear old General Electric, have now taken to telling them to get out and not fight unless threatened with an injunction. "I'd rather go to jail than subscribe to the theory of a competitive economy," has become one of the new slogans of the individual-enterprise system.

Despite this universal trend, however, there are still, in the newspaper field, a few locales that are, at least until the conclusion of negotiations, competitive.

One of these provisionally competitive zones, the top quarter of the New York market for morning papers, provides, at my rough guess, two-thirds of the foreign news reaching the United States that is of any service to a reader who gives a damn. This proceeds from the foreign staffs of the *New York Times* and the *Herald Tribune*, who have about a million readers between them, split 650,000 *Times* and 350,000 *Trib*. The *New York Daily News* and the *New York Daily Mirror*, battling for the low three-quarters of morning circulation, split *three million* readers, in a 2-to-l ratio, but foreign coverage plays no part in their war, which is conducted with comic strips, cheesecake, nudging headlines, and between-us-fellers editorials as weapons. Here rules the classic trichotomy—blood, money, and the female organ of sex—that made good papyrus in Cleopatra's time. It is a kind of journalism that has not changed much since.

The *Times*-versus-*Trib* battleground and the other are more widely separated than San Diego and Long Island. It is impossible that either embattled duo draw a reader from the other's field. The prizes at stake are therefore *two* monopolies. Whoever wins up top, *Times* or *Trib*, will get all the middle-to-high-price advertising and whoever triumphs downstairs will get all the low-to-middle. At this point I take leave of the *News* and *Mirror,* like a big eel and a small eel in a tank. Whenever I look again I expect to see that the big eel has swallowed the small eel, but it hasn't happened yet.

The *Times* has a big lead over the *Trib,* but the *Trib* knows that if it packs in its foreign staff it is through. Consequently it continues to compete, like a down cock hitting back at the bird on top, and not only New York readers benefit. Both papers syndicate their services, each to about 50 clients, out of 1,763 American dailies. The clients include a number of big papers, so that the effect on the total amount of foreign news available to American readers is greater than the discouraging figure would suggest. How long this situation lasts depends on how long the New York department stores find it economic to let it happen. If they clamp down on advertising in the *Trib,* as they did in the poor old *Evening Sun* in 1950, they can put it down instantly, unless its proprietor, John Hay Whitney, consents to carry it purely as a tax-free expenditure on public relations for airlines and railroads. This is hardly likely. The disappearance of the *Trib* would be followed, I would bet confidently, by a heavy cut in the amount of foreign news provided by the *Times.* (Free lunch, principle of.) The Country's present supply of foreign news, therefore, depends largely on how best a number of drygoods merchants in New York think they can sell underwear.

Since competition can no longer be relied upon to produce newspapers that provide news, the mind turns to regulation. In the case of a public monopoly, for example, water supply, there is always a governmental agency to maintain standards of limpidity and taste and its freedom from excess of harmful beasts. But analogies, as Ibn Khaldun, the Tunisian historian, has said, are not to be too far trusted. Public regulation would conflict with the principle of the freedom of the press, which has nothing to do with freedom from impurities or distortion, and still less with clarity or taste. Men of politics cannot be trusted to regulate the press, because the press deals with politics. *Pravda* is even duller than the *Times.*

I abandoned myself long ago to hope, and, so far, luck has always prevented the absolute worst. When I got my first newspaper job in 1925, the drift toward profitable stagnation was already apparent. Frank Munsey, a mass murderer of newspapers, had just burked and buried four New York papers, reducing the number of morning dailies from nine to seven and of evenings from seven to five. We are down to four mornings and three evenings, yet I do not believe that New York will be a one-ownership or even a two-ownership city in my lifetime.

Something will turn up. I remind myself often of the plight of Byzantium at the end of the fifteenth century. The Empire of the East was cooked. The

Emperor wore paste crown jewels because the real ice was in hock to the Venetians. The Turks, on a winning streak that had lasted for three centuries, were about to gobble the imperial capital, and there was nothing the Greeks could do about it. Then along came Timur the Lame out of Central Asia. He hated the Greeks, and he hated the Turks, but the Turks were nearer, so he pulverized them and put the Sultan in a cage in 1402, and then died before he got to Constantinople to do in the Greeks. It saved the empire until 1453, and although the Turks eventually took the Greeks, they were not, for the most part, the same Greeks who worried uselessly in 1402.

It was so in the recent election campaign. The almost monolithic press had Kennedy well screened from public gaze, and was about to misrepresent him as a callow gossoon, hiding a low IQ under his father's thumb. Then television, a crude Timur with a grudge based on the press's ribbing of television payola, came to Kennedy's rescue and exhibited Nixon. He was not in a cage, but exposure to the eye proved sufficient. In performing this kind action, the networks were motivated no kindlier toward the public than Timur toward the Greeks. They just wanted to get even with the newspapers.

Now there is a temporary rift in the clouds. In the next four years the president should be able to do enough favors for individual publishers to set up a small circle of Copperheads in their ranks. These will allow dispatches in their papers to differ from dispatches in other papers until they themselves despair of being named ambassadors. By such small accidents, dissidence survives. Unanimity is delayed, doom postponed, and by 1964 public information may by some other accident again escape extinction.

The Republican Party handles publishers much better. It wastes no time trying to make friends with reporters, knowing they can do nothing their bosses won't let them. Mr. Nixon, after the last campaign, charged that reporters were telling the truth behind their bosses' backs, but this was so inherently improbable that nobody took him seriously. As for the ANPA (without a school for whose members, a wise American once wrote, no school of journalism can have meaning), Republicans treat it fine. (As for the school, it will remain a fantasy, because *a.* the potential students are sure they know everything already, and *b.* there are no entrance examinations they could all pass. The ones who couldn't, though, are precisely those who need the school most.)

The relations between the Grand Old Party and the newspaper owners remind me of a man I saw come into a fine old barroom on a snowy Sunday with a boy about three years old, done up in a snowsuit. Clearly he had told his wife he was taking the kid for a romp. He ordered a sour-mash bourbon, sat the boy on the end of the bar and told the bartender to give him a maraschino cherry. The father pronounced it "Marciano," but that is only an interesting detail. There the two stayed all afternoon, perfectly happy. It was evidently a routine arrangement between the men in the family. Every time the old man took a shot, the boy got a cherry. The boy seemed to feel this was an equitable arrangement. He was so small.

In the same way, while the big Republicans, during a favorable administration, sell themselves national resources, block flood-control because it implies public power projects, take the ceilings off natural-gas rates, perpetuate contracts for the manufacture of obsolete war material *(vide,* General James M. Gavin's book explaining his resignation), give the States (which means their own agents at one remove) tidal oil lands, and resell to the government, at unlimited profit, in the form of machines, patents developed in government laboratories, their administration buys the publishers cherries. These take the form of exempting newsboys from the provisions of the minimum-wage law, making ex-publishers ambassadors to small countries dependent on American goodwill, giving newspapers licenses for local television stations, appointing practicing publishers' wives ambassadors to rather larger countries, permitting newspaper owners to call on the president for five minutes when they want to impress particularly important advertisers, and furnishing the president's *hajib,* or Guardian of Access, with a list of the first names of such publishers, so he can tip off the president when they appear and the President will know whether to say "Roy" or "Bill."

The *hajiba,* or Office of the Doorkeeper, or Guardian of Access, incidentally, reached the highest importance in the last administration than it had attained since the reign of Abu Bakr, the twelfth Sultan of the Hafsid dynasty in Ifrikiyah (Tunis) from 1318 to 1346 A.D. Of the Hafsid system of government Ibn Khaldun, the immortal of Tunisian history, wrote: "The Ruler stayed in seclusion, and the doorkeeper *[hajib]* became the *liaison* officer between the people and all the officials." Naturally, politicians and rich merchants desirous of access or the furtherance of their affairs subjected the *hajib* to temptation in the form of magnificent entertainment at caravanserais and gifts of slave girls rolled in Oriental carpets. No instance is known of the last Republican *hajib,* Llewellyn Sherman Adams, having accepted a slave girl.

Ibu Khaldun is the kind of acquaintance you meet on a street corner when you are hurrying to an appointment, but from whom you find it difficult to break off once he has hooked you in conversation. So I must add here: "Afterwards his [Abu Bakr's] grandson, Sultan Abul'Abbâs, regained control of his affairs. He removed the vestiges of seclusion and outside control by abolishing the office of *hajib,* which had been the stepping-stone toward control of the government. He handled all his affairs himself without asking anybody else for help." Ibn Khaldun does not state whether this was an improvement.

Part 3

Journalists and Their Biases—Conscious or Not?

A familiar argument against the American press is that its leading journalists view the world in a vastly different way from prevailing values. At the core of this deeply resilient critique is the idea that journalists are unhelpful and negative, that their adversarial posture becomes destructive, perhaps unpatriotic.

This view of journalists was powerfully articulated by Theodore Roosevelt, who had been thought to be a friend of the press in general and of individual reporters. In the early years of the twentieth century, President Roosevelt lavished praise on a group of journalists, among them Lincoln Steffens, who had been aggressively exposing abuse in government and business in such publications as *McClure's* and *Everybody's*. Then he turned on his allies in journalism, attacking those very writers who had helped to elevate him to hero status.

Borrowing from John Bunyan's allegory, *Pilgrim's Progress,* published in 1678, Roosevelt compared "these reckless journalists" to the Man with the Muckrake—the person who raked filth, "the man who could look no way but downward, with a muckrake in his hands; who was offered a celestial crown for his muckrake, but who would neither look up nor regard the crown he was offered, but continued to rake to himself the filth on the floor."

In a speech at the dedication of the cornerstone of the new House of Representatives office building, he praised journalists in one breath only to condemn their indiscriminate assaults on public officials in the next breath. Roosevelt read Bunyan's allegory to suggest that the contemporary press, preoccupied with the negative aspects of American life, was contrary to the public's interest.

Roosevelt failed to identify a single story or reporter to support his point. His speech, however, attracted wide attention and was the lead story in the *New York Times* the next day. Although the pejorative connotation of "muckraker" has lingered, journalists have come to embrace that designation as a badge of distinction, and that is how it is commonly understood today.

For many decades after Roosevelt relations between public officials and reporters who covered them were generally cordial. In the turbulent 1960s an adversary press gained traction in a way that had been absent since the muckrakers of Roosevelt's time. Richard Nixon viscerally distrusted the press, although he owed his early political successes to an extremely supportive *Los Angeles Times*. As Nixon's point man in attacking the press, Vice President Spiro Agnew delivered a series of controversial, almost demagogic speeches in which he mastered the memorable phrase, calling journalists "nattering nabobs of negativism" (a phrase coined by William Safire, then a White House speechwriter). In 1969 Agnew began his attack on the press in Des Moines in a speech before Republican officials that had been drafted by Patrick Buchanan, a conservative ideologue who has moved between journalism and politics countless times, and edited by Nixon himself. Agnew asked whether "a form of censorship already exists" when the television news for a nation is "determined by a handful of men responsible only to their corporate employers and filtered through a handful of commentators who admit to their own set of biases."

The Des Moines speech and those that followed inalterably changed the way the media was viewed and how the media viewed itself. Ironically, while Agnew's phrases may have caught on and become part of the nation's vocabulary, his specific criticisms were disingenuous, uninformed, and sometimes just plain inaccurate. For instance, in his Des Moines speech, he singled out for criticism W. Averell Harriman, the veteran diplomat and chief negotiator at the Paris Peace talks, who in response to the president's televised speech on his Vietnam policy concluded by saying: "I wish the president well. I hope he can lead us to peace. But this is not the whole story we've heard tonight." Mild stuff from a mild man, and not, as exaggerated in Agnew's speech, words "encouraging the country not to listen to [the president]."

A more careful contemporary criticism of the press came from Daniel Patrick Moynihan, who was trained as a scholar but became a durable practitioner of traditional politics. Moynihan perceptively wrote of the long-standing conflict between journalists and politicians. Borrowing from the critic Lionel Trilling who spoke of the "adversary culture," Moynihan called journalists "charter members of the adversary culture." With their rising social status, he concluded that the press "grows more and more influenced by attitudes generally hostile to American society and American government."

In the article he listed a series of circumstances that worked to change the old balance of power between the presidency and the press. Journalists were better educated and therefore more distant from their audience. Moreover, journalists promulgated the erroneous notion that the presidential office is all powerful. To get their stories, reporters relied heavily on leaks, which routinely are inimical to the interests of the president in power. For Moynihan, the press is limited in how it reports. For instance, in the name of objectivity, it often prints lies as it did with the false charges made by Senator Joseph McCarthy. Finally, Moynihan complained, journalists lack a tradition of correcting themselves.

In 1976 Moynihan narrowly won the Democratic nomination for Senate from New York, aided decisively by a last-minute endorsement from the *New York Times*. Later, he once wore an apron inscribed with the words of a famous advertisement of the time: "I got my job through the *New York Times*."

Moynihan, as Roosevelt and Agnew before him, falls into a trap of treating the media as a monolith, ignoring fundamental distinctions and shadings. If there is one accurate generalization about the press, it is this: it is unsafe to generalize. Bearing this admonition in mind, the basic formula of newsgathering in the contemporary mainstream media is to report what is said by others— government officials, business executives, experts. Fairness too often means only that an accusation must be balanced by a response, not by independent reporting. Most new organizations share a broad perception of the common interest, skittish about attacking the establishment.

When matters of national interest and security are at stake, the press is usually more complaisant than cantankerous. Evidence of antigovernment bias melts away. The phenomenon was starkly reported by Walter Lippmann and Charles Merz in their stunning and unforgiving reconstruction of how the *New York Times* reported on the Russian Revolution. Lippmann, then thirty years old and Merz, twenty-seven, decoded the coverage brilliantly. Their textual analysis covered a three-year period beginning in 1917 with the overthrow of Czar Nicholas II. The newspaper cited events that did not happen and atrocities that never took place. On nearly one hundred occasions, the *Times* erroneously reported that the Bolshevik regime was about to collapse.

The authors stressed that the future of democracy rested on the delivery by the press of truthful and accurate information. Either out of sloppiness, laziness, patriotism, or excessive reliance on official sources, the *Times,* in the view of the authors, supplied knowledge that was about as useful as "that of an astrologer or an alchemist." A long excerpt from their near book-length article follows.

The Man with the Muckrake

THEODORE ROOSEVELT

O ver a century ago Washington laid the cornerstone of the Capitol in what was then little more than a tract of wooded wilderness here beside the Potomac. We now find it necessary to provide by great additional buildings for the business of the government. This growth in the need for the housing of the government is but proof and example of the way in which the nation has grown and the sphere of action of the national government has grown. We now administer the affairs of a nation in which the extraordinary growth of population has been outstripped by the growth of wealth and the growth in complex interests. The material problems that face us today are not such as they were in Washington's time, but the underlying facts of human nature are the same now as they were then. Under altered external form we war with the same tendencies toward evil that were evident in Washington's time, and are helped by the same tendencies for good. It is about some of these that I wish to say a word today.

In Bunyan's *Pilgrim's Progress* you may recall the description of the Man with the Muckrake, the man who could look no way but downward, with a muckrake in his hands; who was offered a celestial crown for his muckrake, but who would neither look up nor regard the crown he was offered, but continued to rake to himself the filth of the floor.

This speech was delivered in 1906.

In *Pilgrim's Progress* the Man with the Muckrake is set forth as the example of him whose vision is fixed on carnal instead of on spiritual things. Yet he also typifies the man who in this life consistently refuses to see aught that is lofty, and fixes his eyes with solemn intentness only on that which is vile and debasing. Now, it is very necessary that we should not flinch from seeing what is vile and debasing. There is filth on the floor, and it must be scraped up with a muckrake; and there are times and places where this service is the most needed of all the services that can be performed. But the man who never does anything else, who never thinks or speaks or writes save of his feats with the muckrake, speedily becomes, not a help to society, not an incitement to good, but one of the most potent forces of evil.

There are in the body politic, economic and social, many and grave evils, and there is urgent necessity for the sternest war upon them. There should be relentless exposure of and attack upon every evil man, whether politician or businessman, every evil practice, whether in politics, in business, or in social life. I hail as a benefactor every writer or speaker, every man who, on the platform or in book, magazine, or newspaper, with merciless severity makes such attack, provided always that he in his turn remembers that the attack is of use only if it is absolutely truthful. The liar is no whit better than the thief, and if his mendacity takes the form of slander he may be worse than most thieves. It puts a premium upon knavery untruthfully to attack an honest man, or even with hysterical exaggeration to assail a bad man with untruth. An epidemic of indiscriminate assault upon character does not good but very great harm. The soul of every scoundrel is gladdened whenever an honest man is assailed, or even when a scoundrel is untruthfully assailed.

Now, it is easy to twist out of shape what I have just said, easy to affect to misunderstand it, and, if it is slurred over in repetition, not difficult really to misunderstand it. Some persons are sincerely incapable of understanding that to denounce mudslinging does not mean the endorsement of whitewashing; and both the interested individuals who need whitewashing and those others who practice mudslinging like to encourage such confusion of ideas. One of the chief counts against those who make indiscriminate assault upon men in business or men in public life is that they invite a reaction which is sure to tell powerfully in favor of the unscrupulous scoundrel who really ought to be attacked, who ought to be exposed, who ought, if possible, to be put in the penitentiary. If Aristides is praised overmuch as just, people get tired of hearing it; and over-censure of the unjust finally and from similar reasons results in their favor.

Any excess is almost sure to invite a reaction; and, unfortunately, the reaction, instead of taking the form of punishment of those guilty of the excess, is very apt to take the form either of punishment of the unoffending or of giving immunity, and even strength, to offenders. The effort to make financial or political profit out of the destruction of character can only result in public calamity. Gross and reckless assaults on character—whether on the stump or in newspaper, magazine, or book—create a morbid and vicious public sentiment, and at the same time act as a profound deterrent to able men of normal sensitiveness and tend to prevent them from entering the public service at any price. As an instance in point, I may mention that one serious difficulty encountered in getting the right type of men to dig the Panama Canal is the certainty that they will be exposed, both without, and, I am sorry to say, sometimes within, Congress, to utterly reckless assaults on their character and capacity.

At the risk of repetition let me say again that my plea is not for immunity to, but for the most unsparing exposure of, the politician who betrays his trust, of the big businessman who makes or spends his fortune in illegitimate or corrupt ways. There should be a resolute effort to hunt every such man out of the position he has disgraced. Expose the crime and hunt down the criminal; but remember that even in the case of crime, if it is attacked in sensational, lurid, and untruthful fashion, the attack may do more damage to the public mind than the crime itself. It is because I feel that there should be no rest in the endless war against the forces of evil that I ask that the war be conducted with sanity as well as with resolution. The men with the muckrakes are often indispensable to the well-being of society, but only if they know when to stop raking the muck, and to look upward to the celestial crown above them, to the crown of worthy endeavor. There are beautiful things above and round about them; and if they gradually grow to feel that the whole world is nothing but muck their power of usefulness is gone. If the whole picture is painted black there remains no hue whereby to single out the rascals for distinction from their fellows. Such painting finally induces a kind of moral color blindness; and people affected by it come to the conclusion that no man is really black and no man really white, but they are all gray. In other words, they neither believe in the truth of the attack nor in the honesty of the man who is attacked; they grow as suspicious of the accusation as of the offense; it becomes well-nigh hopeless to stir them either to wrath against wrongdoing or to enthusiasm for what is right; and such a mental attitude in the public gives hope to every knave, and is the despair of honest men.

To assail the great and admitted evils of our political and industrial life with such crude and sweeping generalizations as to include decent men in the general condemnation means the searing of the public conscience. There results a general attitude either of cynical belief in and indifference to public corruption or else of a distrustful inability to discriminate between the good and the bad.

Either attitude is fraught with untold damage to the country as a whole. The fool who has not sense to discriminate between what is good and what is bad is well-nigh as dangerous as the man who does discriminate and yet chooses the bad. There is nothing more distressing to every good patriot, to every good American, than the hard, scoffing spirit which treats the allegation of dishonesty in a public man as a cause for laughter. Such laughter is worse than the crackling of thorns under a pot, for it denotes not merely the vacant mind, but the heart in which high emotions have been choked before they could grow to fruition.

There is any amount of good in the world, and there never was a time when loftier and more disinterested work for the betterment of mankind was being done than now. The forces that tend for evil are great and terrible, but the forces of truth and love and courage and honesty and generosity and sympathy are also stronger than ever before. It is foolish and timid no less than a wicked thing to blink at the fact that the forces of evil are strong, but it is even worse to fail to take into account the strength of the forces that tell for good. Hysterical sensationalism is the very poorest weapon wherewith to fight for lasting righteousness. The men who with stern sobriety and truth assail the many evils of our time, whether in the public press or in magazines or in books, are the leaders and allies of all engaged in the work for social and political betterment. But if they give good reason for distrust of what they say, if they chill the ardor of those who demand truth as a primary virtue, they thereby betray the good cause and play into the hands of the very men against whom they are nominally at war.

In his *Ecclesiastical Polity* that fine old Elizabethan divine, Bishop Hooker, wrote:

> He that goeth about to persuade a multitude that they are not so well governed as they ought to be, shall never want attentive and favorable hearers; because they know the manifold defects whereunto every kind of regimen is subject, but the secret lets and difficulties, which in public proceedings are innumerable and inevitable, they have not ordinarily the judgment to consider.

This truth should be kept constantly in mind by every free people desiring to preserve the sanity and poise indispensable to the permanent success of self-government. Yet, on the other hand, it is vital not to permit this spirit of sanity and self-command to degenerate into mere mental stagnation. Bad though a state of hysterical excitement is, and evil though the results are which come from the violent oscillations such excitement invariably produces, yet a sodden acquiescence in evil is even worse. At this moment we are passing through a period of great unrest—social, political, and industrial unrest. It is of the utmost importance for our future that this should prove to be not the unrest of mere rebelliousness against life, of mere dissatisfaction with the inevitable inequality of conditions, but the unrest of a resolute and eager ambition to secure the betterment of the individual and the nation. So far as this movement of agitation throughout the country takes the form of a fierce discontent with evil, of a determination to punish the authors of evil, whether in industry or politics, the feeling is to be heartily welcomed as a sign of healthy life.

If, on the other hand, it turns into a mere crusade of appetite against appetite, of a contest between the brutal greed of the "have-nots" and the brutal greed of the "haves," then it has no significance for good, but only for evil. If it seeks to establish a line of cleavage, not along the line which divides good men from bad, but along that other line, running at right angles thereto, which divides those who are well off from those who are less well off, then it will be fraught with immeasurable harm to the body politic.

We can no more and no less afford to condone evil in the man of capital than evil in the man of no capital. The wealthy man who exults because there is a failure of justice in the effort to bring some trust magnate to an account for his misdeeds is as bad as, and no worse than, the so-called labor leader who clamorously strives to excite a foul class feeling on behalf of some other labor leader who is implicated in murder. One attitude is as bad as the other, and no worse; in each case the accused is entitled to exact justice; and in neither case is there need of action by others which can be construed into an expression of sympathy for crime.

It is a prime necessity that if the present unrest is to result in permanent good the emotion shall be translated into action, and that the action shall be marked by honesty, sanity, and self-restraint. There is mighty little good in a mere spasm of reform. The reform that counts is that which comes through steady, continuous growth; violent emotionalism leads to exhaustion.

It is important to this people to grapple with the problems connected with the massing of enormous fortunes, and the use of those fortunes, both corporate and individual, in business. We should discriminate in the sharpest way between fortunes well won and fortunes ill won; between those gained as an incident to performing great services to the community as whole, and those gained in evil fashion by keeping just within the limits of mere law-honesty. Of course no amount of charity in spending such fortunes in any way compensates for misconduct in making them. As a matter of personal conviction, and without pretending to discuss the details or formulate the system, I feel that we shall ultimately have to consider the adoption of some such scheme as that of a progressive tax on all fortunes, beyond a certain amount, either given in life or devised or bequeathed upon death to any individual—a tax so framed as to put it out of the power of the owner of one of these enormous fortunes to hand on more than a certain amount to any individual; the tax, of course, to be imposed by the national and not the state government. Such taxation should, of course, be aimed merely at the inheritance or transmission in their entirety of those fortunes swollen beyond all healthy limits.

Again, the national government must in some form exercise supervision over corporations engaged in interstate business—and all large corporations are engaged in interstate business—whether by license or otherwise, so as to permit us to deal with the far-reaching evils of over-capitalization. This year we are making a beginning in the direction of serious effort to settle some of these economic problems by the railway rate legislation. Such legislation, if so framed, as I am sure it will be, as to secure definite and tangible results, will amount to something of itself; and it will amount to a great deal more in so far as it is taken as a first step in the direction of a policy of superintendence and control over corporate wealth engaged in interstate commerce, this superinten-dence and control not to be exercised in a spirit of malevolence toward the men who have created the wealth, but with the firm purpose both to do justice to them and to see that they in their turn do justice to the public at large.

The first requisite in the public servants who are to deal in this shape with corporations, whether as legislators or as executives, is honesty. This honesty can be no respecter of persons. There can be no such thing as unilateral hon-esty. The danger is not really from corrupt corporations; it springs from the corruption itself, whether exercised for or against corporations.

The eighth commandment reads, "Thou shalt not steal." It does not read, "Thou shalt not steal from the rich man." It does not read, "Thou shalt not steal from the poor man." It reads simply and plainly, "Thou shalt not steal." No good whatever will come from that warped and mock morality which denounces the misdeeds of men of wealth and forgets the misdeeds practiced at their expense; which denounces bribery, but blinds itself to blackmail; which foams with rage if a corporation secures favors by improper methods, but merely leers with hideous mirth if the corporation is itself wronged. The only public servant who can be trusted honestly to protect the rights of the public against the misdeed of a corporation is that public man who will just as surely protect the corpo-ration itself from wrongful aggression. If a public man is willing to yield to popular clamor and do wrong to the men of wealth or to rich corporations, it may be set down as certain that if the opportunity comes he will secretly and furtively do wrong to the public in the interest of a corporation.

But, in addition to honesty, we need sanity. No honesty will make a public man useful if that man is timid or foolish, if he is a hotheaded zealot or an impracticable visionary. As we strive for reform we find that it is not at all merely the case of a long uphill pull. On the contrary, there is almost as much of breeching work as of collar work; to depend only on traces means that there will soon be a runaway and an upset. The men of wealth who today are trying to prevent the regulation and control of their business in the interest of the public by the proper government authorities will not succeed, in my judgment, in checking the progress of the movement. But if they did succeed they would find that they had sown the wind and would surely reap the whirlwind, for they ultimately provoke the violent excesses which accompany a reform coming by convulsion instead of by steady and natural growth.

On the other hand, the wild preachers of unrest and discontent, the wild agitators against the entire existing order, the men who act crookedly, whether because of sinister design or mere puzzleheadedness, the men who preach destruction without proposing any substitute for what they intend to destroy, or who propose a substitute which would be far worse than the existing evils—all these men are the most dangerous opponents of real reform. If they get their way they will lead the people into a deeper pit than any into which they would fall under the present system. If they fail to get their way they will still do incalculable harm by provoking the kind of reaction which in its revolt against the senseless evil of their teaching would enthrone more securely than ever the very evils which their misguided followers believe they are attacking.

More important than aught else is the development of the broadest sympathy of man for man. The welfare of the wage worker, the welfare of the tiller of the soil, upon these depend the welfare of the entire country; their good is not to be sought in pulling down others; but their good must be the prime object of all our statesmanship.

Materially, we must strive to secure a broader economic opportunity for all men, so that each shall have a better chance to show the stuff of which he is made. Spiritually and ethically we must strive to bring about clean living and right thinking. We appreciate that the things of the body are important; but we appreciate also that the things of the soul are immeasurably more important. The foundation stone of national life is, and ever must be, the high individual character of the average citizen.

Speeches on the Media

SPIRO AGNEW

MID-WEST REGIONAL REPUBLICAN COMMITTEE MEETING, DES MOINES, IOWA

NOVEMBER 13, 1969

Tonight I want to discuss the importance of the television news medium to the American people. No nation depends more on the intelligent judgment of its citizens. No medium has a more profound influence over public opinion. Nowhere in our system are there fewer checks on vast power. So, nowhere should there be more conscientious responsibility exercised than by the news media. The question is, are we demanding enough of our television news presentations? And do the men of this medium demand enough of themselves?

Monday night, a week ago, President Nixon delivered the most important address of his administration, one of the most important of our decade. His subject was Vietnam. His hope was to rally the American people to see the conflict through to a lasting and just peace in the Pacific. For thirty-two minutes, he reasoned with a nation that has suffered almost a third of a million casualties in the longest war in its history.

When the president completed his address—an address he spent weeks preparing—his words and policies were subjected to instant analysis and queru-

---

These speeches were delivered between 1969 and 1971.

lous criticism. The audience of seventy million Americans—gathered to hear the president of the United States—was inherited by a small band of network commentators and self-appointed analysts, the *majority* of whom expressed, in one way or another, their hostility to what he had to say.

It was obvious that their minds were made up in advance. Those who recall the fumbling and groping that followed President Johnson's dramatic disclosure of his intention not to seek reelection have seen these men in a genuine state of non-preparedness. This was not it.

One commentator twice contradicted the president's statement about the exchange of correspondence with Ho Chi Minh. Another challenged the president's abilities as a politician. A third asserted that the president was now "following the Pentagon line." Others, by the expressions on their faces, the tone of their questions, and the sarcasm of their responses, made clear their sharp disapproval.

To guarantee in advance that the president's plea for national unity would be challenged, one network trotted out Averell Harriman for the occasion. Throughout the president's address he waited in the wings. When the president concluded, Mr. Harriman recited perfectly. He attacked the Thieu government as unrepresentative; he criticized the president's speech for various deficiencies; he twice issued a call to the Senate Foreign Relations Committee to debate Vietnam once again; he stated his belief that the Viet Cong or North Vietnamese did not really want a military takeover of South Vietnam; he told a little anecdote about a "very, very responsible" fellow he had met in the North Vietnamese delegation.

All in all, Mr. Harriman offered a broad range of gratuitous advice—challenging and contradicting the policies outlined by the president of the United States. Where the president had issued a call for unity, Mr. Harriman was encouraging the country not to listen to him.

A word about Mr. Harriman. For ten months he was America's chief negotiator at the Paris Peace Talks—a period in which the United States swapped some of the greatest military concessions in the history of warfare for an enemy agreement on the shape of a bargaining table. Like Coleridge's Ancient Mariner, Mr. Harriman seems to be under some heavy compulsion to justify his failures to anyone who will listen. The networks have shown themselves willing to give him all the air time he desires.

Every American has a right to disagree with the president of the United States, and to express publicly that disagreement.

But the president of the United States has a right to communicate directly with the people who elected him, and the people of this country have the right to make up their own minds and form their own opinions about a presidential address without having the president's words and thoughts characterized through the prejudices of hostile critics before they can even be digested.

When Winston Churchill rallied public opinion to stay the course against Hitler's Germany, he did not have to contend with a gaggle of commentators raising doubts about whether he was reading public opinion right, or whether Britain had the stamina to see the war through. When President Kennedy rallied the nation in the Cuban Missile Crisis, his address to the people was not chewed over by a round-table of critics who disparaged the course of action he had asked America to follow.

The purpose of my remarks tonight is to focus your attention on this little group of men who not only enjoy a right of instant rebuttal to every presidential address, but more importantly, wield a free hand in selecting, presenting, and interpreting the great issues of our nation.

First, let us define that power. At least forty million Americans each night, it is estimated, watch the network news. Seven million of them view ABC; the remainder being divided between NBC and CBS. According to Harris polls and other studies, for millions of Americans the networks are the sole source of national and world news.

In Will Rogers's observation, what you knew was what you read in the newspaper. Today, for growing millions of Americans, it is what they see and hear on their television sets.

How is this network news determined? A small group of men, numbering perhaps no more than a dozen "anchormen," commentators, and executive producers, settle upon the twenty minutes or so of film and commentary that is to reach the public. This selection is made from the ninety to one hundred eighty minutes that may be available. Their powers of choice are broad. They decide what forty to fifty million Americans will learn of the day's events in the nation and the world.

We cannot measure this power and influence by traditional democratic standards for these men can create national issues overnight. They can make or break—by their coverage and commentary—a moratorium on the war. They can elevate men from local obscurity to national prominence within a week. They can reward some politicians with national exposure and ignore others. For millions of Americans, the network reporter who covers a continuing issue, like ABMs or civil rights, becomes in effect, the presiding judge in a national trial by jury.

It must be recognized that the networks have made important contributions to the national knowledge. Through news, documentaries, and specials, they have often used their power constructively and creatively to awaken the public conscience to critical problems.

The networks made "hunger" and "black lung" disease national issues overnight. The TV networks have done what no other medium could have done in terms of dramatizing the horrors of war. The networks have tackled our most difficult social problems with a directness and immediacy that is the gift of their medium. They have focused the nation's attention on its environmental abuses...on pollution in the Great Lakes and the threatened ecology of the Everglades.

But it was also the networks that elevated Stokely Carmichael and George Lincoln Rockwell from obscurity to national prominence...nor is their power confined to the substantive.

A raised eyebrow, an inflection of the voice, a caustic remark dropped in the middle of a broadcast can raise doubts in a million minds about the veracity of a public official or the wisdom of a government policy.

One Federal Communications Commissioner considers the power of the networks to equal that of local, state, and federal governments combined. Certainly, it represents a concentration of power over American public opinion unknown in history.

What do Americans know of the men who wield this power? Of the men who produce and direct the network news—the nation knows practically nothing. Of the commentators, most Americans know little, other than that they reflect an urbane and assured presence, seemingly well informed on every important matter.

We do know that, to a man, these commentators and producers live and work in the geographical and intellectual confines of Washington, D.C., or New York City—the latter of which James Reston terms the "most unrepresentative community in the entire United States." Both communities bask in their own provincialism, their own parochialism. We can deduce that these men thus read the same newspapers, and draw their political and social views from the same sources. Worse, they talk constantly to one another, thereby providing artificial reinforcement to their shared viewpoints.

Do they allow their biases to influence the selection and presentation of the news? David Brinkley states, "objectivity is impossible to normal human behavior." Rather, he says, we should strive for "fairness."

Another anchorman on a network news show contends: "You can't expunge all your private convictions just because you sit in a seat like this and a camera starts to stare at you...I think your program has to reflect what your basic feelings are. I'll plead guilty to that."

Less than a week before the 1968 election, this same commentator charged that President Nixon's campaign commitments were no more durable than campaign balloons. He claimed that, were it not for fear of a hostile reaction, Richard Nixon would be giving into, and I quote the commentator, "his natural instinct to smash the enemy with a club or go after him with a meat axe."

Had this slander been made by one political candidate about another, it would have been dismissed by most commentators as a partisan assault. But this attack emanated from the privileged sanctuary of a network studio and therefore had the apparent dignity of an objective statement.

The American people would rightly not tolerate this kind of concentration of power in government. Is it not fair and relevant to question its concentration in the hands of a tiny and closed fraternity of privileged men, elected by no one, and enjoying a monopoly sanctioned and licensed by government?

The views of this fraternity do *not* represent the views of America. That is why such a great gulf existed between how the nation received the president's address—and how the networks reviewed it.

As with other American institutions, perhaps it is time that the networks were made more responsive to the views of the nation and more responsible to the people they serve.

I am not asking for government censorship or any other kind of censorship. I am asking whether a form of censorship already exists when the news that forty million Americans receive each night is determined by a handful of men responsible only to their corporate employers and filtered through a handful of commentators who admit to their own set of biases.

The questions I am raising here tonight should have been raised by others long ago. They should have been raised by those Americans who have traditionally considered the preservation of freedom of speech and freedom of the press their special provinces of responsibility and concern. They should have been raised by those Americans who share the view of the late Justice Learned Hand that "right conclusions are more likely to be gathered out of a multitude of tongues than through any kind of authoritative selection."

Advocates for the networks have claimed the First Amendment right to the same unlimited freedoms held by the great newspapers of America.

The situations are not identical. Where the *New York Times* reaches 800,000 people, NBC reaches twenty times that number with its evening news. Nor can the tremendous impact of seeing television film and hearing commentary be compared with reading the printed page.

A decade ago, before the network news acquired such dominance over public opinion, Walter Lippmann spoke to the issue. He said:

There is an essential and radical difference between television and printing. The three or four competing television stations control virtually all that can be received over the air by ordinary television sets. But, besides the mass circulation dailies, there are the weeklies, the monthlies, the out-of-town newspapers, and books. If a man does not like his newspaper, he can read another from out of town, or wait for a weekly news magazine. It is not ideal. But it is infinitely better than the situation in television. There, if a man does not like what the networks offer him, all he can do is turn them off, and listen to a phonograph.

"Networks," he stated, "which are few in number, have a virtual monopoly of a whole medium of communication." The newspapers of mass circulation have no monopoly of the medium of print.

"A virtual monopoly of a whole medium of communication" is not something a democratic people should blithely ignore.

And we are not going to cut off our television sets and listen to the phonograph because the air waves do not belong to the networks; they belong to the people.

As Justice Byron White wrote in his landmark opinion six months ago, "It is the right of the viewers and listeners, not the right of the broadcasters, which is paramount."

It is argued that this power presents no danger in the hands of those who have used it responsibly.

But as to whether or not the networks have abused the power they enjoy, let us call, as our first witnesses, former vice president Humphrey and the City of Chicago.

According to Theodore H. White, television's inter-cutting of the film from the streets of Chicago with the "current proceedings on the floor of the convention created the most striking and *false* political picture of 1968—the nomination of a man for the American presidency by the brutality and violence of merciless police."

If we are to believe a recent report of the House Commerce Committee, then television's presentation of the violence in the streets worked an injustice on the reputation of the Chicago police.

According to the Committee findings, one network in particular presented "a one-sided picture which in large measure exonerates the demonstrators and protestors." Film of provocations of police that was available never saw the light of day, while the film of the police response which the protestors provoked was shown to millions.

Another network showed virtually the same scene of violence—from three separate angles—without making clear it was the same scene.

While the full report is reticent in drawing conclusions, it is not a document to inspire confidence in the fairness of the network news.

Our knowledge of the impact of network news on the national mind is far from complete. But some early returns are available. Again, we have enough information to raise serious questions about its effect on a democratic society.

Several years ago, Fred Friendly, one of the pioneers of network news, wrote that its missing ingredients were "conviction, controversy, and a point of view." The networks have compensated with a vengeance.

And in the networks' endless pursuit of controversy, we should ask what is the end value ... to enlighten or to profit? What is the end result ... to inform or confuse? How does the ongoing exploration for more action, more excitement, and more drama serve our national search for internal peace and stability?

Gresham's law seems to be operating in the network news.

Bad news drives out good news. The irrational is more controversial than the rational. Concurrence can no longer compete with dissent. One minute of Eldridge Cleaver is worth ten minutes of Roy Wilkins. The labor crisis settled at the negotiating table is nothing compared to the confrontation that results in a strike—or, better yet, violence along the picket line. Normality has become the nemesis of the evening news.

The upshot of all this controversy is that a narrow and distorted picture of America often emerges from the televised news. A single dramatic piece of the mosaic becomes, in the minds of millions, the whole picture. The American who relies upon television for his news might conclude that the majority of American students are embittered radicals, that the majority of black Americans feel no regard for their country, that violence and lawlessness are the rule, rather than the exception, on the American campus. None of these conclusions is true.

Television may have destroyed the old stereotypes—but has it not created new ones in their place?

What has this passionate pursuit of "controversy" done to the politics of progress through logical compromise, essential to the functioning of a democratic society?

The members of Congress or the Senate who follow their principles and philosophy quietly in a spirit of compromise are unknown to many Americans—while the loudest and most extreme dissenters on every issue are known to every man in the street.

How many marches and demonstrations would we have if the marchers did not know that the ever-faithful TV cameras would be there to record their antics for the next news show.

We have heard demands that senators and congressmen and judges make known all their financial connections—so that the public will know who and what influences their decisions or votes. Strong arguments can be made for that view. But when a single commentator or producer, night after night, determines for millions of people how much of each side of a great issue they are going to see and hear; should he not first disclose his personal views on the issue as well?

In this search for excitement and controversy, has more than equal time gone to that minority of Americans who specialize in attacking the United States, its institutions, and its citizens?

Tonight, I have raised questions. I have made no attempt to suggest answers. These answers must come from the media men. They are challenged to turn their critical powers on themselves. They are challenged to direct their energy, talent, and conviction toward improving the quality and objectivity of news presentation. They are challenged to structure their own civic ethics to relate their great freedom with their great responsibility.

And the people of America are challenged, too... challenged to press for responsible news presentations. The people can let the networks know that they want their news straight and objective. The people can register their complaints on bias through mail to the networks and phone calls to local stations. This is one case where the people must defend themselves... where the citizen—not government—must be the reformer... where the consumer can be the most effective crusader.

By way of conclusion, let me say that every elected leader in the United States depends on these men of the media. Whether what I have said to you tonight will be heard and seen at all by the nation is not *my* decision; it is not *your* decision; it is *their* decision.

In tomorrow's edition of the *Des Moines Register* you will be able to read a news story detailing what I said tonight; editorial comment will be reserved for the editorial page, where it belongs. Should not the same wall of separation exist between news and comment on the nation's network.

We would never trust such power over public opinion in the hands of an elected government—it is time we questioned it in the hands of a small and unelected elite. The great networks have dominated America's airwaves for decades; the people are entitled to a full accounting of their stewardship.

MONTGOMERY CHAMBER OF COMMERCE, MONTGOMERY, ALABAMA

NOVEMBER 20, 1969

One week ago tonight I flew out to Des Moines, Iowa, and exercised my right to dissent.

There has been some criticism of what I had to say out there.

Let me give you a sampling.

One congressman charged me with, and I quote, "A creeping socialistic scheme against the free enterprise broadcast industry." That is the first time in my memory anybody ever accused Ted Agnew of entertaining socialist ideas.

On Monday, largely because of this address, Mr. Humphrey charged the Nixon administration with a "calculated attack" on the right of dissent and on the media today. Yet, it is widely known that Mr. Humphrey himself believes deeply that unfair coverage of the Democratic Convention in Chicago, by the same media, contributed to his defeat in November. Now, his wounds are apparently healed, and he casts his lot with those who were questioning his own political courage a year ago. But let us leave Mr. Humphrey to his own conscience. America already has too many politicians who would rather switch than fight.

Others charged that my purpose was to stifle dissent in this country. Nonsense. The expression of my views has produced enough rugged dissent in the last week to wear out a whole covey of commentators and columnists.

One critic charged that the speech was "disgraceful, ignorant, and base," that it "leads us as a nation into an ugly era of the most fearsome suppression and intimidation." One national commentator, whose name is known to everyone in this room, said "I hesitate to get into the gutter with this guy." Another commentator charges that it was "one of the most sinister speeches I have ever heard made by a public official." The president of one network said it was an "unprecedented attempt to intimidate a news medium which depends for its existence upon government licenses." The president of another charged me with "an appeal to prejudice," and said it was evident that I would prefer the kind of television "that would be subservient to whatever political group happened to be in authority at the time."

And they say *I* have a thin skin.

Here are classic examples of overreaction. These attacks do not address themselves to the questions I have raised. In fairness, others—the majority of critics and commentators—did take up the main thrust of my address. And if the debate they have engaged in continues, our goal will surely be reached—a thorough self-examination by the networks of their own policies—and perhaps prejudices. That was my objective then; it is my objective now.

Now, let me repeat to you the thrust of my remarks the other night, and make some new points and raise some new issues.

I am opposed to censorship of television or the press in any form. I don't care whether censorship is imposed by government or whether it results from management in the choice and the presentation of the news by a little fraternity having similar social and political views. I am against censorship in all forms.

But a broader spectrum of national opinion *should* be represented among the commentators of the network news. Men who can articulate other points of view *should* be brought forward.

And a high wall of separation *should* be raised between what is news and what is commentary.

And the American people *should* be made aware of the trend toward the monopolization of the great public information vehicles and the concentration of more and more power over public opinion in fewer and fewer hands.

Should a conglomerate be formed that tied together a shoe company with a shirt company, some voice will rise up righteously to say that this is a great danger to the economy; and that the conglomerate ought to be broken up.

But a single company, in the nation's capital, holds control of the largest newspaper in Washington, D.C., *and* one of the four major television stations, *and* an all-news radio station, *and* one of the three major national news magazines—all grinding out the same editorial line—and this is not a subject you have seen debated in the editorial pages of the *Washington Post* or the *New York Times*.

For the purpose of clarity, before my thoughts are obliterated in the smoking typewriters of my friends in Washington and New York, let me emphasize I am not recommending the dismemberment of the Washington Post Company. I am merely pointing out that the public should be aware that these four powerful voices hearken to the same master.

I am merely raising these questions so that the American people will become aware of—and think of the implications of—that growing monopolization of the voices of public opinion on which we all depend—for our knowledge and for the basis of our views.

When the *Washington Times-Herald* died in the nation's capital, that was a political tragedy; and when the *New York Journal-American,* the *New York World Telegram and Sun,* the *New York Mirror,* and the *New York Herald-Tribune* all collapsed within this decade, that was a great, great political tragedy for the people of New York. The *New York Times* was a better newspaper when they were alive than it is now that they are gone.

What has happened in the city of New York has happened in other great cities in America.

Many, many strong independent voices have been stilled in this country in recent years. Lacking the vigor of competition, some of those that have survived have, let us face it, grown fat and irresponsible.

I offer an example. When three hundred congressmen and fifty-nine senators signed a letter endorsing the president's policy in Vietnam it was news—big news. Even the *Washington Post* and the *Baltimore Sun*—scarcely house organs of the Nixon administration—placed it prominently on the front page.

Yet the next morning the *New York Times,* which considers itself America's paper of record, did not carry a word. Why?

If a theology student in Iowa should get up at a PTA luncheon in Sioux City and attack the president's Vietnam policy, my guess is that you would probably find it reported somewhere the next morning in the *New York Times*. But when three hundred congressmen endorse the president's Vietnam policy, the next morning it is apparently not considered news fit to print.

Just this Tuesday, when the Pope, the spiritual leader of half a billion Roman Catholics applauded the president's efforts to end the war in Vietnam, and endorsed the way he was proceeding—that news was on page eleven of the *New York Times*. But the same day, a report about some burglars who broke into a souvenir shop at St. Peters and stole $9,000 worth of stamps and currency—that story made page three. How's that for news judgment?

A few weeks ago here in the South, I expressed my views about street and campus demonstrations. Here is how the *New York Times* responded:

> He [that's me] lambasted the nation's youth in sweeping and ignorant generalizations, when it is clear to all perceptive observers that American youth today is far more imbued with idealism, a sense of service, and a deep humanitarianism than any generation in recent history, including particularly Mr. Agnew's [generation].

That seems a peculiar slur on a generation that brought America out of the Great Depression without resorting to the extremes of either fascism or communism. That seems a strange thing to say about an entire generation that helped to provide greater material blessings and personal freedom—out of that Depression—for more people than any other nation in history. We are not finished with the task by any means—but we are still on the job.

Just as millions of young Americans in this generation have shown valor and courage and heroism in fighting the longest and least popular war in our history—so it was the young men of my generation who went ashore at Normandy under Eisenhower and with McArthur into the Phillipines.

Yes, my generation, like the current generation, made its own share of great mistakes and blunders. Among other things, we put too much confidence in Stalin and not enough in Winston Churchill.

But whatever freedom exists today in Western Europe and Japan exists because hundreds of thousands of young men in my generation are lying in graves in North Africa and France and Korea and a score of islands in the Western Pacific.

This might not be considered enough of a "sense of service" or a "deep humanitarianism" enough for me; and I am content to let history be the judge. ...

One magazine this week said that I will go down as the "great polarizer" in American politics. Yet, when that large group of young Americans marched up Pennsylvania and Constitution Avenues last week—they sought to polarize the American people against the president's policy in Vietnam. And that was their right.

And so it is my right, and my duty, to stand up and speak out for the values in which I believe. How can you ask the man in the street in this country to stand up for what he believes if his own elected leaders weasel and cringe?

It is not an easy thing to wake up each morning to learn that some prominent man or institution has implied that you are a bigot, a racist, or a fool.

I am not asking any immunity from criticism. That is the lot of the man in politics; we would have it no other way in this democratic society.

But my political and journalistic adversaries sometimes seem to be asking something more—that I circumscribe my rhetorical freedom, while they place no restrictions on theirs.

As President Kennedy once observed in a far more serious matter, that is like offering an apple for an orchard.

We do not accept those terms for continuing the national dialogue. The day when the network commentators and even gentlemen of the *New York Times* enjoyed a form of diplomatic immunity from comment and criticism of what they said—that day is over.

Just as a politician's words—wise and foolish—are dutifully recorded by the press and television to be thrown up to him at the appropriate time, so their words should likewise be recorded and likewise recalled.

When they go beyond fair comment and criticism they will be called upon to defend their statements and their positions just as we must defend ours. And when their criticism becomes excessive or unjust, we shall invite them down from their ivory towers to enjoy the rough and tumble of the public debate.

I do not seek to intimidate the press, the networks, or anyone else from speaking out. But the time for blind acceptance of their opinions is past. And the time for naive belief in their neutrality is gone.

But, as to the future, all of us could do worse than take as our own the motto of William Lloyd Garrison who said: "I am in earnest. I will not equivocate. I will not excuse. I will not retreat a single inch. And I will be heard."

MIDDLESEX CLUB, BOSTON, MASSACHUSETTS

MARCH 18, 1971

There is no doubt that the framers of our Constitution considered the vice presidency an office suitable for men of energy. Until the ratification of the Twelfth Amendment in 1804, the defeated major presidential candidate was usually elected vice president. This created some interesting stresses. Over the years, however, the vice presidency has lost its political punch and has become the most placid and uncontroversial of political positions. Indeed, as presently structured, it may be compared to an adjustable easy chair. The occupant has his choice of either reclining sleepily or sitting up alertly. The posture adopted is inconsequential, because it is virtually certain that no one will notice which attitude has been selected.

Whatever his decision, however—whether he has dozed amiably or listened attentively—it has been traditional for a vice president to be indulged by the intellectuals and opinion makers of his time with nothing harsher than a deprecating comment or a condescending joke.

In recent years, the rules have been amended to allow vice presidents to talk—so long as they are careful to say absolutely nothing. This privilege was heavily exercised and refined to a high degree during the last administration.

And in regard to vice presidential strictures, it seems appropriate to note—on the occasion of a Lincoln Day address before the oldest Republican organization in Massachusetts—that, following four years of lassitude as Abraham Lincoln's vice president, Hannibal Hamlin suddenly found himself Collector for the Port of Boston.

In my own case, I found it an onerous choice between the ennui of easy chair existence and pointless verbosity. And so, quick constitutional research revealing no authoritative reason why a vice president is required to choose between catalepsy and garrulity, I forsook the comfortable code of many of my predecessors, abandoned the unwritten rules—and said something.

Well, in case you haven't heard, my unorthodoxy produced some rather sharp reverberations. It was as though an earthquake, registering eight on the Richter scale, had disturbed the foundations of the *New York Times,* or the funnel of a tornado had dipped into the editorial offices of *Time-Life.* Everywhere, big media referees were flinging down their handkerchiefs and calling foul. The *Washington Post* stepped off fifteen yards for un-vice presidential-like conduct. *Time* magazine waved me to the penalty box. And Eric Sevareid took two free throws at the line—both rolling around the rim and, as usual, dropping out.

Finally the tremors and tumult subsided. Whereupon my critics from all walks of life consulted among themselves and brought forth the strongest indictment they could muster.

"The vice president," they intoned, "just doesn't seem to understand."

If true, the charge would be a serious enough reflection on the condition of the republic. But worse was yet to come. After my speech on the responsibilities of a free news media in a free society, and after the networks had been deluged with mail in support of my conclusions, a noted network newscaster enlarged the indictment by declaring that, not only the vice president, but the American people as a whole simply don't understand.

Let me quote that spokesman directly.

"The public," said Walter Cronkite recently, "does not understand journalism. They"—that means you and me—"do not know how we work, they do not believe we can hold strong private thoughts and still be objective journalists."

And that's the way it was—or at least the way he saw it—in November 1970.

Mr. Cronkite has stated the case well. He has discerned and defined the scope of the widening credibility gap that exists between the national news media and the American people—a gap which has simply been reported, not created, by this non-understanding vice president. By "national news media" I mean the powerful news outlet having not just a regional, but a national, impact.

Now, before I proceed further, let me pause to observe that, in all probability, my mere utterance of the words "national news media" has in the past few minutes again set the ideological Richter needles quivering all along the Manhattan-Washington fault line. For "national news media" is, after all, the forbidden phrase of modern American politics.

To be sure, such is the power of the national media today that of all our political, social, and economic institutions, they seem to be able to cloak themselves in a special immunity to criticism. By their lights, it appears, freedom of expression is fine so long as it stops before any question is raised or criticism lodged against national media policies and practices.

Nor is the national media's refusal to abide criticism reserved for utterances of a vice president or, as I will momentarily point out, a congressman, or a member of a presidential cabinet. Any citizen who has suffered the frustration of being rebuffed when calling or writing to complain about inaccurate or biased news reporting knows exactly what I mean.

Yet, any extremist who dignifies our adversaries and demeans our traditions is sought out and spotlighted for national attention. He is interviewed as though he was representative of a large following and is treated with the utmost deference as he unloads into millions of American living rooms his imprecations against society and disrespect for civilized law. Such attacks against American institutions are editorially lauded as healthy demonstrations of freedom of expression in a free society.

[At this point, the vice president's remarks were interrupted momentarily by a young man who was escorted out by the authorities.]

And, incidentally, ladies and gentlemen, in a graphic and personal demonstration, did you notice where the lights and cameras just went?

Again, when the president of a prestigious university assaults our nation's judiciary by declaring that certain defendants cannot receive a fair trial in an American court, he is not charged with attempting to "intimidate the courts." On the contrary, he is praised by important segments of the national news media for contributing to what they term "the dialogue."

And, as I shall discuss in a few moments, when a major television network delivers a subtle but vicious broadside against the nation's defense establishment, accusing it of disseminating deceptive, self-serving propaganda, contrary to the country's interest, that, too, is considered a legitimate exercise of the right to free expression in the public interest.

But let no man be so bold as even to utter the words "national news media." For, as we are forewarned by the national media themselves, the merest mention of the phrase by a man in government somehow constitutes a form of "intimidation" so great as to pose a fundamental threat to the people's right to know.

And so tonight, in once again taking up matters involving an important segment of the national news media, I believe it only fitting to cite some authority within media ranks to reinforce my right to do so.

Hear now the words of Mr. Frank Stanton, president of the Columbia Broadcasting System.

"No American institution," Mr. Stanton has said, "including network news organizations, should be immune to public criticism or public discussion of its performance."

I wholeheartedly agree. Proceeding from this premise, I therefore intend to discuss the public's right to know more about the performance of Mr. Stanton's network news organization in two cases involving documentaries—instances wherein CBS itself has claimed an immunity from criticism ill-becoming one of the country's major institutional critics.

For those who would challenge a vice president's right to discuss such matters, let me say this: I do so only to raise questions which, if answered, will shed light on an area of network news operations about which the public knows little and needs to know more. These questions do not originate with me, nor do they arise from any partisan political considerations. Others before me, including the Federal Communications Commission, a special subcommittee of the Congress and a former Democratic cabinet member, have asked Mr. Stanton similar questions, to no avail.

However, considering the serious charges leveled recently by the CBS television news organization against the public affairs activities of the Department of Defense, the matter of the network's own record in the field of documentary making can no longer be brushed under the rug of national media indifference.

Little less than a month ago, on the evening of February 23, 1971, CBS television broadcast a one-hour documentary entitled *The Selling of the Pentagon.* The substance of this documentary was that the Department of Defense is subjecting the American people to, I quote, "a propaganda barrage ... the creation of a runaway bureaucracy that frustrates attempts to control it."

"Nothing is more essential to a democracy," read the CBS script, "than the free flow of information. Misinformation, distortion, and propaganda all interrupt that flow."

No one can disagree with the latter statement. But just as he who enters a court of equity should come with clean hands, the news organization that makes such charges should itself be free of any taint of misinformation, distortion, and propaganda in its own operations. In this regard, it is the CBS television network and not the Department of Defense that leaves much to be desired in terms of "the free flow of information."

Let me be specific. What I cite here is not simply the opinion of a single public official, but conclusions drawn by responsible investigative agencies in the government and the Congress. These conclusions are contained in reports, which in themselves would have made excellent documentary exposés, save for the fact that the national news media have given them scant attention. They concern the production and editing techniques employed by CBS personnel in the making of the documentaries *Hunger in America* and *Project Nassau*.

Many in this audience may have been watching on the evening of May 21, 1968, when the attention of millions of Americans tuned to CBS television was drawn to the onscreen image of an infant receiving emergency treatment while a narrator's off-screen voice said:

Hunger is easy to recognize when it looks like this. This baby is dying of starvation. He was an American. Now he is dead.

This was compelling film footage and narration designed to awaken the public conscience to a serious social problem. The only thing wrong with it was that it was untrue—but wait ... let the official Federal Communications Commission report tell the story. I quote from the official report:

Our post-broadcast investigation revealed that the infant who was filmed by CBS in the nursery, and who was shown in the relevant segment of the *Hunger in America* program ... was born prematurely ... the previous day.... . The infant died on October 29, 1967, the death certificate shows the cause of death as "Immediate cause: Septicemia. Due to: Meningitis and Peritonitis. Due to: Prematurity." There is no evidence to show that either the mother or father was suffering from malnutrition.

Thus, although the dramatic footage which opened the documentary *Hunger in America* may have served the network's purpose of whetting viewer interest, the baby shown "dying of starvation" in fact died of other causes.

Nor, as investigation of the production revealed, was this distortion only an incidental aspect in the overall production of *Hunger in America*. Evidence was submitted that CBS personnel had, in the words of the report, "paid participants on the program to appear before its cameras and perform as per their instructions"; that the CBS crew "requested that the doors of the commodity distribution office be closed to allow a line of people to form"; that a physician was asked to make "more dramatic statements" and when he refused, the segment of the program featuring his more balanced view of the problem of malnutrition in the area was edited out for being "too technical."

In a letter to Mr. Stanton, then Secretary of Agriculture Orville Freeman cited numerous other instances of factual misrepresentation and distortion contained in the documentary. He asked for equal time to present a Department of Agriculture response to the network program. The network denied his request.

Now, having myself gained some experience in what to expect by way of negative network response to public criticism, I can fairly predict what Mr. Stanton and other CBS spokesmen are likely to say tomorrow morning concerning my recital of the case history on *Hunger in America*. They will ask why this matter should be brought up again at this time.

My answer is that I believe it both timely and in the public interest to point out that the same CBS employee who wrote the script to the 1968 documentary *Hunger in America* wrote the script to the 1971 documentary *The Selling of the Pentagon*.

A second and even more startling case history of a documentary-in-the making involves the participation of CBS personnel in an aborted effort to film a 1966 invasion of Haiti. The network's role in this effort, called *Project Nassau*, was investigated last year by the Special Subcommittee on Investigations of the House Commerce Committee. Here, again, let the report of the investigative body tell the story. I quote:

> The activities preparatory to *Project Nassau* involved more than the filming of sham events, manipulation of sound tracks, and the like. Underlying the whole activity was the earnest endeavor by a group of dangerous individuals to subvert the laws of the United States. Had it been successful, the conspiracy would have produced a crisis for American foreign policy in the sensitive Caribbean area. Six men have now been convicted for their part in this conspiracy.

Continuing with the House Subcommittee report on CBS's participation in *Project Nassau:*

> CBS funds were provided for the leasing of a 67-foot schooner which was to be utilized by the invasion force; expenses were reimbursed for the transpor-

Barnes & Noble Bookseller
8915 W. Charleston
Las Vegas, NV 89117
702 242-1987
05-04-07 S02128 R005

Killing the Messenger: 1   24.50
9780231118330

SUB TOTAL   24.50
SALES TAX   1.90
TOTAL   26.40
AMOUNT TENDERED
CHECK   26.40
ACCT #   ***********
CHECK #:   3145
AUTH CODE   793796

TOTAL PAYMENT   26.40
      Thank You for shopping at
      Barnes & Noble Booksellers
#221143 05-04-07 06:55P KJY

For merchandise purchased with a check, a store credit will be issu
the first seven days. Without an original receipt, a store credit
at the lowest selling price. With a receipt, returns of new and u
and unopened music from bn.com can be made for store
Textbooks after 14 days or without a receipt are not returnable.
are not returnable.

Valid photo ID required for all returns, (except for credit card purchases)
exchanges and to receive and redeem store credit. With a receipt, a full
refund in the original form of payment will be issued for new and unread
books and unopened music within 30 days from any Barnes & Noble store.
For merchandise purchased with a check, a store credit will be issued within
the first seven days. Without an original receipt, a store credit will be issued
at the lowest selling price. With a receipt, returns of new and unread books
and unopened music from bn.com can be made for store credit.
Textbooks after 14 days or without a receipt are not returnable. Used books
are not returnable.

Valid photo ID required for all returns, (except for credit card purchases)
exchanges and to receive and redeem store credit. With a receipt, a full
refund in the original form of payment will be issued for new and unread
books and unopened music within 30 days from any Barnes & Noble store.
For merchandise purchased with a check a store credit

tation of weapons which were to be subsequently used by the conspirators; various payments were made to ... the leader of the invasion conspiracy, with full knowledge of his identity and his criminal intentions. If these acts did not actually involve the network in the conspiracy to violate the U.S. Neutrality Act, they came dangerously close to doing so.

They're not my words, ladies and gentlemen. They're the words of the man of the House of Representatives charged with this investigation.

Concerning such illegal activities, the House Subcommittee, in the course of its investigation, made public a CBS policy memorandum which, to quote from the views of a bipartisan group of Subcommittee members, "represents a level of irresponsibility which should no longer be tolerated if the public interest is to be served."

Let me read here from that CBS policy statement to its employees and I quote: "CBS personnel will not knowingly engage in criminal activity in gathering and reporting news, nor will they encourage or induce any person to commit a crime."

Now keep in mind, I am directly quoting the network's policy statement to its employees. *"Obviously, there may be exceptions which ought to be made on an ad hoc basis even to so absolute a rule."*

Ladies and gentlemen, exceptions to the prohibition of CBS's employees in engaging in criminal activities, or encouraging or inducing someone to commit a crime! That's unbelievable, but that's what this memorandum says. Small wonder that the House Subcommittee termed the results of its *Project Nassau* investigation "disquieting." The Subcommittee said, quote:

> To the average viewer, unsophisticated in the intricacies of television production, a network news documentary typically represents a scrupulously objective reporting of actual events shown as they actually transpired. If *Project Nassau* is any indication, this is not always true. During the preparation of this news documentary, CBS employees and consultants intermingled and interacted with personages actively engaged in breaking the law. Large sums of money were made available to these individuals with no safeguards as to the manner in which these funds would be put to use. Events were set up and staged solely for the purpose of being filmed by the CBS cameras....
>
> A disturbing conclusion after the inquiry to date with respect to *Project Nassau* is that the CBS News organization, having become elated at the prospect of a sensational news first—a complete documentary of the forcible overthrow of a foreign government—proceeded in a reckless attempt to capture the hoped-for film, and that it did so with no great regard for either accuracy or legality.

Here, again, this investigation of the making of a CBS documentary bears on the network's more recent production, *The Selling of the Pentagon*. For the executive producer of the aborted documentary *Project Nassau* also served as executive producer of *The Selling of the Pentagon*—a documentary, keep in mind, that sought to indict the Department of Defense for "misinformation, distortion," and the alleged staging of events.

But disquieting as the results are of these investigations by the FCC and the House Subcommittee, there is an even more disturbing note to be added here concerning media treatment of the reports themselves.

Who can doubt that had the evidence uncovered and the conclusions drawn by these investigative bodies related to any other industry or institution they would long ago have become, to coin a phrase, household words? The national news media would have made them so—just as CBS even now seeks to exploit its purported "findings" regarding the Pentagon.

Yet, when the industry and institution involved is itself a part of the national news media, a strange silence and rare restraint inhibits the people's right to know. So powerful is this inhibition that neither a cabinet member, nor an executive agency, nor a congressional committee was effective in bringing to public attention the serious matters to which I have addressed these remarks. And I have grave doubts about how much of my criticism tonight will be carried in the national media.

My purpose here, however, has not been to pillory or "intimidate" a network or any segment of the national news media in its effort to enhance the people's right to know. Rather it is, once again, to point out to those in positions of power and responsibility that this right to know belongs to the people. It does not belong to the national networks or any other agency, public or private. It belongs *to the people themselves,* and they are entitled to a fair and full accounting of the truth, and nothing but the truth, by those who exercise great influence with their consent.

The House Subcommittee concluded:

We are living through dangerous times. In these days it does not seem too strong a statement to say that the survival of the American society may depend upon the political and social judgments made during the next few years by the American electorate. Sound judgment presupposes valid information. The American public looks in great measure to the electronic news media to provide that information.

Let the people's representatives—not only in their government but in their national news media—also look, listen, and take heed.

The Presidency and the Press

DANIEL P. MOYNIHAN

A s his years in Washington came to an end, Harry S. Truman wrote a friend:

> I really look with commiseration over the great body of my fellow citizens, who, reading newspapers, live and die in the belief that they have known something of what has been passing in the world in their time.

A familiar presidential plaint, sounded often in the early years of the Republic and rarely unheard thereafter. Of late, however, a change has developed in the perception of what is at issue. In the past what was thought to be involved was the reputation of a particular president. In the present what is seen to be at stake, and by the presidents themselves, is the reputation of government—especially, of course, presidential government. These are different matters, and summon a different order of concern.

There are two points anyone would wish to make at the outset of an effort to explore this problem. First, it is to be acknowledged that in most essential encounters between the presidency and the press, the advantage is with the former. The president has a near limitless capacity to "make" news which must be reported, if only by reason of competition between one journal, or one

From *Commentary*, March 1971.

medium, and another. (If anything, radio and television news is more readily subject to such dominance. Their format permits of many fewer "stories." The president-in-action almost always takes precedence.) The president also has considerable capacity to reward friends and punish enemies in the press corps, whether they are individual journalists or the papers, television networks, news weeklies, or whatever these individuals work for. And for quite a long while, finally, a president who wishes can carry off formidable deceptions. (One need only recall the barefaced lying that went with the formal opinion of Roosevelt's attorney general that the destroyer-naval-base deal of 1940 was legal.)

With more than sufficient reason, then, publishers and reporters alike have sustained over the generations a lively sense of their vulnerability to governmental coercion or control. For the most part, their worries have been exaggerated. But, like certain virtues, there are some worries that are best carried to excess.

The second point is that American journalism is almost certainly the best in the world. This judgment will be disputed by some. There are good newspapers in other countries. The *best* European journalists are more intellectual than their American counterparts, and some will think this a decisive consideration. But there is no enterprise anywhere the like of the *New York Times*. Few capitals are covered with the insight and access of the *Washington Post* or the *Washington Evening Star*. As with so many American institutions, American newspapers tend to be older and more stable than their counterparts abroad. The *Hartford Courant* was born in 1764, twenty-one years before the *Times* of London. The *New York Post* began publication in 1801, twenty years before the *Manchester Guardian*. What in most other countries is known as the "provincial" press—that is to say journals published elsewhere than in the capital—in America is made up of a wealth of comprehensive and dependable daily newspapers of unusually high quality.

The journalists are in some ways more important than their journals—at least to anyone who has lived much in government. A relationship grows up with the reporters covering one's particular sector that has no counterpart in other professions or activities. The relationship is one of simultaneous trust and distrust, friendship and enmity, dependence and independence. But it is the men of government, especially in Washington, who are the more dependent. The journalists are their benefactors, their conscience, at times almost their reason for being. For the journalists are above all others their audience, again especially in Washington, which has neither an intellectual community nor an electorate, and where there is no force outside government able to judge events, much less to help shape them, save the press.

That there is something wondrous and terrible in the intensities of this relationship between the press and the government is perhaps best seen at the annual theatricals put on by such groups of journalists as the Legislative Correspondents Association in Albany or the Gridiron in Washington. To my knowledge nothing comparable takes place anywhere else in the world. These gatherings are a kind of ritual truth telling, of which the closest psychological approximation would be the Calabrian insult ritual described by Roger Vailland in his novel *The Law,* or possibly the group-therapy practices of more recent origin. The politicians come as guests of the journalists. The occasion is first of all a feast: the best of everything. Then as dinner progresses the songs begin. The quality varies, of course, but at moments startling levels of deadly accurate commentary of great cruelty are achieved. The politicians sit and smile and applaud. Then some of them speak. Each one wins or loses to the degree that he can respond in kind; stay funny and be brutal. (At the Gridiron John F. Kennedy was a master of the style, but the piano duet performed by Nixon and Agnew in 1970 was thought by many to have surpassed anything yet done.) A few lyrics appear in the next day's papers, but what the newspapermen really said to the politicians remains privileged—as does so much of what the politicians say to them. The relationship is special.

How is it then that this relationship has lately grown so troubled? The immediate answer is, of course, the war in Vietnam. An undeclared war, unwanted, misunderstood, or not understood at all, it entailed a massive deception of the American people by their government. Surely a large area of the experience of the 1960s is best evoked in the story of the man who says: "They told me that if I voted for Goldwater there would be 500,000 troops in Vietnam within a year. I voted for him, and, by God, they were right." The story has many versions. If he voted for Goldwater we would be defoliating the countryside of Vietnam; the army would he sending spies to the 1968 party conventions; Dr Spock would be indicted on conspiracy charges; and so on. By 1968 Richard Rovere described the capital as "awash" with lies.

The essential fact was that of deceit. How else to carry out a full-scale war that became steadily more unpopular with none of the legally sanctioned constraints on the free flow of information which even the most democratic societies find necessary in such circumstances? This situation did not spring full-blown from the involvement in Southeast Asia. It was endemic to the cold war. At the close of World War II official press censorship was removed, but the kinds of circumstance in which any responsible government might feel that events have to be concealed from the public did not go away. The result was a contradiction impossible to resolve. The public interest was at once served and disserved by secrecy; at once disserved and served by openness. Whatever the case, distrust of government grew. At the outset of the U-2 affair in 1960, the

United States government asserted that a weather plane on a routine mission had been shot down. The *New York Times* (May 6, 1960) reported *not* just that the U.S. government *claimed* it was a weather plane, but simply that it was. Well, it wasn't. Things have not been the same since.

But there are problems between the presidency and the press which have little to do with the cold war or with Vietnam and which—if this analysis is correct—will persist or even intensify should those conditions recede, or even dissolve, as a prime source of public concern. The problems flow from five basic circumstances which together have been working to reverse the old balance of power between the presidency and the press. It is the thesis here that if this balance should tip too far in the direction of the press, our capacity for effective democratic government will be seriously and dangerously weakened.

I

The first of these circumstances has to do with the tradition of "muck-raking"—the exposure of corruption in government or the collusion of government with private interests—which the American press has seen as a primary mission since the period from 1880 to 1914. It is, in Irving Kristol's words, "a journalistic phenomenon that is indigenous to democracy, with its instinctive suspicion and distrust of all authority in general, and of concentrated political and economic power especially." Few would want to be without the tradition, and it is a young journalist of poor spirit who does not set out to uncover the machinations of some malefactor of great wealth and his political collaborators. Yet there is a cost, as Roger Starr suggests in his wistful wish that Lincoln Steffens's *The Shame of the Cities* might be placed on the restricted shelves of the schools of journalism. Steffens has indeed, as Starr declares, continued "to haunt the city rooms of the country's major newspapers." The question to be asked is whether, in the aftermath of Steffens, the cities were better, or merely more ashamed of themselves. Looking back, one is impressed by the energy and capacity for governance of some of the old city machines. Whatever else, it was popular government, of and by men of the people. One wonders: did the middle-and upper-class reformers destroy the capacity of working-class urban government without replacing it with anything better so that half-a-century later each and all bewail the cities as ungovernable? One next wonders whether something not dissimilar will occur now that the focus of press attention has shifted from City Hall to the White House. (And yet a miracle of American national government is the almost complete absence of monetary corruption at all levels, and most especially at the top.)

The muckraking tradition is well established. Newer, and likely to have far more serious consequences, is the advent of what Lionel Trilling has called the "adversary culture" as a conspicuous element in journalistic practice. The appearance in large numbers of journalists shaped by the attitudes of this culture is the result of a process whereby the profession thought to improve itself by recruiting more and more persons from middle- and upper-class backgrounds and trained at the universities associated with such groups. This is a change but little noted as yet. The stereotype of American newspapers is that of publishers ranging from conservative to reactionary in their political views balanced by reporters ranging from liberal to radical in theirs. One is not certain how accurate the stereotype ever was. One's impression is that twenty years and more ago the preponderance of the "working press" (as it liked to call itself) was surprisingly close in origins and attitudes to working people generally. They were not Ivy Leaguers. They now are or soon will be. Journalism has become, if not an elite profession, a profession attractive to elites. This is noticeably so in Washington where the upper reaches of journalism constitute one of the most important and enduring *social* elites of the city, with all the accoutrements one associates with a leisured class. (The Washington press corps is not leisured at all, but the style is that of men and women who *choose to* work.)

The political consequence of the rising social status of journalism is that the press grows more and more influenced by attitudes genuinely hostile to American society and American government. This trend seems bound to continue into the future. On the record of what they have been writing while in college, the young people now leaving the Harvard *Crimson* and the Columbia *Spectator* for journalistic jobs in Washington will resort to the Steffens style at ever-escalating levels of moral implication. They bring with them the moral absolutism of George Wald's vastly popular address, "A Generation in Search of a Future," that describes the Vietnam War as "the most shameful episode in the whole of American history." Not tragic, not heartbreaking, not vastly misconceived, but *shameful.* From the shame of the cities to the shame of the nation. But nobody ever called Boss Croker any name equivalent in condemnatory weight as the epithet "war criminal."

II

An ironical accompaniment of the onset of the muckraking style directed toward the presidency has been the rise of a notion of the near-omnipotency of the office itself. This notion Thomas E. Cronin describes as the "textbook president." Cronin persuasively argues that in the aftermath of Franklin Roosevelt a view of the presidency, specifically incorporated in the textbooks of recent decades, was developed which presented seriously "inflated and unrealistic interpretations of presidential competence and beneficence," and which grievously "overemphasized the policy change and policy accomplishment capabilities" of the office. Cronin cites Anthony Howard, a watchful British commentator:

For what the nation has been beguiled into believing ever since 1960 is surely the politics of evangelism: the faith that individual men are cast to be messiahs, the conviction that presidential incantations can be substituted for concrete programs, the belief that what matters is not so much the state of the nation as the inspiration-quotient of its people.

In his own research among advisers of Kennedy and Johnson, Cronin finds the majority to hold "tempered assessments of presidential determination of 'public policy.'" Indeed, only 10 percent would describe the president as having "very great impact" over such matters.

Working in the White House is a chastening experience. But it is the experience of very few persons. Watching the White House, on the other hand, is a mass occupation, concentrated especially among the better-educated, better-off groups. For many the experience is one of infatuation followed much too promptly by disillusion. First, the honeymoon—in Cronin's terms, the "predictable ritual of euphoric inflation." But then "the Camelot of the first few hundred days of all Presidencies fades away.... . Predictably, by the second year, reports are spread that the president has become isolated from criticism." If this is so, he has only himself to blame when things go wrong. And things do go wrong.

If the muckraking tradition implies a distrust of government, it is nonetheless curiously validated by the overly trusting tradition of the "textbook presidency" which recurrently sets up situations in which the presidency will be judged as having somehow broken faith. This is not just the experience of a Johnson or a Nixon. Anyone who was in the Kennedy administration in the summer and fall of 1963 would, or ought to, report a pervasive sense that our initiative had been lost, that we would have to get reelected to get going again.

Here, too, there is a curious link between the presidency and the press. The two most important presidential newspapers are the *New York Times* and the *Washington Post* (though the *Star* would be judged by many to have the best reporting). Both papers reflect a tradition of liberalism that has latterly been shaped and reinforced by the very special type of person who *buys* the paper. (It is well to keep in mind that newspapers are capitalist enterprises which survive by persuading people to buy them.) Theirs is a "disproportionately" well-educated and economically prosperous audience. The geographical areas in which the two papers circulate almost certainly have higher per-capita incomes and higher levels of education than any of comparable size in the nation or the world. More of the buyers of these two papers are likely to come from "liberal" Protestant or Jewish backgrounds than would be turned up by a random sample of the population; they comprise, in fact, what James Q. Wilson calls "the Liberal Audience." Both the working-class Democrats and the conservative Republicans, with exceptions, obviously, have been pretty much driven from office among the constituencies where the *Times* and the *Post* flourish. It would be wrong to ascribe this to the influence of the papers. Causality almost certainly moves both ways. Max Frankel of the *Times,* who may have peers but certainly no betters as a working journalist, argues that a newspaper is surely as much influenced by those who read it as vice versa.

The readers of the *New York Times* and the *Washington Post,* then, are a special type of citizen: not only more affluent and more liberal than the rest of the nation but inclined also to impose heavy expectations on the presidency, and not to be amused when those expectations fail to be met. Attached by their own internal traditions to the "textbook presidency," papers like the *Times* and the *Post* are reinforced in this attachment by the temperamental predilections of the readership whose character they inevitably reflect. Thus they help to set a tone of pervasive dissatisfaction with the performance of the national government, whoever the presidential incumbent may be and whatever the substance of his policies.

III

A third circumstance working to upset the old balance of power between the presidency and the press is the fact that Washington reporters depend heavily on more or less clandestine information from federal bureaucracies which are frequently, and in some cases routinely, antagonistic to presidential interests.

There is a view of the career civil service as a more or less passive executor of policies made on high. This is quite mistaken. A very great portion of policy ideas "bubble up" from the bureaucracy, and, just as important, a very considerable portion of the "policy decisions" that go down never come to anything, either because the bureaucrats cannot or will not follow through. (The instances of simple inability are probably much greater than those of outright hostility.) Few modern presidents have made any *impact* on the federal bureaucracies save by creating new ones. The bureaucracies are unfamiliar and inaccessible. They are quasi-independent, maintaining, among other things, fairly open relationships with the congressional committees that enact their statutes and provide their funds. They are usually willing to work with the president, but rarely to the point where their perceived interests are threatened. Typically these are rather simple territorial interests: not to lose any jurisdiction and, if possible to gain some. But, recurrently, issues of genuine political substance are also involved.

At the point where they perceive a threat to those interests, the bureaucracies just as recurrently go to the press. They know the press; the press knows them. Both stay in town as presidential governments come and go. Both cooperate in bringing to bear the most powerful weapons the bureaucracies wield in their own defense, that of revealing presidential plans in advance of their execution. Presidents and their plans are helpless against this technique. I have seen a senior aide to a president, sitting over an early morning cup of coffee, rise and literally punch the front page of the *New York Times*. A major initiative was being carefully mounted. Success depended, to a considerable degree, on surprise. Someone in one of the agencies whose policies were to be reversed got hold of the relevant document and passed it on to the *Times*. Now everyone would know. The mission was aborted. There was *nothing* for the presidential government to do. No possibility of finding, much less of disciplining, the bureaucrat responsible. For a time, or rather from time to time, President Johnson tried the technique of *not* going ahead with any policy or appointment that was leaked in advance to the press. Soon, however, his aides began to suspect that this was giving the bureaucracy the most powerful weapon of all, namely, the power to veto a presidential decision by learning of it early enough and rushing to the *Times* or the *Post*. (Or, if the issue could be described in thirty seconds, any of the major television networks.)

What we have here is disloyalty to the presidency. Much of the time what is involved is no more than the self-regard of lower-echelon bureaucrats who are simply flattered into letting the reporter know how much *they* know, or who are just trying to look after their agency. But just as often, to repeat, serious issues of principle are involved. Senator Joseph McCarthy made contact with what he termed "the loyal American underground"—State Department officials, and other such, who reputedly passed on information to him about communist infiltration of the nation's foreign-policy and security systems. President Johnson made it clear that he did not trust the Department of State to maintain "security" in foreign policy. Under President Nixon the phenomenon has been most evident in domestic areas, as OEO warriors struggle among themselves to be the first to disclose the imminent demise of VISTA, or HEW functionaries reluctantly interpret a move to close some fever hospital built to accommodate an 18th-century seaport as the first step in a master plan to dismantle public medicine and decimate the ranks of the elderly and disadvantaged.

It is difficult to say whether the absolute level of such disloyalty to the presidency is rising. One has the impression that it is. No one knows much about the process of "leaking" except in those instances where he himself has been involved. *(Everyone* is sooner or later involved. That should be understood.) The process has not been studied and little is known of it. But few would argue that the amount of clandestine disclosure is decreasing. Such disclosure is now part of the way we run our affairs. It means, among other things, that the press is fairly continuously involved in an activity that is something less than honorable. Repeatedly it benefits from the self-serving acts of government officials who are essentially hostile to the presidency. This does the presidency no good, and if an outsider may comment, it does the press no good either. Too much do they traffic in stolen goods, and they know it.

This point must be emphasized. The leaks which appear in the *Post* and the *Times*—other papers get them, but if one wants to influence decisions in Washington these are clearly thought to be the most effective channels—are ostensibly published in the interest of adding to public knowledge of what is going on. This budget is to be cut; that man is to be fired; this bill is to be proposed. However, in the nature of the transaction the press can only publish half the story—that is to say the information that the "leaker" wants to become "public knowledge." What the press *never* does is say who the leaker is and why he wants the story leaked. Yet, more often than not, this is the more important story: that is to say, what policy wins if the one being disclosed loses, what individual, what bureau, and so on.

There really are ethical questions involved here that have not been examined. There are also serious practical questions. It would be my impression that the distress occasioned by leaks has used up too much presidential energy, at least from the time of Roosevelt. (Old-time brain-trusters would assure the Johnson staff that nothing could compare with FDR's distractions on the subject.) The primary fault lies within government itself, and one is at a loss to think of anything that might be done about it. But it is a problem for journalism as well, and an unattended one.

IV

The fourth of the five conditions making for an altered relation between the presidency and the press is the concept of objectivity with respect to the reporting of events and especially the statements of public figures. Almost the first canon of the great newspapers, and, by extension, of the television news networks which by and large have taken as their standards those of the best newspapers, is that "the news" will be reported whether or not the reporter or the editor or the publisher likes the news. There is nothing finer in the American newspaper tradition. There is, however, a rub and it comes when a decision has to be made as to whether an event really is news or simply a happening, a non-event staged for the purpose of getting into the papers or onto the screen. The record of our best papers is not reassuring here, as a glance at the experience of the Korean and the Vietnam wars will suggest. Beginning a bit before the Korean hostilities broke out, but in the general political period we associate with that war, there was a rise of right-wing extremism, a conspiracy-oriented politics symbolized by the name of Senator Joseph McCarthy and directed primarily at the institution of the presidency. There was, to be sure, a populist streak to this movement: Yale and Harvard and the "striped-pants boys" in the State Department were targets, too. But to the question, "Who promoted the Press?" there was only one constitutional or—for all practical purposes—political answer, namely, that the president did. McCarthy went on asking such questions, or rather making such charges, and the national press, which detested and disbelieved him throughout, went on printing them. The American style of objective journalism made McCarthy. He would not, I think, have gotten anywhere in Great Britain, where, because it would have been judged he was lying, the stories would simply not have been printed.

Something not dissimilar has occurred in the course of the Vietnam War, only this time the extremist, conspiracy-oriented politics of protest has been putatively left-wing. Actually both movements are utterly confusing if one depends on European analogues. McCarthy was nominally searching out Communists, but his preferred targets were Eastern patricians, while his supporters were, to an alarming degree, members of the Catholic working class. The Students for a Democratic Society [SDS], if that organization may be used as an exemplar, was (at least in its later stages) nominally revolutionist, dedicated to the overthrow of the capitalist-imperialist-fascist regime of the United States. Yet, as Seymour Martin Lipset, Nathan Glazer, and others have shown, its leadership, and perhaps also its constituency, was disproportionately made up of upper-class Jewish and Protestant youth. By report of Steven Kelman, who lived as a contemporary among them at Harvard, the SDS radicals were "undemocratic, manipulative, and self-righteous to the point of snobbery and elitism." Peter Berger, a sociologist active in the peace movement, has demonstrated quite persuasively—what others, particularly persons of European origin like himself have frequently seemed to sense—that despite the leftist ring of the slogans of SDS and kindred groups, their ethos and tactics are classically fascist: the cult of youth, the mystique of the street, the contempt for liberal democracy, and the "totalization of friend and foe [with] the concomitant dehumanization of the latter," as in the Nazi use of "*Saujuden*" ("Jewish pigs").

In any case, the accusations which have filled the American air during the period of Vietnam have been no more credible or responsible than those of McCarthy during the Korean period, and the tactics of provocation and physical intimidation have, if anything, been more disconcerting. Yet the national press, and especially television, has assumed a neutral posture, even at times a sympathetic one, enabling the neo-fascists of the Left to occupy center stage throughout the latter half of the 1960s with consequences to American politics that have by no means yet worked themselves out. (It took Sam Brown to point out that one consequence was to make the work of the antiwar movement, of which he has been a principal leader, vastly more difficult.)

Would anyone have it otherwise? Well, yes. Irving Kristol raised this question in an article that appeared before the New Left had made its presence strongly felt on the national scene, but his views are doubtless even more emphatic by now. He wrote of the "peculiar mindlessness which pervades the practice of journalism in the United States," asserting that the ideal of objectivity too readily becomes an excuse for avoiding judgment. If McCarthy was lying, why print what he said? Or why print it on the front page? If the SDS stages a confrontation over a trumped-up issue, why oblige it by taking the whole episode at face value? Here, let it be said, the editorials of the *Times* and the *Post* have consistently served as a thoughtful corrective to the impressions inescapably conveyed by the news columns. But the blunt fact is that just as the news columns were open to astonishingly false assertions about the nature of the American national government during the McCarthy period, they have been open to equally false assertions—mirror images of McCarthyism indeed—during the period of Vietnam. And although it is impossible to prove, one gets the feeling that the slanderous irresponsibilities now being reported so dutifully are treated with far more respect than the old.

The matter of a policy of "genocide" pursued by the national government against the Black Panthers is a good example. By late 1969, preparing a preface to a second edition of *Beyond the Melting Pot*, Nathan Glazer and I could insist that the charge that twenty-eight Panthers had been murdered by the police was on the face of it simply untrue. Yet in that mindless way of which Kristol writes, the *Times* kept reprinting it. Edward Jay Epstein has brilliantly explained the matter in a recent article in the *New Yorker*. What he finds is an immense fraud. No such policy existed. There was no conspiracy between the Department of Justice, the FBI, and various local police forces to wipe out the

Panthers. Yet that fraudulent charge has so profoundly affected the thinking of the academic and liberal communities that they will probably not even now be able to see the extent to which they were deceived. The hurt that has been done to blacks is probably in its way even greater. None of it could have happened without the particular mind-set of the national press.

If the press is to deserve our good opinion, it must do better in such matters. And it should keep in mind that the motivation of editors and reporters is not always simply and purely shaped by a devotion to objectivity. In the course of the McCarthy era James Reston recalled the ancient adage which translated from the Erse proposes that, "if you want an audience, start a fight." This is true of anyone who would find an audience for his views or simply for himself. It is true also of anyone who would find customers for the late city edition. T. S. Matthews, sometime editor of *Time,* retired to England to ponder the meaning of it all. In the end, all he could conclude was that the function of journalism was entertainment. If it is to be more—and that surely is what the Rosenthals and Bradlees and Grunwalds and Elliotts want—it will have to be willing on occasion to forgo the entertainment value of a fascinating but untruthful charge. It will, in short, have to help limit the rewards which attend this posture in American politics.

V

The final, and by far the most important, circumstance of American journalism relevant to this discussion is the absence of a professional tradition of self-correction. The mark of any developed profession is the practice of correcting mistakes, by whomsoever they are made. This practice is, of course, the great invention of Western science. Ideally it requires an epistemology which is shared by all respected members of the profession, so that when a mistake is discovered it can be established as a mistake to the satisfaction of the entire professional community. Ideally, also, no discredit is involved: to the contrary, honest mistakes are integral to the process of advancing the field. Journalism will never attain to any such condition. Nevertheless, there is a range of subject matter about which reasonable men can and will agree, and within this range American journalism, even of the higher order, is often seriously wide of the mark. Again Irving Kristol:

> It is a staple of conversation among those who have ever been involved in
> a public activity that when they read the *Times* the next morning, they will
> discover that it has almost never got the story quite right and has only too

frequently got it quite wrong.

Similar testimony has come from an editor of the *New York Times* itself. In an article published some years ago in the magazine of the Sunday *Times*, A. H. Raskin had this to say:

> No week passes without someone prominent in politics, industry, labor or civic affairs complaining to me, always in virtually identical terms: "Whenever I read a story about something in which I really know what is going on, I'm astonished at how little of what is important gets into the papers—and how often even that little is wrong." The most upsetting thing about these complaints is the frequency with which they come from scientists, economists and other academicians temporarily involved in government policy but without any proprietary concern about who runs the White House or City Hall.

This is so, and in part it is unavoidable. Too much happens too quickly: that the *Times* or the *Post* or the *Star* should appear once a day is a miracle. (Actually they appear three or four times a day in different editions.) But surely when mistakes are made they ought to be corrected. Sometimes they are but not nearly enough. It is in this respect that Kristol is right in calling journalism "the underdeveloped profession."

Assertions that the press has a flawed sense of objectivity, or that it enjoys too cozy a relationship with the civil service, are not easily proved or disproved. But to say that mistakes are repeatedly made and not corrected is to say something which ought to be backed up with specific instances. Let me, then, offer two, taken from stories which appeared in the *New York Times* during the second half of 1970. (I was serving in the White House at the time, though I was not directly involved in any of the matters to be described.)

The first of my two examples is a long article which appeared in the *Times* on Sunday, November 15, 1970, under the headline, "Blacks Seek Tougher Equality Standards for Federal Hiring and Promotion." This story was not hostile to the administration; rather the contrary. It noted that the president had earlier signed an executive order requiring each department and agency to maintain an "affirmative" equal-opportunity program, and that the number of blacks in the top grades of the civil service had gone up almost by half under the "low-key approach of the Nixon administration." The number of black lawyers in the Justice Department had declined somewhat. There were said to have been 61 (out of a total of 1,900 to 2,000) under the Democrats. This figure had dropped under the Republicans to 45, but it also appeared that the difference was lo be made up by new recruits. In the meantime the Department of Transportation was promulgating new rules, the Bureau of Prisons had eliminated the written test for correction officers, and similar activity aimed at increasing the number of blacks in the higher levels of the federal government was to be encountered elsewhere. All this, however, was going on in the context of a federal employment system whose patterns of practice were lamentably at odds with its profession of being an "equal-opportunity employer," to use the federal phrase. In the words of the *Times* story:

> The most recent figures show 137,919 blacks among the 1,289,114 government employees covered by Civil Service regulations. That is about 10.7 percent, less than the black proportion of the population, estimated in the 1970 census as 12.9 percent.

The story went on to note that a number of black activists doubted that the federal government ever had been an equal-opportunity employer. One was particularly skeptical of executive orders: "This friendly persuasion thing has never worked in the history of our government." Next came the question of quotas:

> Although little support for a formal quota system is evident, there is a widely held belief that presidential statements of policy should be supplemented by more detailed instructions as to how the policies should be implemented.

There is little to take exception to in the foregoing. The official census figures for 1970 show blacks to be 12.4 percent of the population, *not* 12.9 percent, but newspapers routinely make such mistakes. It should also have been pointed out that blacks constitute only 10.9 percent of the civilian non-institutional population of sixteen years of age or older, which is to say the population available for employment. In that sense, even accepting the figures used by the *Times,* blacks might be seen as having almost exactly "their" proportion of government employment, although an inadequate number of top positions.

The difficulty in this instance lies not with what was in the story but what was not. What was not in the story was the fact that the category of federal worker—"General Schedule"—of which Negroes do indeed comprise 10.7 percent is only one of three categories. In the other two categories of federal employee, the Postal Service and Wage System employees, Negroes made up 19.5 percent and 19.7 percent, respectively. In rough terms, federal jobs are about equally divided among the three categories. Small wonder, then, that the *Times* reported an absence of much discussion about establishing racial quotas for federal employment. Altogether, blacks have more than 15 percent of federal jobs. If quotas were established according to the black proportion of the adult population, almost a third of black federal employees would have to be fired!

What all this comes to is that the very considerable achievement of blacks in qualifying for federal jobs and getting them far in excess of their proportion in the work force is in effect concealed and a legitimate source of black pride thereby denied. So, too, we are denied a legitimate sense of national progress in combating discrimination. And thus we are fed the tendentious allegations of those who wish to discredit the American "system" as inherently and irrevocably racist.

With respect to the role of the *Times* reporter, it must be said that it is simply not possible for him to have gotten the data on Classified Service employment from the Civil Service Commission releases on the subject without knowing that this is but one of three categories of employment, and that in the other categories blacks do exceptionally well. The truth would have made things look better than the reporter wished them to look. One fears it is as simple as that.

The second instance is rather more complicated. On September 14, 1970 a front-page story was published in the *Times* under the headline, "Negro College Heads Say Nixon Ignores Their Plight." The lead paragraph declared: "The presidents of nine financially troubled Negro colleges accused the Nixon administration today of intensifying racial tensions by falling to support black education." The presidents felt that massive grants were needed, and one was reported as saying that "it's five minutes before doomsday in this country." Dr. Vivian Henderson, president of Clark College in Atlanta, was reported as notably disturbed, asserting that "the Nixon administration's utter lack of sensitivity on this point, purposeful or otherwise, is feeding the flames that already roar in the hearts of many black students."

All this seemed routine enough. From the onset of mass urban rioting in the mid-1960s all manner of requests for federal funds have been backed up by not especially subtle threats of violence. Nor was it unfamiliar to learn a few weeks later that the tactic had worked. On October 2, the front page of the *Times* carried a story from the Associated Press which began: "The Nixon administration responded to complaints that it is insensitive to Negro education by announcing today a 30 percent increase in Federal aid for predominantly black colleges." The next paragraph explained: "The Secretary of Health, Education, and Welfare, Elliot L. Richardson, said in a statement that the $30 million increase was ordered by President Nixon after he heard appeals from Negro educators."

The story bumped around in the press for the next few months, culminating in a way on January 3, 1971, when another *Times* story reported that the Negro colleges were not finding it possible to draw on all of the additional $30 million. Some college presidents were reportedly angry to have learned that the law provides for a 30 percent matching requirement for construction aid, which made up $20 million of the additional $30 million. But the basic theme of the *Times's* coverage of this episode remained the same. The January 3 story began: "For two years, Negro colleges called on the Nixon administration for substantial financial help. Last September, the administration responded, releasing $30 million for use by the schools." There are problems of detail here. The Nixon administration had not been in office for two years in September 1969; the first *Times* report of an appeal appeared (as best I can determine) that very month, and the response came a month later, in October. Be that as it may, the January 3 story declared: "Black educators have severely criticized President Nixon for allegedly ignoring the plight of their schools. The educators charged that black schools have not shared in the money and grants that go out to American educational institutions."

To repeat a familiar theme: the way to get something out of the federal government is to blast it out. Left to itself, government would never have given these financially weak institutions a break. If you want action—especially if you are black—raise hell, right?

Wrong.

At least wrong in this instance. The true sequence of events which made up this story was turned literally upside down by the *Times*. The initiative to aid black colleges had been voluntarily taken by the administration a year before the *Times* got onto the issue. The increased support was announced months before the *Times* reported it. Far from having denounced the administration, the black college presidents had been praising it. And, for good measure, far from getting less than their share of federal aid, the black colleges had all along been getting rather more.

There are124 "predominantly black colleges" in America, most of them small, and most in the South. They enroll somewhat more than 2 percent of the college population, but this includes more than half of all black undergraduates. They live with many difficulties, of which the most important—as is true of almost all colleges, large and small—is money. In 1969, they organized themselves as the National Association for Equal Opportunity in Higher Education and set out, as well they might, to get more federal funds. On October 23, 1969, a meeting on this subject was held in the Executive Office Building presided over by Robert J. Brown, a special assistant to the president, who as a southern Negro was much interested in the problems of the predominantly black colleges. As a result of this meeting the Federal Interagency Committee on Education (FICE) was directed to find out what was already being done for these colleges by the considerable array of federal agencies involved in supporting education and what plans existed for the future. A preliminary report was sent to the White House in February 1970, and in June a 45-page document entitled "Federal Agencies and Black Colleges" was printed. It was a good report full of information concerning what was being done and of recommendations for doing more. (One does not commission such reports with the expectation of being advised to do less.) In the meantime, on May 25, 1970, the president had met with a group of black college presidents, apparently the first such meeting ever to be held. In the aftermath of the Cambodian invasion, Dr. James Cheek, president of Howard University, which is basically a federal institution, served temporarily in the White House as an associate of Chancellor Alexander Heard. During that time he made recommendations directly to the president on the subject of the black colleges. Much attention, then, was being given to this matter in the White House.

On July 23. 1970, a White House press conference was held by Brown and Robert Finch, formerly Secretary of HEW, now counsellor to the president. The main purpose of the occasion was to release a statement by Heard on the completion of his advisory work on campus unrest. Obviously seeking to strike a positive note about the Heard-Cheek effort, the two White House men also brought up the subject of black colleges. The FICE report was given to the press, and Finch announced that, on departing, Dr. Cheek had filed a "separate document" on this "Very unique" problem. He continued: "That just came in today. The president read it today. The president asked him to write such a report, and I am authorized to say, after discussing it with the president, that in HEW ... we are going to increase [aid] ... from $80 million to $100 million." Finch's numbers were somewhat garbled. HEW aid to black colleges at the time was $96 million for the fiscal year. The additional sum now being reallocated was between $29 million and $30 million. In any event, the *Times* report of the press conference did not mention this subject.

On July 31, Dr. Herman R. Branson, president of Central State University in Wilberforce, Ohio, and the new head of the National Association for Equal Opportunity in Higher Education, wrote the president expressing appreciation for his move. On August 10 the president replied:

The present financial plight of many of our small and the overwhelming majority of our black colleges clearly demonstrates to me that the federal government must strengthen its role in support of these institutions.

I have commuted this administration to the vigorous support of equal educational opportunity. At the same time, we are encouraging excellence in all of our institutions of higher education.

In a release dated August 11, 1970, the National Association for Equal Opportunity in Higher Education formally responded to the administration's move. In the accepted and understood manner of interest groups, the association expressed gratitude for what it had been given but assured the government that it was not, of course, enough. On the other hand, it was confident that more would be forthcoming:

> We do not view this excellent first step as adequate to all our needs but rather as a model of what all agencies can do.... With the forthright statement of the president in his letter to Dr. Branson, we are very much encouraged and heartened about the future.

The *Times* reported nothing of this statement, as it had reported nothing of the original announcement from the White House that an extra $30 million or so was being made available to black colleges. White House announcements, presidential letters, Washington press conferences—all were ignored. The subject was not dealt with at all until the following month when, as noted earlier, a story depicted the black college presidents as denouncing the administration's "utter lack of sensitivity" on this matter. *This* story made the front page.

The day after it appeared Dr. Vivian Henderson, of Clark College in Atlanta, to whom the remark about "utter lack of sensitivity'" had been attributed, sent the following unequivocal denial to the *Times:*

> I am deeply disturbed by the inaccurate reporting of the conference of Presidents of Negro Colleges that appeared in the September 14 issue of the *New York Times.* The following statement is attributed to me: "Instead the Nixon administration's utter lack of sensitivity on this point, purposeful or otherwise, is feeding the flames that already roar in the hearts of many black students." This is a gross error and misrepresentation of what actually went on at the meeting. To be sure, we were concerned with the limited response of President Nixon to our problems. The fact is, however, that President Nixon has responded. He has not been silent with regard to concerns expressed by the presidents in the meeting with him last May. Since the meeting with Mr. Nixon, about $27 million additional funds have been made available to black colleges. It would be unfair on our part not to recognize this response, limited though it is.
>
> I did not make the statement your reporter attributes to me. I do not recall such a statement being made during the course of the conference.

The *Times* did not print this letter. Instead it went on to repeat the theme of the original story and gradually to establish it elsewhere as truth. In the end a small bit of history had been rewritten: even the wire services followed the *Times's*, version. No one intended this. That should be clear. It is simply that the journalistic system preferred a confrontation-capitulation model of events, and there was no internal corrective procedure to alert the editors to the mistakes being made.

There are true social costs in all this. For one thing, a paper like the *Times* is a prime medium for internal communication within the government itself. Any Washington official following this story in the *Times* would have had to assume that the administration's attitude toward black colleges was just about opposite to what in fact it was. Such a reversal of signals can have serious consequences. Similarly there are consequences to the principals involved, in this case the college presidents who had been acting with skill and discipline and reasonable success (most notably in having gained access: within hours of the appearance of the first *Times* story a black college president was in the White House seeking reassurance that the $27–30 million had not been jeopardized) but who found themselves represented as stereotypical confrontationists. Everyone in a sense lost because the *Times* got the story wrong.

VI

In the wake of so lengthy an analysis, what is there to prescribe? Little. Indeed, to prescribe much would be to miss the intent of the analysis. I have been hoping to make two points—the first explicitly, the second largely by implication. The first is that a convergence of journalistic tradition with evolving cultural patterns has placed the national government at a kind of operating disadvantage. It is hard for government to succeed: this theme echoes from every capital of the democratic world. In the United States it is hard for government to succeed and just as hard for government to appear to have succeeded when indeed it has done so. This situation can be said to have begun in the muckraking era with respect to urban government; it is now very much the case with respect to national government, as reflected in the "national press" which primarily includes the *New York Times,* the *Washington Post, Time, Newsweek,* and a number of other journals.

There is nothing the matter with investigative reporting; there ought to be more. The press can be maddeningly complacent about real social problems for which actual countermeasures, even solutions, exist. (I spent a decade, 1955–65, trying to obtain some press coverage of the problem of motor vehicle design, utterly without avail. The press, from the most prestigious journals on down, would print nothing but the pap handed out by the automobile companies and wholly owned subsidiaries such as the National Safety Council.) The issue is not one of serious inquiry but of an almost feckless hostility to power.

The second point is that this may not be good for us. American government will only rarely and intermittently be run by persons drawn from the circles of those who own and edit and write for the national press; no government will ever have this circle as its political base. Hence the conditions are present for a protracted conflict in which the national government keeps losing. This might once have been a matter of little consequence or interest. It is, I believe, no longer such, for it now takes place within the context of what Nathan Glazer has so recently described in these pages as an "assault on the reputation of America ... which has already succeeded in reducing this country, in the eyes of many American intellectuals, to outlaw status." In other words, it is no longer a matter of this or that administration; it is becoming a matter of national morale, of a "loss of confidence and nerve," some of whose possible consequences, as Glazer indicates, are not pleasant to contemplate.

Some will argue that in the absence of a parliamentary question-time only the press can keep the presidency honest. Here we get much talk about presidential press conferences and such. This is a serious point, but I would argue that the analogy does not hold. Questions are put in Parliament primarily by members of an opposition party hoping to replace the one in office. Incompetent questions damage those chances; irresponsible questions damage the office. Indeed, British politicians have been known to compare the press lords to ladies of the street, seeking "power without responsibility." It would, of course, be better all around if Congress were more alert. Thus the *Times* has reported that the GNP estimate in the 1971 Budget Message was not that of the Council of Economic Advisers, but rather a higher figure dictated by the White House for political purposes. This is a profoundly serious charge. Someone has a lot to explain. It could be the administration; it could be the *Times*. Congress should find out.

Obviously the press of a free country is never going to be and never should be celebratory. Obviously government at all levels needs and will continue to get criticism and some of it will inevitably be harsh or destructive, often enough justifiably so. Obviously we will get more bad news than good. Indeed the content of the newspapers is far and away the best quick test of the political structure of a society. Take a morning plane from Delhi to Karachi. One leaves with a sheaf of poorly printed Indian papers filled with bad news; one arrives to find a small number of nicely printed Pakistani papers filled with good news. One has left a democracy and has entered a country that is something less than a democracy. Nonetheless there remains the question of balance. Does not an imbalance arise when the press becomes too willing an outlet for mindless paranoia of the Joseph McCarthy or New Left variety? Does it not arise when the press becomes too self-satisfied to report its own mistakes with as much enterprise as it reports the mistakes of others?

Norman E. Isaacs, a working journalist, has written thoughtfully about the possibility of establishing a "national press council." This, in effect, was proposed by Robert M. Hutchins's Commission on Freedom of the Press in 1947: "A new and independent agency to appraise and report annually upon the performance of the press." There are press councils in other democratic countries which hear complaints, hand down verdicts, and even, as in Sweden, impose symbolic fines. There is a case to be made here, but I would argue that to set up such a council in this country at this time would be just the wrong thing to do. There is a statist quality about many of the press councils abroad: often as not they appear to have been set up to ward off direct government regulation. Freedom of the press is a constitutional guarantee in the United States: how that freedom is exercised should remain a matter for the professional standards of those who exercise it. Here, however, there really is room for improvement. First in the simple matter of competence. The very responsibility of the national press in seeking to deal with complex issues produces a kind of irresponsibility. The reporters aren't up to it. They get it wrong. It would be astonishing were it otherwise.

Further, there needs to be much more awareness of the quite narrow social and intellectual perspective within which the national press so often moves. There are no absolutes here; hardly any facts. But there *is* a condition that grows more, not less, pronounced. The national press is hardly a "value-free" institution. It very much reflects the judgment of owners and editors and reporters as to what is good and bad about the country and what can be done to make things better. It might be hoped that such persons would give more thought to just how much elitist criticism is good for a democracy. Is this a shocking idea? I think not. I would imagine that anyone who has read Peter Gay or Walter Laqueur on the history of the Weimar Republic would agree that there are dangers to democracy in an excess of elitist attack. A variant of the Jacksonian principle of democratic government is involved here. Whether or not ordinary men are capable of carrying out any governmental task whatsoever, ordinary men are going to be given such tasks. That is what it means to be a democracy. We had best not get our expectations too far out of line with what is likely to happen, and we had best not fall into the habit of measuring all performance by the often quite special tastes, preferences, and interests of a particular intellectual and social elite. (Perhaps most important, we must be supersensitive to the idea that if things are not working out well it is because this particular elite is not in charge. Consider the course of events that led to the war in Indochina.)

As to the press itself, one thing seems clear. It should become much more open about acknowledging mistakes. The *Times* should have printed Dr. Henderson's letter. Doubtless the bane of any editor is the howling of politicians and other public figures claiming to have been misquoted. But often they *are* misquoted. Not the very least, should more space be allotted to rebuttals and exchanges in which the issue at hand is how the press performed?

Another possibility is for each newspaper to keep a critical eye on itself. In the article previously cited which he did for the Sunday *Times Magazine*, A. H. Raskin called for "a Department of Internal Criticism" in every paper "to put all its standards under reexamination and to serve as a public protection in its day-to-day operations." The *Times* itself has yet to establish such a department but the *Washington Post* has recently set a welcome example here by inaugurating a regular editorial-page feature by Richard Harwood entitled "The News Business." Harwood's business is to check up on what his paper runs, and he is finding a good deal to check up on. (To all editors: *Please* understand there is nothing wrong with this. It is a routine experience of even the most advanced sciences. Perhaps especially of such.) Harwood has made a useful distinction between mistakes of detail—the ordinary garbles and slips of a fast-moving enterprise—and mistakes of judgment about the nature of events:

> The mistakes that are more difficult to fix are those that arise out of our selection and definition of the news. Often we are unaware of error until much time has passed and much damage has been done.
>
> In retrospect, it seems obvious that the destructive phenomenon called "McCarthyism"—the search in the 1950s for witches, scapegoats, traitors— was a product of this kind of error. Joseph McCarthy, an obscure and mediocre senator from Wisconsin, was transformed into the Grand Inquisitor by publicity. And there was no way later for the newspapers of America to repair that damage, to say on the morning after: "We regret the error."

Which will turn out "in retrospect" to seem the obvious errors of the 1960s? There were many, but they are past. The question now is what might be the errors of the 1970s and whether some can be avoided. One Richard Harwood does not a professional upheaval make, but he marks a profoundly important beginning. All major journals should have such a man in a senior post, and very likely he should have a staff of reporters to help him cover "the news business."

As for government itself, there is not much to be done, but there is something. It is perfectly clear that the press will not be intimidated. Specific efforts like President Kennedy's to get David Halberstam removed as a *Times* correspondent in Vietnam almost always fail, as they deserve to do. Nonspecific charges such as those leveled by Vice President Agnew get nowhere either. They come down to an avowal of dislike, which is returned in more than ample measure, with the added charge that in criticizing the press the government may be trying to intimidate it which is unconstitutional.

What government can do and should do is respond in specific terms to what it believes to be misstatements or mistaken emphases; it should address these responses to specific stories in specific papers, and it should expect that these will be printed (with whatever retort the journal concerned wishes to make). Misrepresentations of government performance must never be allowed to go unchallenged. The notion of a "one-day story," and the consoling idea that yesterday's papers are used to wrap fish, are pernicious and wrong. Misinformation gets into the bloodstream and has consequences. The *Times* ought by now to have had a letter from the Chairman of the Civil Service Commission pointing out the mistakes in the November 15 story on minority employment, and the even more important omissions. If the first letter was ignored, he should have sent another. Similarly the *Times* ought long since have had a letter from an HEW official exposing the errors of its coverage of federal aid to black colleges. Failing that, someone should have called in the education writers of the *Times* and asked why they let other men misreport their beat. Etc. Hamilton's formulation has not been bettered: the measure of effective government is energy in the executive.

In the end, however, the issue is not one of politics but of culture. The culture of disparagement that has been so much in evidence of late, that has attained such an astonishing grip on the children of the rich and the mighty, and that has exerted an increasing influence on the tone of the national press in its dealings with the national government is bad news for democracy. Some while ago the late Richard Hofstadter foresaw what has been happening:

> Perhaps we are really confronted with two cultures (not Snow's), whose spheres arc increasingly independent and more likely to be conflicting than to be benignly convergent: a massive adversary culture on the one side, and the realm of socially responsible criticism on the other.

But given what has been happening to the press in recent years and what is likely to go on being the case if current trends should continue on their present path, where is such "socially responsible criticism" to come from? Or, rather, where is it to appear in a manner that will inform and influence the course of public decision making?

A Test of the News

WALTER LIPPMANN AND CHARLES MERZ

INTRODUCTION

It is admitted that a sound public opinion cannot exist without access to the news. There is today a widespread and growing doubt whether there exists such an access to the news about contentious affairs. This doubt ranges from accusations of unconscious bias to downright charges of corruption, from the belief that the news is colored to the belief that the news is poisoned. On so grave a matter, evidence is needed. The study which follows is a piece of evidence. It deals with the reporting of one great event in the recent history of the world. That event is the Russian Revolution from March 1917 to March 1920. The analysis covers thirty-six months and over one thousand issues of a daily newspaper. The authors have examined all news items about Russia in that period in the newspaper selected; between three and four thousand items were noted. Little attention was paid to editorials.

The *New York Times* was selected as the medium through which to study the news, first because the *Times,* as great as any newspaper in America, and far greater than the majority, has the means for securing news; second, because the makeup of the news in the *Times* is technically admirable; third, because the *Times* index is an enormous convenience to any student of contemporary history; fourth, because the bound volumes are easily ac-

From the *New Republic,* August 4, 1920.

cessible; and, fifth, because the *Times* is one of the really great newspapers of the world.

The Russian Revolution was selected as the topic because of its intrinsic importance, and because it has aroused the kind of passion which tests most seriously the objectivity of reporting.

The first question, naturally, is what constitutes the test of accuracy? A definitive account of the Russian Revolution does not exist. In all probability it will never exist in this generation. After a hundred years there is no undisputed history of the French Revolution, and scholars are still debating the causes and the meaning of the revolt of the Gracchi, the fall of Rome, and even of the American Revolution and the American Civil War. A final history of the Russian Revolution may never be written, and even a tolerably settled account is not conceivable for a long time. It would be footless, therefore, to propose an absolute measurement of news gathered amid such excitement and confusion. It would be equally vain to accept the account of one set of witnesses in preference to any other set.

The "whole truth" about Russia is not to be had, and consequently no attempt is made by the authors to contrast the news accounts with any other account which pretends to be the "real truth" or the "true truth." A totally different standard of measurement is used here. The reliability of the news is tested in this study by a few definite and decisive happenings about which there is no dispute. Thus there is no dispute that the offensive of the Russian army under Kerensky in July 1917 was a disastrous failure; no dispute that the Provisional Government was overthrown by the Soviet power in November 1917; no dispute that the Soviets made a separate peace with Germany at Brest-Litovsk in March 1918; no dispute that the campaigns of Kolchak, Denikin, and Yudenitch were a failure; no dispute that the Soviet government was still in existence in March 1920. Against such salient facts the daily reports about Russia in this period are measured. The only question asked is whether the reader of the news was given a picture of various phases of the revolution which survived the test of events, or whether he was misled into believing that the outcome of events would be radically different from the actual outcome.

The question of atrocities and of the merits or demerits of the Soviets is not raised. Thus, for example, there was a Red Terror officially proclaimed by the Soviet government in the summer of 1918; and apart from the official terror, excesses occurred in many parts of Russia. No attempt is made here to sift the truth of the accounts, to determine whether there were exaggerations, or how far the White Terror equaled the Red Terror. The attempt is not made because no dependable account is available with which to measure the news reports. There was a round measure of truth in the report of terror and atrocity. For analogous reasons no discussion of the virtues and defects of the Soviet system is attempted. There are no authoritative reports. Able and disinterested observers furnish contradictory evidence out of which no objective criteria emerge. Under these circumstances an accurate report of the Soviet government and the Terror is no doubt more than could have been expected from a newspaper.

But what might more reasonably have been expected, and what was more immediately important for Americans, was to know in the summer of 1917 whether the Russian army would fight, and whether the Provisional Government would survive. It was important to know in the winter of 1917–18 whether the Soviet government would make a separate peace. It was important to know in the spring and early summer of 1918 whether the Russian people would support allied intervention. It was important to know whether the Soviet government was bound to collapse soon under Allied pressure. It was important to know whether the White Generals—Kolchak, Denikin, Yudenitch—were, or were not, winning their campaigns. It was important to know whether Poland was defending herself or invading Russia. It was important to know the disposition of the Soviet government toward peace at the time of the peace conference. It was important to know whether there was a Red Peril before Allied troops entered Russia, or whether that peril dates from the German surrender. It was important to know whether the Red regime was tottering to its fall or marching to the military conquest of the world. On each one of these questions depended some aspect of policy involving lives, trade, finance, and national honor. It is important now to know what the net effect was of the news on these points.

For the reader's convenience certain tentative conclusions from the evidence are stated here:

1. From the overthrow of the czar to the failure of the Galician offensive in July 1917. The difficulties in Russia, and especially in the Russian army, are not concealed from the attentive reader, but the dominant tendency of the captions and the emphasis is so optimistic as to be misleading.

2. From the military disaster in July 1917 to the Bolshevik revolution of November. The difficulties of the regime play a bigger part in the news, but a misleading optimism still continues. In this period, the tendency to seek a solution through a dictator-savior appears in the mistaken hope placed upon the Kornilov adventure, a hope quickly falsified by his collapse. It may fairly be said that the growth of the Bolshevik power from July to November must have been seriously underestimated in view of the success of the November coup.

3. From the Bolshevik Revolution to the ratification of the Treaty of Brest-Litovsk. This period is on the whole the best in the three years. Different points

of view are given, and the emphasis is generally neutral. After the recovery from the shock of the second revolution, the reports are inspired by an eager curiosity about the diplomatic battle between the Bolsheviks and the enemy. At the height of this diplomatic battle the news is handled in a rather uncritically pro-Bolshevik fashion, as a result of the optimistic assumption that the Soviets would refuse to make peace with Germany.

4. From the ratification at Brest-Litovsk, which coincided approximately with the Great German offensive in March 1918, to the decision for Allied intervention in August 1918. Under the stress of disappointment and danger the tone and quality of the news change radically. Organized propaganda for intervention penetrates the news. This propaganda has two phases. There is a short and intense period in late March and early April, which stops rather suddenly with the announcement that the president has decided against intervention. There is a prolonged and intense period beginning about May which culminates in the American approval of intervention.

5. The months immediately following the signing of the armistice. The Red Peril, which had hitherto played only an insignificant role, now takes precedence in the news from Russia and serves as a new motive for Allied intervention.

6. Spring, summer, and autumn of 1919. Kolchak, Denikin, and Yudenitch are heralded as dictator-saviors of Russia; for their campaigns, extravagant claims are made when they are moving forward; in retreat there is a steady assurance that a better turn is coming. Meantime the world is warned against a Russian invasion of Poland—though Polish troops are as a matter of fact deep in Russian soil.

7. Winter of 1919–20 and spring of 1920. Once more, with the failure of the White Armies, the Red Peril reappears.

The news as a whole is dominated by the hopes of the men who composed the news organization. They began as passionate partisans in a great war in which their own country's future was at stake. Until the armistice they were interested in defeating Germany. They hoped until they could hope no longer that Russia would fight. When they saw she could not fight, they worked for intervention as part of the war against Germany. When the war with Germany was over, the intervention still existed. They found reasons then for continuing the intervention. The German Peril as the reason for intervention ceased with the armistice; the Red Peril almost immediately afterwards supplanted it. The Red Peril in turn gave place to rejoicing over the hopes of the White Generals. When these hopes died, the Red Peril reappeared. In the large, the news about Russia is a case of seeing not what was but what men wished to see.

This deduction is more important, in the opinion of the authors, than any other. The chief censor and the chief propagandist were hope and fear in the minds of reporters and editors. They wanted to win the war; they wanted to ward off Bolshevism. These subjective obstacles to the free pursuit of facts account for the tame submission of enterprising men to the objective censorship and propaganda under which they did their work. For subjective reasons they accepted and believed most of what they were told by the State Department, the so-called Russian Embassy in Washington, the Russian Information Bureau in New York, the Russian Committee in Paris, and the agents and adherents of the old regime all over Europe. For the same reason they endured the attention of officials at crucial points like Helsingfors, Omsk, Vladivostok, Stockholm, Copenhagen, London, and Paris. For the same reason they accepted reports of governmentally controlled news services abroad, and of correspondents who were unduly intimate with the various secret services and with members of the old Russian nobility.

From the point of view of professional journalism the reporting of the Russian Revolution is nothing short of a disaster. On the essential questions the net effect was almost always misleading, and misleading news is worse than none at all. Yet on the face of the evidence there is no reason to charge a conspiracy by Americans. They can fairly be charged with boundless credulity, and an untiring readiness to be gulled, and on many occasions with a downright lack of common sense.

Whether they were "giving the public what it wants" or creating a public that took what it got, is beside the point. They were performing the supreme duty in a democracy of supplying the information on which public opinion feeds, and they were derelict in that duty. Their motives may have been excellent. They wanted to win the war; they wanted to save the world. They were nervously excited by exciting events. They were baffled by the complexity of affairs, and the obstacles created by war. But whatever the excuses, the apologies, and the extenuation, the fact remains that a great people in a supreme crisis could not secure the minimum necessary information on a supremely important event. When that truth has burned itself into men's consciousness, they will examine the news in regard to other events, and begin a searching inquiry into the sources of public opinion. That is the indispensable preliminary to a fundamental task of the twentieth century: the insurance to a free people of such a supply of news that a free government can be successfully administered.

In devoting so long a study to the work of a single newspaper the authors have proceeded without animus against the *Times,* and with much admiration for its many excellent qualities. They trust that the readers of this report, among them the proprietors and editors of the *Times,* will not regard it as an "exposure" of the *Times* but as a piece of inductive evidence on the problem of the news. The authors do not wish to imply, because honestly they do not believe, that the less conservative press is necessarily more reliable. As editors of a liberal weekly journal they know from experience that there are large glass windows in their own house, and they are keenly aware of the fact that reliability is harder to attain in the haste of a daily newspaper than in the greater deliberation of a periodical. If, consequently, nothing were at stake but the question of praise and blame, if nothing were to be accomplished beyond a score in the duel between liberal and conservative, then this report would not have been made. Something much greater is at issue, for the reliability of the news is the premise on which democracy proceeds. A great newspaper is a public service institution. It occupies a position in public life fully as important as the school system or the church or the organs of government. It is entitled to criticism, and subject to criticism, as they are. The value of such criticism is directly proportionate to the steadiness with which the ultimate end of a better news system is clearly and dispassionately kept in mind.

I. TO THE JULY OFFENSIVE

The Russian Revolution occurred during the war with Germany. It was an event that affected immediately and directly the lives, the fortunes, and the dearest hopes of all nations engaged in the war. The Revolution began during the second week of March in the year 1917. This date is highly significant. It is about six weeks after the German government had announced unlimited submarine war, and six weeks after the rupture of diplomatic relations by America. The Allies were confronted at the same moment by the uncertainty as to what Russia and what the United States would do. The United States was in the act of making up its mind to begin to fight. The question which dominated all the news out of Russia was whether the Russians would continue to fight.

Thus, the circumstances of the Revolution were not such as to invite impartial inquiry. What the reader of newspapers was chiefly concerned about was the fighting power of Russia on the great eastern front. He could hardly have expected a current history of so vast a revolution. He did expect, and he had reason to demand, reliable reports about the morals and strength of Russia's armies. For on those reports he had to arrive at judgments of supreme practical importance.

The reliability of the news for the first four months can fairly be measured by this one concrete test: did it give a tolerably true account of Russia's military strength? Did the news lead to correct or incorrect expectations?

The actual military power of Russia was tested against Germany just once. In July 1917, about three and a half months after the Revolution, the army attacked on a wide front in Galicia. After a small initial success the offensive collapsed, the Germans attacked and pierced the Russian front; there were mutinies followed by a rout. The official Russian communiqué (per British Admiralty per Wireless press, Petrograd, July 22) said of the disaster: "This is the result of the instability of our troops, disregard for military orders, and the propaganda of the Maximalists." What had the news for the weeks from March to July been?

TWO VIEWS OF RUSSIA'S POWER

The *Times* of March 16 published the report of the successful revolution. Together with admirably full accounts of events in Petrograd, there began a series of semi-editorial news dispatches. Thus (special cable to the *New York Times,* London, March 16):

> As the situation is explained to the *New York Times* correspondent, the Revolution *simply means* (italics ours) that German sympathizers within the Russian government have been overthrown, and that no chance remains for a separate peace being secretly arranged with Germany. This, it is felt, is the real basis of the Revolution.

Such was the official public British theory. In the same issue Mr. Bonar Law (unidentified dispatch from London, March 15) was quoted as saying that the Revolution was due to Russia's purpose to fight the war out. This was, of course, not a statement of fact, but the expression of a wish.

This wish was father to much of the news which followed for several months. Concurrently, there were, however, other interpretations of the Revolution. On March 16 the *Times* published, of course obscurely, an interview with Leon Trotzky:

CALLS PEOPLE WAR WEARY
But Leo Trotzky Says They Do Not Want Separate Peace

Leo Trotzky, a Russian revolutionist now in America, said last night in the office of the *Novy mir*... that the committee which has taken the place of the deposed Ministry in Russia did not represent the interests or the aims of the revolutionists, that it would probably be short-lived, and step down in favor of men who would be more sure to carry forward the democratization of Russia.... That the cause of the revolution was the unrest of the mass of the people who were tired

of war and that the real object … was to end war … throughout Europe. They
do not favor Germany … but wish to stop fighting.

Two days later, in the issue of March 18 (Berlin, March 17, by wireless to the
New York Times via Tuckerton, N.J.), the *Times* printed a report saying that
the general opinion in Berlin was that the new government could not last long
and that the lower classes were wishing for peace at any price.

There were thus two alternative theories: one, the official Allied theory that
Russia would fight; the other, the theory of an unknown Russian revolutionist
in New York and of "general opinion in Berlin" that Russia would not fight. The
bulk of the news which followed appeared to sustain the official theory.

Three and a half months elapsed to the offensive of July. The reader had
by that time perused 107 issues of his paper, practically all of them containing
news of the Russian Revolution. He had received hints of profound economic
disorder, of demoralization in the army, and of confused dissatisfaction with the
Allies. He was in a position to guess that the striking power of Russia was not
great, if he read all the obscurely placed dispatches, read between the lines of the
other dispatches, and sternly declined to let his hopes govern his judgment.

But if he read casually, and chiefly the captions and emphasized news, the
impression of hopefulness or at least of whistling to keep up hope, would have
been strong. Captions or prominent news on the following days all stated or
implied a Russian will to fight.

MARCH 16^2, 19, 20, 21, 23, 27, 28, 29, 30^2—9 issues, 11 items.

APRIL 2, 10, 12, 14, 18, 19_2, 20^2, 21, 22, 24^2, 28, 29, 30^2—13 issues, 17 items.

MAY 3, 4, 7, 9, 12, 13, 17, 18, 19, 20, 21^2, 23, 25, 28^2, 29^2, 31—16 issues, 19 items.

JUNE 2, 3, 4^2, 5, 6^2, 7, 8^2, 9, 11, 13^2, 15, 16, 17, 18^2, 19, 21^2, 22, 23, 24^2, 25^2, 27^2, 28^2,
  29, 30^2—24 issues, 35 items.

Total 62 issues, 82 items.

Thus oftener than every other day for the whole period the reader was assured
that Russia would fight or that the Russian army was strong, or that the difficulties were being surmounted. Ordeal by battle proved all these assurances
to be false.

Was a darker picture ever suggested? It was. In 49 different issues of the
Times were perhaps 66 items of a pessimistic character. Numerically this seems
to strike a tolerably even balance:

Optimistic: 62 issues, 82 items
Pessimistic: 49 issues, 66 items

REPUTABLE AND DISREPUTABLE

But closer examination of what has been included under "optimistic" and "pessimistic" reveals a far greater discrepancy than the figures show. Take, for example, the first day's news (March 16). We have called optimistic and unidentified the London dispatch (March 15) quoting Mr. Bonar Law that the revolution was due to Russia's purpose to fight the war out; we have also called optimistic the dispatch from London (March 16) printed on the first page saying:

> As the situation is explained to the *New York Times* correspondent, the revolution simply means that German sympathizers within the Russian government have been overthrown.

Compare these authoritative pronouncements with the "pessimistic" item printed at the foot of the fifth column of the fourth page quoting Leo [*sic*] Trotzky from his New York office as saying that the people wished to stop fighting. Trotzky happened to be right, Mr. Bonar Law and the people who interpreted the Revolution in London to the *Times* correspondent happened to be dead wrong. But which interpretation was emphasized and given the authority of the editors? The official and the optimistic, of course, against the obscure and the unpleasant. The unsatisfactory view was not suppressed, but it was ignored or played down. This is characteristic of the news of the period we are considering. The values placed upon news items were wrong, wrong by the ultimate test of battle.

It is easy to see how this came about. There was an initial desire, shared by the editors and readers of the *Times,* to have Russia fight, to secure the military assistance of Russia without opening up contentious questions of war aims, to smother pacifist agitation. Conflicting estimates of Russian strength and weakness came to the *Times* office. One series was optimistic, the other pessimistic. The optimistic series had the right of way.

Then, too, the sources of the optimistic reports were such as to commend themselves more readily to the credulity of men who have high respect for prestige. Out of 82 optimistic items, approximately 49 emanated directly from official sources including the Provisional Government, the American State Department, Ambassador Francis, the Root mission, etc. The remaining 33 are from sources including 4 Reuters, 1 Harold Williams, 2 Herbert Bailey, 1 Special *New York Times,* 1 London *Times,* 5 London *Daily Chronicle,* 13 unidentified, the rest scattered.

When there were at least 49 official assurances and thirty-odd more from sources of recognized authority in a period of 107 days it is not surprising that the net tone of the news about Russia was optimistic. It is even less surprising when the character of the 66 pessimistic items is examined. If we add together the distinctly unpopular and therefore incredible sources, that is, the German, the Bolshevik, the Council of Workmen's and Soldiers' Deputies, and the items tagged and peppered with epithets, the total is 36.

Thus, out of 82 optimistic items, 49 are from friendly official sources, and the rest from respectable ones; out of 66 pessimistic items, 36 are distinctly disreputable, and, of the thirty remaining, practically none contains more than a fragmentary hint of the real difficulty in Russia as later revealed by the collapse of the July offensive, the first Bolshevik rebellion, and the ultimate fall of the Provisional Government.

It remains to be noted, however, that the optimistic items carried their own antidote to the sophisticated reader. The very fact that it was necessary to proclaim the solidarity and strength of Russia every other day was a suspicious fact. Reiteration emphasized doubt, and trained readers were enabled to reach conclusions quite opposite from those insisted upon in the general intent of the news. But what chance had they of persuading the casual reader that Russian affairs required his earnest attention. Was the casual reader, absorbed in our own war activities, not told about every other day that he could afford to be complacent?

II. THE PRELUDE TO BOLSHEVISM

MISLEADING OPTIMISM

The military weakness of Russia was clear to all observers on the spot after what Kerensky calls the "Tranopol disgrace" of July 19. The condition of the army was explained by the Russian official communiqué (British Admiralty per Wireless press, Petrograd, July 22); the condition behind the lines was indicated by the abortive Bolshevik rebellion of July 16–18. The most obvious facts no longer justified the complacency which had dominated the news. "Something" had to be done by somebody.

There were, roughly speaking, three parties contending for power; the Left led by the Bolsheviks, the Center led by Kerensky, and the Right led by someone in the role of a Dictator-Savior. The Bolshevik uprising of July was suppressed by Kerensky's government. For the next two months the contenders, on the surface at least, are the Right and the Center parties. The Kornilov rebellion in September was the first of the many efforts of the Right to establish a Dictator-Savior. The rebellion was easily put down by Kerensky. The government had thus survived first an attack from the Left, and then an attack from the Right. But within a few days of the supression of Kornilov there is unmistakable evidence of the rise of the third power—that of the Bolsheviks. On September 29, six days after the general's capitulation, the Petrograd Soviet passed from Menshevik and Social Revolutionary control into Bolshevik hands, and the next day (September 20) the Moscow Soviet for the first time refused a vote of confidence in the government of Kerensky. In five weeks that government had fallen.

Every shred of justification for complacent optimism had ceased by July 19. The correspondents in Russia abandoned it. Mr. Harold Williams, in the *Times* of July 28, speaks of "this hour of national disgrace ... how can Russia be saved ... the shameful collapse of (the) armies." But though the *Times* of July 23 had printed a three column head saying,

MUTINY ON RUSSIAN FRONT SPREADS
Whole Line Giving Way

Nevertheless the *Times* of July 28 carried the following dispatch from Washington: "The State Department has advices by cable that the defeat of the Russian Army on the Galician front has had a wholesome effect in Petrograd."

Meantime the headlines showed a continued optimism, as the following samples show:

JULY 30 ARMY NOW RECOVERING

JULY 31 RUSSIAN ARMIES NOW STRIKING BACK

AUG. 1 RUSSIANS THROW GERMANS BACK

AUG. 2 RUSSIANS ATTACK ON GALICIAN FRONT

AUG. 4 MINIMIZES CABINET CRISIS

AUG. 5 ROOT HAS FAITH RUSSIA WILL STAND

AUG. 7 TO FIGHT ON, SAYS FRANCIS NO EVIDENCE
          THAT RUSSIA INTENDS TO QUIT

AUG. 8 SEES RUSSIA SOON AS STRONG AS EVER

AUG. 9 WE CAN DEPEND ON RUSSIA WITH AID FROM U.S.,
          ROOT SAYS

AUG. 9 RUSSIANS AGAIN ATTACK IN GALICIA

AUG. 9 KORNILOV FIRM FOR WAR

AUG. 14 RUSSO-RUMANIANS TAKE 1,100 TEUTONS

AUG. 15 PRESS TEUTONS BACK ON RUMANIAN FRONT

AUG. 15 TELLS KING GEORGE RUSSIA WILL FIGHT ON

AUG. 18 RUSSO-RUMANIANS REPEL ALL ATTACKS

AUG. 20 RUSSIANS REPULSE ATTACKS EVERYWHERE

Thus, from the military rout in July to the verge of the Kornilov conspiracy, on average once every other day a certain show of optimism is made. It is derived from official reports of minor engagements, from advice to the State Department, and from the Russian government. The persistent will to believe is illustrated by the *Times* of July 24. The captions read as follows:

RUSSIANS TAKE 1,000 PRISONERS
BREAK GERMAN LINE IN VILNA REGION DESPITE DEFECTION
OF SOME REGIMEMTS BUT COLLAPSE IN GALICIA
WHOLE FRONT DOWN TO THE CARPATHIANS IN RETREAT—
TARNOPOL GONE

Is it not just to say that the newspaper is a misleading optimist which re-gards the capture of 1,000 prisoners as of greater significance than the collapse of the whole front down to the Carpathians? It was not always possible, of course, to extract hope out of a desperate situation, but on fourteen days out of twenty-two the captions writer succeeds. On the following dates he announces reverses: July 20, 21, 23, 26, 27, 28, 31, Aug. 2, 17, 23, 24. No doubt there were minor successes, but the net disaster was indisputable. Therefore the interlard-ing of the news of big defeats with little resistances and verbal optimism must be described as confusing in its total effect. The presentation of news values is eccentric and distorts the main picture.

THE QUEST OF A DICTATOR-SAVIOR

But parallel with all this runs a great theme of the Russian news: the theme of the Dictator-Savior and the strong man. This quest appears many times throughout the three years of the Revolution dealt with in this study. It cul-minates, as all the world knows, in Kolchak, Denikin, and Yudenitch, but it emerges long before. The first choice of the correspondents, curiously enough, is Kerensky himself. The faith in Kerensky is short-lived but strenuous while it lasts:

JULY 24 KERENSKY MADE DICTATOR OF RUSSIA
Peasants Yearn for New Monarchy

Kerensky, who possesses all Peter the Great's energy and twice his wisdom, is the national hero.... It [a new czardom] would give the imaginative peasants some one in whom to place that loyalty which they could never accord with the same enthusiasm to a black-coated president. (Herbert Bailey, Special to the *New York Times,* Petrograd, July 21)

That Kerensky did not altogether disdain the role of strong man is indicated by his interview to the Associated Press (issue of July 25) which the *Times* heads:

KERENSKY'S RULE TO BE MERCILESS
WILL BEAT RUSSIA INTO UNITY WITH BLOOD AND IRON
IF NECESSARY, HE SAYS

Mr. Harold Williams has at this time begun to cast about for a savior. Being better informed than Mr. Bailey, he has never taken very seriously the dictatorship of Kerensky. In the *Times* of July 26, he notes that the Council of Workmen's and Soldiers' Delegates attached a string to Kerensky's unlimited power by demanding an accounting not less than twice a week. And two days later, he is aware of "the brave commander on the southwestern front, General Kornilov." Other correspondents present other guesses as to where the saving force is to be found. Thus, in the issue of August 31, the *London Times* correspondent (Moscow, August 28), makes what appears to be the first sketch of the geographical area on which the counterrevolutions of Kolchak and Denikin were later organized. Over a year before the event he discovers that,

The Knights of St. George, representing 80,000,000 acres, [*sic*] have combined in military leagues... here is a *solid* (italics ours) block far exceeding in size and population the combined strength of the Central Empires. From Lake Bikal to the Dniester, from the Don to the Persian border, loyal sons of Russia are ready to rise against the forces of disintegration and defeat.

The *Times* heads this dispatch:

GREAT NEW POWER RISING IN RUSSIA

No less interesting and prophetic is the appearance of the first argument for external military intervention in Russia. While Messrs. Bailey and Williams and the London *Times* correspondent are looking for loyal Russians, the French authorities are thinking of the Japanese army. The *Times* of August 23, in a box on the first page, prints an unidentified dispatch from Paris, August 22, which says:

The *Figaro* today asks if the moment has not arrived for Japan to take further steps in the war....

The *Petit Journal,* in an editorial along the same lines…adds that never will the Japanese troops be more needed on the Russian front than they are today. (Italics ours)

The reader will note the common inspiration of these French newspapers and the synchronism of the publication with the bad news of the German offensive against Riga. With such estimates of the Russian problem in their minds, and with such prepossessions, it is not surprising that the newsmen were completely taken in by the Kornilov fiasco.

THE KORNILOV REBELLION

The historical evidence about the affair is still a matter of hot dispute, and there is much mystery about the role of the various personalities who figured prominently in the intrigue. This aspect of the affair the correspondents did not report at length, and could not have been expected to report. But the facts which concerned the American reader were simple. Did Kornilov represent the power of Russia? Were those who gathered about him the effective substance of the nation? Was he, in brief, the real thing, or a flash in the pan? He was a distinguished officer of the General Staff, a Cossack, who had been appointed commander-in-chief by Kerensky himself after the defeat of July. According to his own proclamation (in *The Prelude to Bolshevism,* by A. F. Kerensky; Dodd, Mead, 1919) issued September 9, his purpose in rebelling against the Provisional Government of Kerensky and starting to march on Petrograd, was "the preservation of a Great Russia." He swore "to carry over the people, by means of a victory over the enemy, to the Constituent Assembly to which it will decide its own fate and choose the order of the new state life." He was, in other words, to be a temporary military dictator acting as a savior of his country. Kerensky in a proclamation (in *The Prelude to Bolshevism*) also issued September 9, denounced him as a counter-revolutionist, representing "a desire of some circles of Russian society to take advantage of the grave condition of the state for the purpose of establishing in the country a state of authority in contradiction to the conquests of the Revolution." The rebellion was proclaimed on September 9. By September 12 the Associated Press correspondent in Petrograd described the coup as a failure. Kornilov was suppressed practically without bloodshed.

Nevertheless the special correspondents showed their credulity about the possibilities of a military dictator. As early as July 31, the reporter of the *London Morning Post* cables (*New York Times,* August 3) that "from intimations I have received I gather that the fighting generals have placed before Kerensky what amounts to an ultimatum from the officers of Russia's armies." Note that the soldiers of Russia's armies do not appear. On August 29 the *Times* carried, under headlines announcing "Hailed as Russia's Savior," a Moscow dispatch reporting that "at present the name of General Kornilov is on every tongue." Mr. Harold Williams, to be sure, noted in a cable published the next day that the executives of the Council of Workmen's and Soldiers' Delegates refused to stand or to greet Kornilov at the Moscow Congress.

But the bulk of the dispatches during the two weeks following were highly optimistic. The counter-revolutionists were described as riding on to glory. "Great New Power Rising in Russia" said a headline in the *Times,* August 31. "Kornilov commands confidence in military circles," cabled Mr. Charles H. Grasty on September 11, "not only on his record as an officer, *but because he is a Cossack.* This is the tribe around which *intelligent opinion* in Western Europe has been clustering hopefully *for several months past*" (Italics ours).

News of the actual revolt was cabled that same day from London. "There is yet no indication of General Kornilov's intentions," said a special dispatch to the *Times,* "but it is known that the Cossacks, the backbone of the Russia army, are his strong adherents." Yet two days later the Kornilov revolt was a confessed fiasco. "Kornilov Gives Up, Revolt Ends," said a headline in the *Times,* September 14. Where, one wonders, were the Cossacks who three days before were "known" in London to be Kornilov's "strong adherents" and "the backbone of the Russian army"? A fortnight later Mr. Harold Williams, in a special to the *Times* from Petrograd dated September 26, blurted out the following:

> The Kornilov affair has intensified mutual distrust and completed the work of destruction. The government is shadowy and unreal, and what personality it had has disappeared before the menace of the democratic conference. Whatever power there is, is again concentrated in the hands of the Soviets, and, as always happens when the Soviets secure a monopoly of power, the influence of the Bolsheviks has increased enormously. (Italics ours.)

So runs the obituary by a friend of the first Dictator-Savior.

In view of the fact that the Soviets seized the government six weeks after this dispatch was filed, Mr. Williams had reported news of the first importance. Does the news for the next six weeks, the last weeks before the triumph of Bolshevism, follow the lead given so clearly by Mr. Williams?

THE END OF KERENSKY

The news out of Russia for the first ten days of October does not minimize the increasing difficulties of the existing regime. But the news comment out of

Washington on October 10 (unidentified dispatch from Washington, October 9), is this:

> Russian diplomats here appear to be convinced now that the Bolsheviks have been finally overthrown and that Premier Kerensky is once more firmly established in the supreme power.
>
> It was said at the embassy today that the Bolsheviks were greatly discouraged by their first attempt to obtain control of the government, on July 8, when disturbances caused by them were suppressed by the provisional authorities, and again during the Kornilov movement, when the Bolsheviks seized upon that occasion to overthrow the coalition administration. The action of the democratic conference in upholding the principle of a coalition Cabinet was asserted to reveal the total defeat of the extreme radicals.

Nevertheless the correspondents in Russia are agreed as to the crisis, thus:

OCT. 13   RUSSIAN CABINET IN HARD POSITION

OCT. 15   DISORDERS GROWING AMONG THE PEASANTS

OCT. 16   RUSSIAN FLEET IS DEMORALIZED

OCT. 25   "The evening newspapers which publish the program for the meeting of the Central Council of Soldiers' and Workmen's Delegates on Nov. 2 are filled with rumors of a Bolshevik demonstration and an attempt to seize the government. ..."

OCT. 28   RUSSIAN ROADS PARALYZED
HANDLED LESS TRAFFIC IN SUMMER THAN THEY DID LAST WINTER

NOV. 2   (This was the day on which the *Times* printed briefly Kerensky's historic interview to the Associated Press: Petrograd, November 1. The longer text was printed November 3.)
RUSSIA WORN OUT, ALLIES MUST TAKE UP BURDEN, KERENSKY SAYS

But the State Department in Washington knew better: It issued a statement that,

> There has been absolutely nothing in the dispatches received by the Department of State from Russia, nor in information derived from any other source whatever, to justify the impression created by the *Washington Post* today ... that Russia is out of the conflict.

NOV. 3   (Special to the *New York Times*, Washington, November 2.) "Russia is not out of the war. She is to make no separate peace. The Russian Embassy and the State Department made this clear today."

NOV. 4   From London, Kerensky's interview was deprecated. (London, November 3.)

The Petrograd correspondent of the *Daily Telegraph*, who is now in London, writes: "Premier Kerensky's statement seems to have been taken a little too seriously in some quarters."

The *Graphic* (London) is quoted: "*We should hate to regard the statements as authentic. They have the ring of pro-German propaganda.*" (Italics ours.)

On November 6 the *Times* printed obscurely on the fourth column of the fourth page the following news of worldwide importance:

BOLSHEVIK PERIL ACUTE
Russian Radical Pacifists Expect to Come into Power

(London, Nov. 5). At a meeting in Petrograd on Saturday, as reported in an Exchange Telegraph dispatch from that city, representatives of the whole Petrograd garrison passed under the guidance and influence of the Bolsheviks....

The issues of November 7 and 8 carry the news of the Bolshevik Revolution, culminating on November 9, with the six-column headline on the first page:

REVOLUTIONISTS SEIZE PETROGRAD; KERENSKY FLEES
Pledge Is Given to Seek "An Immediate Peace"

The reader who had ignored the State Department and the Russian Embassy for the preceding six weeks, and had read the news dispatches from Russia, had no reason to be surprised. The reader who had trusted official pronouncements was misled.

The Provisional Government having been overthrown by the Soviets, the reader was concerned in the weeks that followed, first, as to whether the Bolsheviks would last and, second, as to what they would do about the war.

DEDUCTIONS

Assuming that the preceding sections constitute at least a prima facie case for saying that the run of the news on one matter of transcendent importance to Americans has been dubious, what deductions are there to be drawn by the constructive critic of the press? Primarily, we believe that the professional standards of journalism are not high enough, and the discipline by which standards are maintained not strong enough, to carry the press triumphantly through a test so severe as that provided by the Russian Revolution.

First as to standards. The analysis shows how seriously misled was the *Times* by its reliance upon the official purveyors of information. It indicates that statements of fact emanating from governments and the circles around governments as well as from the leaders of political movements cannot be taken as judgments of fact by an independent press. They indicate opinion, they are controlled by special purpose, and they are not trustworthy news. If, for example, the Russian Minister of War says that the armies of Russia were never stronger, that cannot be accepted by a newspaper as news that the armies of Russia *are* stronger than ever. The only news in the statement is that the Minister *says* they are stronger. By any high journalistic standard, the Minister's statement if it deals with a matter of vital importance is a challenge to independent investigation.

The analysis shows that even more misleading than the official statement purporting to be a statement of fact is the semi-official and semi-authoritative but anonymous statement. Such news is fathered by such phrases as:

Officials of the State Department
government and diplomatic sources
reports reaching here
it is stated on high authority that

Behind those phrases may be anybody, a minor bureaucrat, a dinner table conversation, hotel lobby gossip, a chance acquaintance, a paid agent. Dispatches of this type put the editor at home and the reader at the mercy of opinion that he cannot check, and it is time to demand that the correspondent take the trouble to identify his informants sufficiently to supply the reader with some means of estimating the character of the report. He need not name the individual source but he can "place" him.

The analysis shows that certain correspondents are totally untrustworthy because their sympathies are too deeply engaged. Mr. Harold Williams's reports from Denikin's army were obviously queer at the time and are ridiculous in the light of events. A reporter is not entitled to hold an assignment when his disinterestedness is open to question. One is not able to avoid the impression that in the selection of correspondents the virtue of conformity is at least balanced against the virtues of objectivity, insight, and credibility.

The analysis indicates also that even so rich and commanding a newspaper as the *Times* does not take seriously enough the equipment of the correspondent. For extraordinarily difficult posts in extraordinary times, something more than routine correspondents are required. Reporting is one of the most difficult professions, requiring much expert knowledge and serious education. The old contention that properly trained men lack the "news sense" will not stand against the fact that improperly trained men have seriously misled a whole nation. It is habit rather than preference which makes readers accept news from correspondents whose usefulness is about that of an astrologer or an alchemist. Important as it is for the press to read lessons in efficiency to workingmen, employees, and politicians, it is no less important for the press to study those lessons itself. Measured by its responsibility and pretensions the efficiency of the newspapers is not what determined men could make it.

The analysis shows further that at critical periods the time-honored tradition of protecting news against editorials breaks down. The Russian policy of the editors of the *Times* profoundly and crassly influenced their news columns. The office handling of the news, both as to emphasis and captions, was unmistakably controlled by other than a professional standard. So obvious is this fact, so blatant is the intrusion of an editorial bias, that it will require serious reform before the code which has been violated can be restored.

Where is the power to be found which can define the standards of journalism and enforce them? Primarily within the profession itself. We do not believe that the press can be regulated by law. Our fundamental reliance must be on the corporate tradition and discipline of the newspaper guild. It is for them to agree on a code of honor, as the Bar Associations and Medical Societies have agreed, and for them to watch vigilantly for infractions of that code. As citizens they cannot escape this duty, and as members of a profession they are forced to it by the growing distrust which everywhere greets them. They know that today they are feared but not intimately respected, and the sins of some are visited upon all.

But while the technical code of journalistic standards, the tradition and the discipline belong to the guild, newspapers must be prepared for an increasing supervision from the readers of the press. Those readers will not simply "write letters to the editor," effective as such letters are. They will speak through organizations which will become centers of resistance. The report on the steel strike made by the Inter-church World Movement is an example of such resistance to the newspaper reports of that strike. The report on the activities of the attorney-general by twelve lawyers for the Popular Government League is an example of resistance to the Red hysteria of 1919–20. They illustrate the point that a powerful engine of criticism is appearing in the community which will no longer naively accept the current views on contentious questions; with that fact the profession of journalism will have to make a reckoning.

Part 4
Telling Stories: Facts, Truth, and the News

In contrast to the strong, often over-the-top language of contemporaries like Upton Sinclair, Frederick Lewis Allen wrote with restrained anger about the limitations of the press and the factors that rendered objective reporting so difficult. Less concerned with the political content of stories than with the larger reality reporters portrayed, Allen emphasized the need for reporting that was unencumbered by personal opinions. Nothing, he wrote, is more important than reporters presenting "not a distorted picture, but the reality."

For him, facts should never be embellished. The line between journalism and fiction should never be blurred. In the introduction to a recent biography about Allen, Russell Lynes, his long-time colleague at Harper's magazine, recalled: "He would have been appalled at what is called "the new journalism" in which fact is embellished and beclouded and often falsified by fantasy."

By the middle 1960s, a growing dissatisfaction with the standard twentieth-century form of journalism emerged. Rebelling at the thought that they were mere stenographers devoid of opinions and feelings, many journalists embraced a "new journalism." Yet long before a phrase was attached to it, new journalism was being practiced. In 1721, it was the style used by Daniel Defoe in his *Journal of the Plague Year*. In the 1960s, the phrase "new journalism" evoked a number of different styles. It was saturation reporting, advocacy journalism, participatory journalism, underground journalism, or the nonfiction novel.

Its practitioners sought to make reporting as interesting and as artistic as fiction. In the introduction to *The Best American Essays, 1987*, Gay Talese, one of the most talented of the new breed of journalists, reminisced: "Since my earliest days in journalism, I was far less interested in the exact words that came out of people's mouths than in the essence of their meaning." New journalists relied on the narrative form, and they used extensive dialogue and evocative adjectives and verbs. They took the freedom to express their points of view, and they often were given the space to do so. While many writers injected novelistic techniques into their daily writing, only a few could pull it off. The next selection in this section was written by John Hersey, who many new journalists credited with founding the latter-day version of "new journalism," particularly in his post–World War II novel, *Hiroshima.* Hersey, who is difficult to categorize by narrow definitions of genre, began as a wartime correspondent for *Life* and *Time* and alternated between fiction and stylish journalism. In this essay, written for the *Yale Review,* Hersey most vigorously disavows any patrimony linking him to the birth of new journalism, clearly demarcating what for him separates journalism from fiction. The one sacred rule of journalism, he writes, is "The writer must not invent. The legend on the license must read: NONE OF THIS WAS MADE UP."

Most often, criticism of journalism comes from those who are outside the process looking in. Occasionally someone inside the process will look out, and, rarer still, a self-examination of this kind rises above the mundane. One of the best insider accounts of life inside a newspaper—in this instance, the *Newark Star Ledger* and the *New York Times*—comes from Robert Darnton, a historian of the French Revolution who teaches at Princeton and had worked briefly at newspapers in the mid-1960s. Darnton wrote of a time of transition in newsrooms. Darnton, after graduating from Harvard and receiving a doctorate from Oxford where he was a Rhodes scholar, spent a year at the *New York Times,* where he astutely wrote of the cultural mores among reporters who bristled under the traditional strictures of a paper that still thought of itself as the paper of record.

Darnton's article appeared in *Daedulus,* ostensibly in response to an academic study of the media. "Whatever its contribution may have been to the field of communications theory, it was so astute about *Times* affairs that it was passed around among reporters as a kind of in-house Masters and Johnson," wrote Elizabeth Kolbert in the *New Yorker* in 2003.

Writing News and Telling Stories

ROBERT DARNTON

All the news that fits we print.
—From the graffiti in the pressroom of police headquarters, Manhattan, 1964

This essay is a personal report on the experience of writing news. It resulted from an attempt to circumnavigate the literature on communication
theory, diffusion studies, and the sociology of the media, which I under-
took in the expectation of finding a new approach to the French Revolution.
As a historian of propaganda and radical ideology, I have always held onto the
hope that the social sciences will provide a kind of Northwest Passage to the
past. I ran aground, however, while reading "Newsmen's Fantasies, Audiences,
and Newswriting" by Ithiel de Sola Pool and Irwin Shulman in *Public Opinion
Quarterly* (summer 1959). That article touched off an analysis of my earlier
experience as a reporter, which I offer with the wish that it may point to some
fruitful lines of inquiry, despite its subjective character.

THE POOL-SHULMAN STUDY

Pool and Shulman got newspapermen to conjure up images of their public
through a process of free association. They asked thirty-three reporters to
name persons who came to mind as they were going over stories they had just
completed. Some reporters named persons whom they liked and whom they

From *Daedalus,* Spring 1975.

expected to react warmly to stories conveying good news. Others imagined hostile readers and took a certain pleasure in providing them with bad news. Comparison of the fantasies about "supportive" and "critical" readers suggested that the affective component in a reporter's image of his public might influence the accuracy of his writing. Pool and Shulman tried to test this distortion factor by supplying four groups of thirty-three journalism students each with scrambled facts taken from stories that communicated both good news and bad news. Each student assembled the facts into his own version of the story and then listed persons who came to mind while thinking back over the writing. He then was interviewed to determine the degree of approval or criticism that he attributed to the persons on his list, and his story was checked for accuracy. The experimenters found that writers with supportive "image persons" reported good news more accurately than they reported bad news, and that writers with critical "image person" reported bad news with more accuracy. Pool and Shulman concluded that accuracy was congruent with a reporter's fantasies about his public.

The experiment suggests how current theories about mass communication may be applied to research on the media. Now that sociologists no longer think of communication as a one-way process of implanting messages in a relatively passive "mass" audience, they can analyze the audience's influence on the communicator. Having become sensitive to the importance of feedback and noise, they can understand how a writer's image of his public shapes his writing. But they sometimes fail to take into consideration another element, which is conspicuously absent from the Pool-Shulman study, namely, the communicator's milieu. Reporters operate in city rooms, not in classrooms. They write for one another as well as for the public. And their way of conceiving and communicating news results from an apprenticeship in their craft. Translated into sociological language, those observations suggest four hypotheses: in order to understand how newspapermen function as communicators, one should analyze (1) the structure of their milieu, the city room; (2) their relation to primary reference groups, i.e., editors, other reporters, and news sources; (3) their occupational socialization, or the way they get "broken in" as reporters; and (4) the cultural determinants of their encoding, or how standardized techniques of telling "stories" influence their writing of "news." By ignoring the milieu of the city room and by dealing with students who had not undergone an apprenticeship, Pool and Shulman neglected the most important elements in newswriting. In order to indicate the importance of the four elements named above, I have tried to analyze my recollections of my brief career as a reporter for the *Newark Star Ledger* and the *New York Times* from 1959 to 1964.

THE STRUCTURE OF THE NEWSROOM

Reporters on the *New York Times* used to believe that their editors expected them to aim their stories at an imaginary twelve-year-old girl. Some thought that she appeared in the *Style Book of the New York Times,* although she only existed in our minds. "Why twelve years old?" I used to ask myself. "Why a girl? What are her opinions on prison reform and the Women's House of Detention?" This mythical creature was the only "audience image" I ever ran across in my newspaper work, and she merely functioned as a reminder that we should keep our copy clear and clean. We really wrote for one another. Our primary reference group was spread around us in the newsroom or the "snake pit," as some called it. We knew that no one would jump on our stories as quickly as our colleagues, for reporters make the most voracious readers and they have to win their status anew each day as they expose themselves before their peers in print.

There arc structural elements to the status system of the newsroom, as its layout indicates. The managing editor rules from within an office; and lesser editors command clusters of "desks" (foreign desk, national desk, city or "metropolitan" desk) at one end of the room, an end that stands out by the different orientation of the furniture and that is enclosed behind a low fence. At the other end, row upon row of reporters desks face the editors across the fence. They fall into four sections. First, a few rows of star reporters led by luminaries like Homer Bigart, Peter Kihss, and McCandlish Phillips. Then three rows of rewrite men, who sit to the side of the stars at the front of the room so that they can be near the command posts during deadline periods. Next a spread of middle-aged veterans, men who have made their names and can be trusted with any story. And, finally, a herd of young men on the make in the back of the room, the youngest generally occupying the remotest positions. Function determines some locations: sports, shipping, "culture," and "society" have their own corners, and copyreaders sit accessibly to the side. But to the eye of the initiate, the general lines of the status system stand out as clearly as a banner headline.

The most expert eye in the city room belongs to the city editor. From his point of maximal visibility, he can survey his entire staff and put each man in his place, for he alone knows the exact standing of everyone. The "staffer" is only aware of occupying an indeterminate position in one of the four sections. He therefore tries to trace the trajectory of his career by watching the key variable in the functioning of the city room: the assignment. A reporter who keeps a string of good assignments going for several weeks is destined to move up to a desk nearer the editor's end of the room, while a man who constantly bungles stories will stagnate in his present position or will be exiled to Brooklyn or "society" or "the West Side shack" (a police beat now extinct and replaced, functionally, by New Jersey). The daily paper shows who has received the best assignments. It is a map which reporters learn to read and to compare with their mental map of the city room in an attempt to know where they stand and where they are headed.

But once you have learned to read the status system, you must learn to write. How do you know when you have done a good job on a story? When I was a greenhorn on the *Times,* I began one week with a "profile" or man-in-the-news, which won a compliment from the assistant city editor and a coveted out-of-town assignment for the next day. Half the police force of a small town had been arrested for stealing stolen goods and I found a cop who was willing to talk, so the story made the "second front," the front page of the second section, which attracts a good deal of attention. On the third day, I covered the centenary celebrations at Cornell. They satisfied my ego (I rode back to New York in the private plane that normally served the president of the university) but not my editor: I filed seven hundred and fifty words, which were cut down to five hundred. Next, I went to a two-day convention of city planners at West Point. Once again my ego swelled as the planners scrambled to get their names in the *Times,* but for the life of me I could not find anything interesting to say about them. I filed five hundred words, which did not even make the paper. For the next week I wrote nothing but obituaries.

Assignments, cuts, and the situating or "play" of stories therefore belong to a system of positive and negative reinforcements Bylines come easily on the *Times,* unlike many papers, so reporters find gratification in getting their stories past the copy desk unchanged and into a desirable location in the paper, that is, close to the front and above the fold. Every day every foreign correspondent gets his reinforcement in the form of "frontings," a cable telling him which stories have made the front page and which have been "insided. " Compliments also carry weight, especially if they come from persons with prestige, like the night city editor, the stars, or the most talented reporters in one's own territory. The city editor and managing editor dispense pats on the back, occasional congratulatory notes, and lunches, and every month the publisher awards cash prizes for the best stories. As the reinforcements accrue, one's status evolves. A greenhorn may eventually become a veteran or embark on more exotic channels of upward mobility by winning a national or foreign assignment. The veterans also include a sad collection of men on the decline, foreign correspondents who have been sent home to pasture, or bitter, ambitions men who have failed to get editorships. I often heard it said that reporting was a young man's game, that you passed your prime by forty, and that as you got older all stories began to seem the same.

Reporters naturally write to please the editors manipulating the reward system from the other end of the room, but there is no straightforward way of winning reinforcement by writing the best possible story. In run-of-the-mill assignments, a voice over the public address system—"Jones, city desk"—summons the reporter to the assignment editor, who explains the assignment: "The Kiwanis Club of Brooklyn is holding its annual luncheon, where it will announce the results of this year's charity drive and the winner of its Man of the Year Award. It's probably worth a good half-column, because we haven't done anything on Brooklyn recently, and the drive is a big deal over there." The editor tries to get the best effort from Jones by playing up the importance of the assignment, and he plants a few clues as to what he thinks "the story" is. A potential lead sentence may actually rattle around in Jones's head as he takes the subway to Brooklyn: "This year's charity drive in Brooklyn produced a record-breaking $, the Kiwanis Club announced at its annual luncheon meeting yesterday." Jones arrives, interviews the president of the club, sits through a chicken dinner and several speeches, and learns that the drive produced a disappointing $300,000 and that the club named a civic-minded florist as its man of the year. "So what's the story?" the night city editor asks him upon his return. Jones knows better than to play up this non-event to the night city editor, but he wants something to show for his day's work; so he explains the unspectacular character of the drive, adding that the florist seemed to be an interesting character. "You'd better lead with the florist, then. Two hundred words," says the night city editor. Jones walks off to the back of the room and begins the story: "Anthony Izzo, a florist who has made trees grow in Brooklyn for a decade, received the annual Man of the Year Award from the Brooklyn Kiwanis Club yesterday for his efforts to beautify the city's streets. The club also announced that its annual charity drive netted $300.000, a slight drop from last year's total, which the Club's president, Michael Calise, attributed to the high rate of unemployment in the area." The story occupies a mere fourth of a column well back in the second section of the paper. No one mentions it to Jones on the following day. No letters arrive for him from Brooklyn. And he feels rather dissatisfied about the whole experience, especially as Smith, who sits next to him in the remote centerfield section of the city room, made the second front with a colorful story about garbage dumping. But Jones consoles himself with the hope that he might get a better assignment today and with the reflection that the allusion to the tree growing in Brooklyn was a nice touch, which might have been noticed by the city editor and certainly had been appreciated by Smith. But Jones also knows that the story did not make his stock rise with the assignment editor, who had had a different conception of it, nor with the night city editor, who had not had time to devote more than two or three minutes' thought to it, nor with the other editors, who must have perceived it as the hack job that it was.

In the case of an important assignment, like a multicolumn "take out," the city editor might walk over to Jones's desk and discuss the story with him in a kind of conspiratorial huddle before a sea of eyes. Jones contacts a dozen different sources and writes a story that differs considerably from what the editor had in mind. The editor who gets a carbon copy of everything submitted to the copy desk, disapproves of the text and has Jones summoned to him by the public address system. After huddling in alien territory, Jones negotiates his way back to his desk through the sea of eyes and tries again. Eventually he reaches a version that represents a compromise between the editor's preconceptions and his own impressions—still he knows that he would have won more points if his impressions had come closer to the mark imagined by the editor in the first place. And he did not enjoy walking the tightrope between his desk and the city editor before the crowd of reporters waiting for his status to drop.

Like everyone else, reporters vary in their sensitivity to pressure from their peer group, but I doubt that many of them—especially from the ranks of the greenhorns—enjoy being summoned to the city desk. They learn to escape to the bathroom or to crouch behind drinking fountains when the hungry eye of the editor surveys the field. When the fatal call comes over the public address system—"Jones, city desk"—Jones can feel his colleagues thinking as he walks past them, "I hope he gets a lousy assignment or that he gets a good one and blows it." The result will be there for everyone to see in tomorrow's paper. Editors sometimes try to get the best effort out of their men by playing them off against one another and by advocating values like competitiveness and "hustling." "Did you see how Smith handled that garbage story?" the city editor will say to Jones. "That's the kind of work we need from the man who is going to fill the next opening in the Chicago bureau. You should hustle more." Two days later, Jones may have outdone Smith. The immediacy and the irregularity of reinforcement in the assignment-publication process mean that no one, except a few stars, can be sure of his status in the newsroom.

Chronic insecurity breeds resentment. While scrambling over one another for the approval of the editors, the reporters develop great hostility to the men at the other end of the room, and some peer-group solidarity develops as a counterforce to the competitiveness. The reporters feel united by a sentiment of "them" against "us" which they express in horseplay and house jokes. (I remember a clandestine meeting in the men's room, where one reporter gave a parody of urinating techniques among "them.") Many reporters, especially among the embittered veterans, deride the editors, who are mostly former reporters, for selling out to the management and for losing contact with the down-to-earth reality that can only be appreciated by honest "shoe-leather men." This anti-management ideology creates a barrier to the open courting of editors and makes some reporters think that they write only to please themselves and their peers.

The feeling of solidarity against "them" expresses itself most strongly in the reporters' taboo against "piping" or distorting a story so that it fits an editor's preconceptions. Editors apparently think of themselves as "idea men," who put a reporter on the scent of a story and expect him to track it down and bring it back in publishable form. Reporters think of editors as manipulators of both reality and men. To them an editor is a person who cares mainly about improving his position in his own separate hierarchy by coming up with bright ideas and getting his staff to write in conformity to them. The power of editor over reporter, like that of publisher over editor, does indeed produce bias in newswriting, as has been emphasized in studies of "social control in the newsroom." [Bibliograhical note omitted.] But the reporters' horror of "piping" acts as a countervailing influence. For example, an assistant city editor on the *Times* once got an inspiration for a pollution story from his son who complained that, as he walked down the street, an ice-cream cone had become so filthy that he had had to throw it into a trash can. The reporter dutifully built the story around the anecdote, adding as an embellishment that the unnamed little boy missed the trash can and walked away. The editor did not delete this last touch. He was delighted with the story, which presumably improved his standing with the other editors and the reporter's standing with him. But it made the reporter's reputation plummet among her peers and served as a deterrent against further "piping" on the other side of the fence.

The peer group's own standards of craftsmanship also pit reporters against copy editors. Copy editors tend to be a separate breed among newspapermen. Quiet, intense, perhaps more eccentric and more learned than most reporters, they are cast in the role of being sticklers for language. They go by the book—*The Style Book of the New York Times*—and they have their own hierarchy, which leads from the lowly members of their desk to the "slot man," who apportions the copy among them, to the "bull pen," where the final tailoring of each edition takes place, and ultimately to an assistant managing editor, who in my day was Theodore Bernstein, a man of great power and prestige. Copy editors apparently think of themselves as second-class citizens in the newsroom: everyday, as they see it, they save the reporters from dozens of errors of fact and grammar; yet the reporters revile them. "The game is to sneak some color or interpretation past that line of humorless zombies," one reporter explained to me. Copy editors seem to view stories as segments in an unremitting flow of "copy," which cries out for standardization, while reporters regard each piece as their own. Personal touches—bright quotations or observations—satisfy the reporter's sense of craftsmanship and provoke the blue penciling instinct of the copy editor. Lead sentences produce the worst injuries in the reporter's unending battle with his editors and copy editors; he may attribute cuts and poor play of his stories to the pressure of circumstances, but a change in his lead is a challenge to his news judgment, the ineffable quality that marks him as a "pro." To reverse the order of a reporter's first two paragraphs is to wound his professional identity. He will even take offense at slight changes of phrasing in his first sentence that he would hardly notice further down in the story. And a really bad lead can damage a man's career. A friend of mine once led a story with a remark about a baby who had been burned "to an almost unrecognizable crisp." It was the "almost" that especially outraged the editors. That lead cost him ten years in the lowliest position of the newsroom, or so we believed.

Reporters are held together by subgroups, which also mitigate competitiveness and insecurity and influence ways of writing. Clusters of reporters form according to age, life-style or cultural background (City College vs. Harvard in the early sixties at the *Times*). Some have lunch together, buy each other drinks in certain bars, or exchange family visits. A reporter develops trust in his subgroup. He consults it while working on stories and pays attention to its shop talk. A reporter in my group once had to do a rushed story about a confusing change in the city's incomprehensible welfare programs. Four or five of us went over his material, trying to extract some meaning from it, until one person finally pronounced: "It's a holding operation." That became the lead of the story and the idea around which the entire article was organized. Almost every article develops around a core conception of what constitutes "the story," which may emerge from the reporter's contacts with allies in the city room as well as from his dialogue with the editors. Just as messages pass through a "two-step" or multi-step communication process on the receiving end, they pass through several stages in their formation. If the communicator is a city reporter, he filters his ideas through reference groups and role-sets in the city room before turning them loose on "the public."

The adjustment of writer to milieu is complicated by a final factor: institutional history. Long-term shifts in the power structure of a newspaper affect the way reporters write, even though the rank and file does not know exactly what goes on among editors and executives. Many papers are divided into semi-autonomous dukedoms ruled by the city editor, the foreign editor, and the national editor. Each of these men commands clusters of assistant editors and owes fealty to the managing editor, who in turn shares power with other executives, such as the business manager, and submits to the supreme sovereign of all, the publisher. At the *Times,* each editor dominates a certain proportion of the paper, so that, in an issue of *n* columns, the city editor can expect to command x columns, the foreign editor *y* columns, and so forth. Of course the proportions vary every day according to the importance of events, but in the long run they are determined by the ability of each potentate to defend and extend his domain. Changes in territoriality often take place at the "four o'clock conference" in the managing editor's office, where the day's paper takes shape. Here each editor summarizes the output of his staff and, day after day, builds up a case for the coverage of his area. A forceful city editor can get more space for city-room reporters and can inspire them with a fresh sense of the newsworthiness of their subjects

City news underwent such a revival during my period at the *Times,* owing to the influence of a new city editor, A.M. Rosenthal. Before Rosenthal's editorship, New York stories tended to be thorough, reliable, conventional, and dull. Rosenthal wanted snappier, more original copy, and he wanted his men to "hustle." He therefore gave the best assignments to the reporters who conformed most closely to his standards, regardless of their position in the city room. This policy infuriated the veterans, who had learned to write according to the old rules and who believed in the established principle that one earned the right to the best assignments by years of solid service. They complained about trendiness, jazziness, superficiality, and sophomorism. Some resigned, some succeeded in brightening up their copy, and many withdrew into a world of private or peer-group bitterness. Most of the greenhorns responded by exuberant hustling. An alliance grew up between them and Rosenthal, a poor boy from the Bronx and City College, who had hustled his way to the top of the *Times.* The qualities that had made him succeed—talent, drive, and enthusiasm—now made for success in the city room. Of course, those qualities were recognized under the old seniority system (otherwise Rosenthal himself would never have had such a spectacular career), but the new editor shifted the balance among the norms. The emphasis on hustling at the expense of seniority meant that achievement outweighed ascription in the determination of status

The institutionalization of this new value system created more confusion and pain than can be conveyed by sociological terminology. In disturbing the established routes of mobility, Rosenthal did not completely cut himself off from the veterans. He did not interfere with the stars, and he did not win over all the greenhorns. Instead, he produced status anxiety everywhere, perhaps even for himself, for he seemed to have been surprised at the hostility he evoked from men who had been his friends, and he probably had worries about his own standing among the other editors and executives. The first months of his editorship constituted a difficult, transitional period in the city room. While the rules of the game were changing, no one knew where he stood; for standing seemed to fluctuate as erratically as the apportionment of assignments. A reporter might keep a string of good assignments going for a week, while a deadly rain of obituaries fell all around him, but he could also be banished overnight to the obit page or the "caboose" (the last news section of the Sunday paper). Hence the dread character of the summons over the public address system. Eventually, however, a new status system became established according to the new norms. Bolstered by raises and promotions, the bright, aggressive young men set the tone in the newsroom and moved on to more prestigious posts. By now several of them have become stars. Changes also occurred throughout the executive ranks. The paper acquired a new foreign editor, city editor, national editor, Washington bureau chief, and, ultimately, a new managing editor—A.M. Rosenthal. Gossips attributed these changes to personal machinations, but in its brutal, awkward way *The Times* was really rejuvenating itself by putting power into the hands of the generation that was ready and eager to succeed those who had reached their prime during World War II. Institutional evolution—the redistribution of power, the disturbance of role-sets, and the modification of norms—had an important influence on the way we wrote news, even though we were only half aware of the forces at work.

SECONDARY REFERENCE GROUPS AND THE PUBLIC

Whatever their subliminal "images" and "fantasies," newspapermen have little contact with the general public and receive almost no feedback from it. Communication through newspapers is far less intimate than through specialized journals, whose writers and readers belong to the same professional group. I have received many more responses from articles in scholarly journals with tiny readerships than from front page stories in the *Times* that must have been read by half a million persons. Even well-known reporters do not receive more than one or two letters a week from their readers, and very few reporters are really well known. The public rarely reads bylines and is not apt to know that Smith has taken over the city-hall beat from Jones

It may be misleading to talk of "the public" as if it were a meaningful entity, just as it is inadequate, according to diffusion studies, to conceive of a "mass" audience of undifferentiated, atomistic individuals. The management of the *Times* assumes that its readers consist of heterogeneous groups: housewives, lawyers, educators, Jews, suburbanites, and so on. It calculates that certain groups will read certain parts of the paper, and not that a hypothetical general reader will read everything. It therefore encourages specialization among reporters. It hires a physician to cover medical news; it sends a future Supreme

Court reporter to law school for a year; and it constantly opens up new beats such as advertising, architecture, and folk music. A serious sociology of news-writing ought to trace the evolution of beats and the branching out of special-izations. It might also profit from the market research done by newspapers themselves which hire specialists to devise sophisticated strategies for increas-ing their circulation

The tendency toward specialization within newspapers encourages report-ers to write for particular publics. City Hall took notice when Smith replaced Jones, and Smith expected city hall to give his stories a careful reading. When Tom Wicker was covering the Kennedy White House, he not only knew that Kennedy read his stories attentively, he also knew exactly when and where Kennedy read them. The Pentagon correspondent, I was told, knew that Mac-Namara read defense stories between 7:00 and 8:00 AM every day while being driven to the office. Those reporters must have had vivid images of Kennedy and MacNamara scowling or smiling at the prose at certain times in certain places, and those images probably had more effect on their writing than any fuzzy view of the general public. For a reporter with a beat, "the morning after" begins to exist, psychologically, in the early afternoon, when he turns in a sum-mary of the story he is about to write; for he knows that he must confront his news sources on the next day and that they can hurt his attempt to cover sub-sequent stories if he wounds them in writing this one. A reporter on general assignment suffers less from anticipatory retaliation, because he develops fewer stable relationships with the subjects of his stories.

I got the impression that newspapermen were very sensitive to the danger of becoming captives of their informants and of slipping into self-censorship. Conventional news sources, especially in government, struck me as being so-phisticated about the give-and-take with reporters. Press spokesmen and pub-lic relations men are often former reporters, who adopt a tone of "we are all in this together" and try to seem frank or even irreverent in their off-the-re-cord comments. In this way they can influence the "angle" or the "slant" of a story—the way it is handled and the general impression it creates—rather than its substance, which is often beyond their control. They attempt to influence the reporter during the stage before "the story" has congealed in his mind, when he is casting about for a central, organizing conception. If his lead sen-tence begins "The decline in unemployment" instead of "The rise in inflation," they have succeeded in their task. Some press spokesmen hoard big stories and dispense them to reporters who write favorably; but that strategy can backfire, because reporters are sensitive to favoritism and, in my experience, tend to be cliquish rather than competitive. Outright manipulation may be less effective than the establishment of a certain amicable familiarity over a long period of daily contact. They develop sympathy for the complexities of the mayor's job, the pressures on the police commissioners, and the lack of room for maneuver in the welfare department. The head of the London bureau of the *Times* when I worked there was vehemently pro-British, while the head of the Paris bureau was pro-French. They wrote against each other, while reporting Britain's negotiations to enter the Common Market. The *Times* is so wary of the tendency among its foreign correspondents to develop a bias in favor of the countries they inhabit that it shifts them around every three years. On a humbler level, the veteran crime reporters who dominate the press rooms in most police headquarters develop a symbiotic relationship with the police. In Newark there were four tough old reporters who had done more time in headquarters than most of the cops. They knew everyone of importance on the force; they drank with cops, played poker with cops, and adopted the cops' view of crime. They never wrote about police brutality.

The sociology of newswriting ought to analyze the symbiosis as well as the antagonisms that grow up between a reporter and his sources, and it ought to take account of the fact that those sources constitute an important element of his "public."

The reporting of news runs in closed circuits: it is written for and about the same people, and it sometimes is written in a private code. After finishing a story by James Reston, which mentions "concern" about the Middle East situation among "the highest sources," the initiate knows that the president has confided his worries to "Scotty" in an interview. It used to be said that the defense correspondent of the *Manchester Guardian* wrote in a code that could be understood only by the defense minister and his entourage, while the ostensible message of the articles was intended for the general public. The sense of belonging to a common in-group with the persons who figure in their stories—the tendency toward sympathy and symbiosis—creates a kind of conservatism among reporters. You often hear that newsmen tend to be liberals or Democrats, and as voters they may indeed belong to the Left. But, as reporters, they generally struck me as hostile to ideology, suspicious of abstractions, cynical about principles, sensitive to the concrete and the complex, and therefore apt to understand, if not condone, the status quo. They seemed scornful of preachers and professors and quick with pejoratives like "do-gooder" and "egg-head." Until some social psychologist devises a way to make an inventory of their value system, I am inclined to disagree with the common contention that journalism suffers from a liberal or left-wing bias. It does not follow, however, that the press consciously favors "the establishment." The "shoe-leather man" and the "flatfoot," the diplomatic correspondent and the foreign minister, are bound together by the nature of their jobs, and inevitably develop some common points of view.

The producer/consumers of news who make up the inner circle of a report-er's public also includes reporters from other papers who constitute his wider, occupational reference group. He knows that the competition will give his sto-ries a careful going over, although, paradoxically nothing could be less competi-tive than a group of reporters on the same story. The greenhorn may arrive on the scene with his editor's injunction to hustle ringing in his ears, but he soon will learn that the greatest of all sins is to scoop the other side—and that the penalty can be ostracism on the next assignment. If he works from a pressroom outside his paper, he may become totally absorbed in a group of inter-paper peers. "Them" then becomes the city desks of all the papers and news services in town, who invade the repose and security of the men on the beat. Under those conditions, the failure to share information is such a crime that some reporters leak "exclusives" to colleagues on their own paper, so that the story will seem to come from "them" and will not disturb relations in the pressroom. In some pressrooms, one man does all the "leg work" or research, while the others play poker. Once he has collected the facts, he dictates them to the group, and each man writes his own version of the story or phones it in to a rewrite man in his city room. If a man is being pushed by his desk, he may by tacit agreement make extra phone calls to dig up exclusive quotes, "color," and "angles," but he would be condemned for doing this digging on his own initiative. An independent hustler can force hustling upon everyone else and will certainly break up the poker game, which is an important institution in many pressrooms. In the old press shack (now destroyed) behind police headquarters in Manhattan, the pot often came to fifty dollars, and the gamblers gathered around it included an assortment of cops and robbers. At critical moments, a cop who had dropped out of a hand would take calls from city desks. Reporters would suppress stories in order to avoid interrupting the game. The group was cohesive enough to keep "them" from discovering the news, except in the case of big stories, which threatened every reporter's security by arousing the appetite for "angles" and "exclusives" among his editors. To protect themselves, the reporters shared leads as well as details of their stories. After a news conference, they would mingle, filtering impressions and sounding one another out as to what the "story" was, until they reached a consensus and were able to file variants on the same lead: "Well, what d'ya think?" "Don't know." "Not much new, was there?" "Naw, that bit about weeding out corruption, he's said that before." "Maybe the part about civilizing the force…." "Yeah, civilizing…."

Competitiveness has also declined as a result of the attrition rate among newspapers. Reporters in one-newspaper cities only need to keep ahead of the wire services and television, which represent different genres of reporting and do not provide real competition. But if they work out of an important bureau, they are bound to be read by reporters who cover the same stories for papers in other towns. They know that the way those colleagues judge their work will determine their position in the status hierarchy of the local press corps. Professional reputation is an end in itself for many reporters, but it also leads to job offers. Recruiting often takes place through reporters who learn to respect one another by working together, just as promotions result from impressions created within a reporter's paper. The *Times* has a tenure system: once one has "made staff," he can remain there for life, but many lifers never make it out of the veterans' ranks in the city room. Professionalism is therefore an important ingredient in reportage: stories establish status, and reporters write to impress their peers.

They also get some feedback from friends and family, who look out for their bylines and who provide such comments as: "That was a nice piece on Kew Gardens. I was down there last week, and the place really is going to hell"; or "Is Joe Namath really as obnoxious as he sounds?" Such remarks carry less weight than the reaction of fellow professionals, but they give reporters a reassuring sense that the message got through. "Mom may not be a critical reader, but she is comforting. Without her, publishing a story can be like dropping a stone in a bottomless pit: you wait and wait, but you never hear the splash. Reporters also can expect some reaction from special segments of the public—from some readers in Kew Gardens or from some football players. Much of this kind of feedback tends to be negative, but reporters learn to discount for discontent among special interest groups. What they have difficulty in imagining is the effect of their stories upon the "mass" public, which probably is no mass at all but a heterogeneous collection of groups and individuals.

In short, I think Pool and Shulman err in assuming that newswriting is determined by a reporter's image of the general public. Newspapermen may have some such image, though 1 doubt it, but they write with a whole series of reference groups in mind: their copyreaders, their various editors, their different sets of colleagues in the city room, the sources and subjects of their articles, reporters on other papers, their friends and family, and special interest groups. Which of these readers takes precedence may vary from writer to writer and from story to story. They can make competing and contradictory demands upon a reporter. He may even find it impossible to reconcile the conception of "the story" that he gets from the assignment editor, the city editor, the night city editor, the copyreader, and his colleagues. Most of the time he tries to minimize "noise" and muddle through.

Although some reporters may learn to write in journalism schools, where Pool-Shulman selected the subjects for the student group in their experiment, most of them (including many journalism school graduates) pick up newswriting in the course of an apprenticeship. They acquire attitudes, values, and a professional ethos while serving as copyboys in the city room; and they learn to perceive news and to communicate while being "broken in" as rookie reporters.

By watching the smoke rise from Homer Bigart's typewriter near deadline time, by carrying his hot copy to the editors, and by reading it in cold print on the next day, the copyboy internalizes the norms of the craft. He acquires the tone of the newsroom by listening. Slowly he learns to sound more like a New Yorker, to speak more loudly, to use reporter's slang, and to increase the proportion of swear words in speech. These techniques ease communication with colleagues and with news sources. It is difficult, for example, to get much out of a telephone conversation with a police lieutenant unless you know how to place your mouth close to the receiver and shout obscenities. While mastering these mannerisms, the copyboy stocks his mind with values. I remember vividly the disgust on a copyreader's face when he read a dispatch from a correspondent in the Congo that contained some hysterical phrases about bullets whizzing through the hotel room. It did not do to lose one's cool. Another correspondent, who had seen some rough fighting during the Algerian revolution, impressed me with a story about a lizard that got caught in the fan of his cooling unit in the Algiers bureau. He did not mention the slaughter of Algerians, but he had a great deal to say about the difficulty of writing while being sprayed with chopped lizard. One does not have to eavesdrop very hard to get the gist of reporters talk. They talk about themselves, not the personages of their stories—just as history professors talk about history professors, not about Frederick II. It takes only a few weeks of carrying copy to learn how Mike Berger interviewed Clare Booth Luce, how Abe Rosenthal anatomized Poland, and how Dave Halberstam scored against the Diems in South Vietnam. In fact, the talk of the *Times* is institutionalized and appears as *Times Talk,* a house publication in which reporters describe their work. So even if you feel timid about approaching Tom Wicker, you may read his own version of how he covered the assassination of President Kennedy. Like other crafts, newspapering has its own mythology. Many times have I heard the tale of how Jamie MacDonald covered a raid over Germany from the turret of an R.A.F. bomber and how his wife, Kitty, the greatest telephone operator of all time, put Mike Berger, the greatest city reporter, in touch with the governor of New York by establishing a radio link-up to a yacht in the middle of the Atlantic, where the governor was trying to remain incommunicado. The newsroom will not soon forget the day that Edwin L. James took up his duties as managing editor. He arrived in his fabled coat, sat down at the poker game that was always under way behind the rewrite desk, cleaned everybody out, and then joined "them" at the other end of the room, where he reigned thenceforth with supreme authority. Reporters sense an obligation to "measure up" to standards set in the past, though they know that they must look small in comparison with their mythical titans. It does not matter that Gay Talese can never write about New York as well as Mike Berger or that Abe Rosenthal cannot command the managing editorship with the intelligence and flair of Edwin L. James. The cult of the dead gives life to the quick. We wrote for Berger and James as well as for the living members of the city room.

Reporters' talk also concerns the conditions of their work: the problems of telephone and telegraph communication in underdeveloped countries, the censorship in Israel and the U.S.S.R, expense accounts. (I was so obtuse about filing for expenses in London that I did not even get the point of the classic stories about the Canadian correspondent who put in for a dogsled or the African correspondent who invited reporters to spend weekends in his villa and then presented them with fake hotel bills to be filed with their expense accounts. I had to be told that my paltry expenses were lowering the living standard of the whole bureau.) One city room reporter told me that his proudest moment came when he was sent to cover a fire, discovered it was a false alarm, and returned with a story about false alarms. He felt he had transformed the humdrum into "news" by finding a new "angle." Another reporter said that he felt he had crossed the line dividing greenhorns and veterans one day when he was covering the civil war in the Congo. He got an open line to London at an unexpectedly early moment, when he had hardly finished reading over his notes. Knowing that he could not postpone communication and that every minute was terribly expensive, he wrote the story at great speed directly on the teletype machine. Some reporters remarked that they did not feel fully professional until they had completed a year on night rewrite, an assignment that requires great speed and clarity in writing. Others said that they gained complete confidence after successfully covering a big story that broke right on deadline.

Reporters gradually develop a sense of mastery over their craft—of being able to write a column in an hour on anything, no matter how difficult the conditions. The staff in London had great respect for Drew Middleton's ability to dictate a new lead to a story immediately after being awakened in the middle of the night and informed of a major new development. Failure to make a deadline is considered unspeakably unprofessional. One man near me in the city room had missed several deadlines. At about 4.00 PM when he had a big story, he would furtively gulp down a Dixie Cup full of bourbon from a bottle that he hid in the bottom drawer of his desk. The copyboys knew all about him. In one sweep of the eye, they could take in the deadline agonies of dozens of men. Their job virtually forces anticipatory socialization upon them, for they have no fixed position but rove all over the city room, working with editors and copyreaders as well as reporters. They quickly learn to read the status system and have no difficulty in choosing positive and negative identity models. By listening to shop talk and observing behavior patterns, they assimilate an ethos: unflappability, accuracy, speed, shrewdness, toughness, earthiness, and hustle. Reporters seem somewhat cynical about the subjects of their stories and sentimental about themselves. They speak of the "shoe-leather man" as if he were the only honest and intelligent person in a world of rogues and fools. While everyone about him manipulates and falsifies reality, he stands aside and records it. I remember how one reporter introduced the figure of the newspaperman into an anecdote about politicians' ad men and P.R. men, "and then there was this guy in a trench coat." I never saw a trench coat anywhere in the *Times*. The reporters tended to outfit themselves at Brooks Brothers, which may have been a sign of ambivalence about an "establishment" that they pretended to despise. But they had a trench-coat image of themselves. In fact, they had a whole repertory of stylized images that shaped the way they reported the news, and they acquired this peculiar mental set through their on-the-job training.

STANDARDIZING AND STEREOTYPING

Although the copyboy may become a reporter through different rites of passage, he normally undergoes a training period at police headquarters. After this "probation," as it is known at the *Times*, he is supposed to be able to handle anything; for the police story passes as an archetypical form of "news," and he is ready for the White House if he has survived headquarters—a parallel, incidentally, that suggests something of the spirit in which reporters approach their material.

I was inducted at the police headquarters of Newark, New Jersey, in the summer of 1959, when I worked for the *Newark Star Ledger*. On my first day of work, a veteran reporter gave me a tour of the place, which came to a climax in the photographic section. Since a police photographer takes a picture of every corpse that is found in Newark, the police have developed a remarkable collection of pictures of ripped-open and decomposed cadavers (the corpses of drowned persons are the most impressive), and they enjoy showing it off to greenhorns from the press. Press photographers build up their own collections, sometimes with help from the police, who get arrested prostitutes to pose for them. When I returned to the pressroom, a photographer from the *Mirror* gave me one of his obscene mug shots and showed me his homemade pin-up collection, which featured his fiancée. A woman reporter then asked me whether

I was a virgin, which produced a round of laughs from the men at the poker game. She was leaning back in her chair with her feet on the desk and her skirt around her hips, and my face changed instantly from green to red. Once the initiation was over, the poker game resumed, and I was left to do the "leg work" for everyone. That meant collecting the "squeal sheets," or summary reports of every action by the police, from an office upstairs. The reporters depended on the police radio and on tips from friends on the force to inform them of big stories, but they used the squeal sheets to check out the odd, man-bites-dog occurrence that has potential news value. Every hour or so I would bring a batch of squeal sheets down to the pressroom and would read them aloud to the poker game, announcing anything that struck me as a potential story. I soon discovered that I was not born with a nose for news, for when I smelled something newsworthy, the veterans usually told me that it was not a story, while they frequently picked up items that seemed unimportant to me. I knew, of course, that no news is good news and that only something awful could make a really "good" story. But it took some time before I learned not to get excited at a "DOA" (dead on arrival—a notation that often refers to heart attacks) or a "cutting" (a stabbing, usually connected with minor thefts or family squabbles that were too numerous to be newsworthy). Once I thought I had found such a spectacular squeal sheet—I think it included murder, rape, and incest—that I went directly to the homicide squad to check it out. After reading the sheet, the detective looked up at me in disgust, "Can't you see that it's a 'black' kid? That's no story." A capital "B" followed the names of the victim and the suspect. I had not known that atrocities among black persons did not constitute "news."

The higher the victim's status, the bigger the story: that principle became clear when Newark was lucky enough to get the biggest crime story of the summer. A beautiful, wealthy debutante disappeared mysteriously from Newark Airport, and immediately the pressroom filled with hot-shot reporters from all over the East, who filed such stories as NEWARK HUNTS THE MISSING DEB, FIANCÉE DISAPPEARS IN BROAD DAYLIGHT, AND FATHER GRIEVES KIDNAPPED HEIRESS. We had not been able to get our desks to take more than a paragraph on the best muggings and rapes, but they would accept anything about the missing deb. A colleague and I filed a long report on HER LAST STEPS, which was nothing more than a description of the airport's floor plan with some speculation as to where the girl could have gone, but it turned out that "side bars" (stories devoted to secondary aspects of an event) about last steps often accompany stories about kidnappings and vanishings. We simply drew on the traditional repertory of genres. It was like making cookies from an antique cookie cutter.

Big stories develop in special patterns and have an archaic flavor, as if they were metamorphoses of *Ur*-stories that have been lost in the depths of time. The first thing a city-room reporter does after receiving an assignment is to search for relevant material among earlier stories filed in the "morgue." The dead hand of the past therefore shapes his perception of the present. Once he has been through the morgue, he will make a few phone calls and perhaps do some interviewing or observing outside the office. (I found that reporters consumed little shoe leather and ran up enormous telephone bills.) But the new information he acquires must fit into categories that he has inherited from his predecessors. Thus many stories are remarkably similar in form, whether they concern "hard news" or more stylized "features." Historians of American journalism—with the exception of Helen MacGill Hughes, a sociologist—seem to have overlooked the long-term cultural determinants of "news." French historians, however, have observed some remarkable cases of continuity in their own journalistic tradition. One story concerns a case of mistaken identity in which a father and mother murder their own son. It first was published in a primitive Parisian news-sheet of 1618. Then it went through a series of reincarnations, appearing in Toulouse in 1848, in Angouleme in 1881, and finally in a modern Algerian newspaper, where Albert Camus picked it up and reworked it in existentialist style for *L'Etranger* and *Le Malentendu*. Although the names, dates, and places vary, the form of the story is unmistakably the same throughout those three centuries.

Of course, it would be absurd to suggest that newsmen's fantasies are haunted by primitive myths of the sort imagined by Jung and Levi-Strauss, but newswriting is heavily influenced by stereotypes and by preconceptions of what "the story" should be. Without pre-established categories of what constitutes "news," it is impossible to sort out experience. There is an epistemology of the *fait divers*. To turn a squeal sheet into an article requires training in perception and in the manipulation of standardized images, clichés, "angles," "slants," and scenarios, which will call forth a conventional response in the minds of editors and readers. A clever writer imposes an old form on new matter in a way that creates some tension—will the subject fit the predicate?—and then resolves it in falling back on the familiar. Hence Jones's satisfaction with his lead sentence. Jones began by summoning up a standard image, the tree growing in Brooklyn, and just when the reader began to feel uneasy about where it might be going, Jones snapped it on the "peg" or the event of the day: the man-of-the-year award. "A florist gets a prize for making trees grow in Brooklyn," the reader thinks. "That's neat." It is the neatness of the fit that produces the sense of satisfaction, like the comfort that follows the struggle to force one's foot into a tight boot. The trick will not work if the writer deviates too far from the conceptual repertory that he shares with his public and from the techniques of tapping it that he has learned from his predecessors.

The tendency toward stereotyping did not mean that the half-dozen reporters in Newark police headquarters wrote exactly the same thing, though our copy was very similar and we shared all our information. Some reporters favored certain slants. One of the two women regulars in the pressroom frequently phoned around district police stations asking, "Any teenage sex parties lately?" As the acknowledged expert in her field, she filed stories on teenage sex that the rest of us would not touch. Similarly, a fire-buff among the Manhattan reporters—a strange man with a wooden leg, who wore a revolver around his chest—reported more fires than anyone else. To remain as a "regular" in a police pressroom probably calls for some congruity in temperament and subject matter, and also for a certain callousness. I learned to be fairly casual about "cuttings" and even "jumpers" (suicides who leap off buildings), but I never got over my amazement at the reporters' ability to get "reaction" stories by informing parents of their children's death. "He was always such a good boy, exclaimed Mrs. MacNaughton, her body heaving with sobs." When I needed such quotes I used to make them up, as did some of the others—a tendency that also contributed toward standardization, for we know what "the bereaved mother" and "the mourning father" should have said and possibly even heard them speak what was in our minds rather than what was on theirs. "Color" or feature stories left more room for improvisation but they, too, fell into conventional patterns. Animal stories, for example, went over very well with the city desk. I did one on policemen's horses and learned after its publication that my paper had carried the same story, more or less, at least twice during the previous ten years.

By the end of my summer in Newark, I had written a great many stories but had not received a byline One day, when I had nothing better to do, I checked out a squeal sheet about a boy who had been robbed of his bicycle in a park. I knew that my desk would not take it, but I produced four paragraphs on it anyway, in order to practice writing, and I showed it to one of the regulars during a lull in the poker game. You can't write that kind of a story straight as if it were a press release, he explained. And in a minute or so he typed out an entirely different version, making up details as he needed them. It went something like this:

Every week Billy put his twenty-five-cent allowance in his piggy bank. He wanted to buy a bike. Finally, the big day came. He chose a shiny red Schwinn and took it out for a spin in the park. Every day for a week he rode proudly around the same route. But yesterday three toughs jumped him in the middle of the park. They knocked him from the bike and ran off with it. Battered and bleeding, Billy trudged home to his father, George F. Wagner of 43 Elm Street. "Never mind, son," his dad said. "I'll buy you a new bike, and you can use it on a paper route to earn the money to pay me back." Billy hopes to begin work soon. But he'll never ride through the park again.

I got back on the phone to Mr. Wagner with a new set of questions: Did Billy get an allowance? Did he save it in a piggy bank? What was the color of the bicycle? What did Mr. Wagner say to him after the robbery? Soon I had enough details to fit the new pattern of the story. I rewrote it in the new style, and it appeared the next day in a special box above the fold, on the front page, and with a byline. The story produced quite a response, especially on Elm Street, where the Wagners' neighbors took up a collection for a new bicycle, as Mr. Wagner told me later. The commissioner of parks was upset and telephoned to explain how well the parks were patrolled and how new measures were being taken to protect citizens in the Elm Street area. I was astonished to discover that I had struck several chords by manipulating stock sentiments and figures: the boy and his bike, piggy-bank saving, heartless bullies, the comforting father. The story sounded strangely old-fashioned. Except for the bicycle, it might have come out of the mid-nineteenth century. Several years later, when I did some research on popular culture in early modern France and England, I came across tales that bore a striking resemblance to the stories that we had written from the pressroom of police headquarters in Newark. English chapbooks, broadside ballads, and penny dreadfuls, French *canards, images d'Epinal,* and the *bibliotheque bleue* all purvey the same motifs, which also appear in children's literature and probably derive from ancient oral traditions. A nursery rhyme or an illustration from Mother Goose may have hovered in some semiconscious corner of my mind while I wrote the tale of Billy and the Bullies:

> I had a little moppet [doll]
> I kept in my pocket
> And fed it on corn and hay;
> Then came a proud beggar
> And said he would have her,
> And stole my little moppet away.

In their original version, nursery rhymes were often intended for adults. When journalists began to address their stories to a "popular" audience, they wrote as if they were communicating with children, or "le peuple, ce grand enfant," as the French say. Thus the condescending, sentimental, and moralistic character of popular journalism. It would be misleading, however, to conceive of cultural diffusion exclusively as a "trickle-down" process, for currents move up from the common people as well as down from the elite. The *Tales* of Perrault, *The Magic Flute* by Mozart, and Courbet's *Burial at Omans* illustrate the dialectical play between "high" and "low" culture in three genres during three centuries. Of course, we did not suspect that cultural determinants were shaping the way we wrote about crimes in Newark, but we did not sit down at our typewriters with our minds a *tabula rasa*. Because of our tendency to see immediate events rather than long-term processes, we were blind to the archaic element in journalism. But our very conception of "news" resulted from ancient ways of telling "stories."

Tabloid stories and crime reporting may be more stylized than the writing that goes into the *New York Times,* but I found a great deal of standardization and stereotyping in the stories of the *Times* London bureau, when I worked there in 1963–64. Having spent more time in England than the other correspondents in the bureau, I thought I could give a truer picture of the country; but my copy was as stylized as theirs. We had to work within the conventions of the craft. When we covered diplomatic stories, the press spokesman for the Foreign Office would provide an official statement, an off-the-record explanation, and a background analysis for anything we needed to know. The information came so carefully packaged that it was difficult to unwrap it and to put it together in another way; as a result, diplomatic stories all sounded very much alike. In writing "color" stories, it was almost impossible to escape American clichés about England. The foreign desk devoured everything about the royal family, Sir Winston Churchill, cockneys, pubs. Ascot, and Oxford. When Churchill was ailing, I wrote a story about the crowds that gathered outside his window and quoted one man who had caught a glimpse of him as saying, "Blimey, he's beautiful." The cockney-Churchill combination could not be resisted. The *Times* put it on the front page, and it was picked up by dozens of other papers, wire services, and news magazines. Few foreign correspondents speak the language of the country they cover. But that handicap does not hurt them because, if they have a nose for news, they do not need a tongue or ears; they bring more to the events they cover than they take away from them. Consequently, we wrote about the England of Dickens, and our colleagues in Paris portrayed the France of Victor Hugo, with some Maurice Chevalier thrown in.

After leaving London, I returned to the newsroom of the *Times.* One of my first stories concerned a "homicidal maniac" who had scattered his victims' limbs under various doorsteps of the West Side. I wrote it up as if I were composing an ancient *canard:* "Un homme de 60 ans coupe en morceaux.... Details horribles!!!" When I had finished the story, I noticed one of the graffiti scribbled on the walls of the pressroom in the headquarters of the Manhattan police: "All the news that fits we print." The writer meant that one can only get articles into the paper if there is enough space for them, but he might have been expressing a deeper truth: newspaper stories must fit cultural preconceptions of news. Yet eight million people live out their lives every day in New York City, and I felt overwhelmed by the disparity between their experience, whatever it was, and the tales that they read in the *Times.*

CONCLUSION

One man's encounter with two newspapers hardly provides enough material to construct the sociology of newswriting. I would not presume to pronounce on the meaning of other reporters' experience, because I never got beyond the greenhorn stage and because I did not work on papers that typify either "yellow" or "quality" journalism. Styles of reporting vary according to time, place, and the character of each newspaper. The American way of writing news differs from the European and has differed throughout American history. Benjamin Franklin probably did not worry about an occupational ethos when he wrote the copy, set the type, pulled the sheets, distributed the issues, and collected the revenue of the *Pennsylvania Gazette.* But since Franklin's time, newspapermen have become increasingly enmeshed in complex professional relationships, in the newsroom, in the bureau, and on the beat. With specialization and professionalization, they have responded increasingly to the influence of their professional peer group, which far exceeds that of any images they may have of a general public

In emphasizing this influence, I do not mean to discount others. Sociologists, political scientists, and experts on communication have produced a large literature on the effects of economic interests and political biases on journalism. It seems to me, however, that they have failed to understand the way reporters work. The context of work shapes the content of news, and stories also take form under the influence of inherited techniques of storytelling Those two elements of newswriting may seem to be contradictory, but they come together during a reporter's "breaking in," when he is most vulnerable and most malleable. As he passes through this formative phase, he familiarizes himself with news, both as a commodity that is manufactured in the newsroom and as a way of seeing the world that somehow reached the *New York Times* from *Mother Goose.*

Newspapers and the Truth

FREDERICK LEWIS ALLEN

I

It is a significant fact that public interest in newspaper ethics and the conduct of the press was never as widespread in this country as it is today. Before
the war, people who discussed the subject concerned themselves primarily
with the question of whether the newspapers degraded public morals by their
exploitation of divorce scandals and their general preoccupation with men's
misdeeds, and the question of whether large advertisers, and especially department stores, could bring about the suppression or distortion of news affecting
their financial interests. The war, however, with its censorship, its development of the art of propaganda, and the improvement which it brought about
in methods of swaying masses of men by controlling or doctoring the news,
has made us realize that the problem of newspaper conduct is larger and more
fundamental than we had supposed it to be. We now see that it is immensely
important that the press shall give us the facts straight, and not merely the
facts relating to department stores and other large business concerns but the
entire mass of facts about the world in which we live—political, economic,
religious, scientific, social, and industrial.

From *The Atlantic Monthly,* January 1922.

It is beginning to be understood that, as Mr. Walter Lippmann ably argued in his recent book on *Liberty and the News,* access to accurate accounts of what is going on about us is one of the indispensable conditions of freedom. We talk a great deal about the right of the individual to express his opinions, and somewhat less about the advantage to the community, or the nation, or the world, of determining its collective action after the freest discussion; but we are just beginning to see that it is still more vital that the individual shall be able to form his opinion upon the facts. If these facts are withheld from him or misrepresented to him, his opinion is as valueless as that of a judge who has heard incomplete or false evidence in a case. Though the individual may be at liberty to shout his ideas from the housetops, he is still a slave to illusion; and all the more completely a slave than if he were in bonds, because he fancies that he walks freely in the light.

There never was such an age of newspaper-reading as the present. Most of us read—or at least glance at—one, two, or more newspapers a day. They are the eyes through which largely we see the life of our time, and the news that they print is in great measure the raw material of our ideas. Nothing is more important than that through these eyes we shall see not a distorted picture but the reality. It is often contended in England, where the Northcliffe Press wields far more power than any existing group of American newspapers, and it is occasionally contended in this country by those who take a gloomy view of affairs, that the public is at the mercy of the lords of the press, who feed it such garbled news as will best serve their own selfish purposes. Other critics, such as Professor James Melvin Lee, the author of an illuminating history of American journalism, assure us that the ethics of the newspaper profession are higher today than those of any other. It would seem worthwhile to consider the whole matter afresh, and decide for ourselves what the public interest requires of the press in the interest of truth, and how far these requirements are being met.

The public interest requires that all unsigned news on the news pages—all news, in other words, which does not bear its own tag, to warn the reader that he is seeing the facts through the spectacles of somebody's personal opinion— shall be presented as accurately and impartially as is humanly possible. On the editorial page every newspaper proprietor or editor has a right to state his views as forcibly as he wishes; and I for one do not believe, as some people do, that it is necessary for editorials to be individually signed, provided the names of the proprietor and editor are regularly printed somewhere in the paper; for editorials are usually, to some extent, the work of a group rather than of an individual; and, in any case, the fact that they appear on the editorial page is fair warning that they are to be regarded as comment rather than as sheer fact.

Papers also have an unquestionable right to commission correspondents to include in their dispatches their personal view of events, provided these dispatches are signed. The imperative thing is that what the press presents as fact shall be fact, given correctly and without bias.

Bias is all the more completely the enemy of truth on account of the slovenly way in which most of us are accustomed to read the papers. For every report that we read through thoroughly and weigh for ourselves, checking the generalizations and summaries in headline and leading paragraph by the details which follow, there are ten that we only glance at. Usually we carry away nothing but the dim impression that Mr. X has done something disastrous or that Governor Y has made another fine speech; we retain the bias, and little else. If you doubt that you yourself skim the paper in this way, try handing it to somebody else after you have finished, and making him examine you on the contents of an important article. You will probably soon realize how vaguely most of your news-reading is done, and understand how easily the twist of a phrase in headline or leading paragraph, by giving a biased impression, may cause thousands of readers to form opinions based not on the facts but on somebody else's view of the facts.

This cardinal rule of newspaper ethics—that what is presented as sheer fact should be accurate and without bias—is easy to state. It is harder to live up to than anybody can imagine who has not faced the newspaperman's problem for himself.

In the first place, it is hard for a reporter, just as for any other person, to give an absolutely accurate account of any event, even when he has seen it with his own eyes. The fallibility of even firsthand evidence from eyewitnesses is well known; no one can read a book like the late Professor Munsterberg's *On the Witness Stand* without appreciating what the reporter is up against. Furthermore, it is also exceedingly hard to write an account of any event without coloring it with one's own opinions. Though the reporter has every intention of stating only the clear facts, he may give them bias simply through his choice of language.

Suppose one senator denounces another in a speech. Shall the reporter write, "Senator A—sternly rebuked Senator B—," or shall he use the words "vigorously attacked," or "sharply attacked," or "fiercely attacked"? If he decides upon "sternly rebuked," he seems to favor Senator A—, who uttered the rebuke; if he says "fiercely attacked," he gives no favorable impression, and the reader tends instinctively to side with the senator who was attacked. Shall he, in describing an automobile accident, say, "The truck was going at a terrific rate," or content himself with, "The truck was said to have been going thirty miles an hour," and leave the reader to decide whether this was a "terrific" rate for a truck to be going at in that place at that time?

Or suppose he must give an account of something really difficult to record objectively—the applause, let us say, which greeted the closing sentence of President Harding's inaugural address. Was it enthusiastic or perfunctory; was it general or half-hearted and scattered? The truth here is a matter of judgment. One man thinks the applause large, because he knows beforehand how hard it is to hear a public speech out-of-doors without distractions, and therefore expects something less impressive than actually occurs. Another man, who comes to the inaugural expecting an ovation, is disappointed. Then again the reporter's political sympathies, his personal opinion of Mr. Harding, and his own enthusiasm or lack of enthusiasm for the address are almost sure to influence his judgment of the facts.

If he were the crack reporter of an opposition paper, he might, with every intention of giving the exact truth, write something like this, which appeared in the *New York Times* on the morning of March 5, 1921:

> Mr. Harding has a good voice, and the amplifier in the roof of the kiosk carried his voice as far as the House and Senate office buildings. Considering that the average inaugural address is audible only to those who stand within fifteen feet of the president, this was an enormous improvement and enabled the crowd to manifest its feelings, when it had any, with something like spontaneity.
>
> The address was only thirty-seven minutes long, and Mr. Harding delivered its final pledge with a devout solemnity which did not fail to have its effect on the crowd.
>
> There was a roar of applause as he concluded and turned to receive the congratulations of those nearby, Vice President Coolidge being the first to shake hands with him.

Another reporter of Democratic sympathies might regard the applause as Mr. Louis Seibold did in his dispatch to the *New York World*. After noting earlier in his account that "five times his [President Harding's] reading was interrupted by applause, but at no time was there a demonstration in which all of the people gathered in front of him united," he quoted the president's peroration and then wrote:

> The applause that approved this sentiment was rather more general than had followed any other statement made by the new President. Before it had died away, and while the Marine Band was rendering the national anthem, the crowd began to melt away. Mr. Harding acknowledged the congratulations that were showered upon him by the members of his Cabinet and the leaders of the two Houses.

If, on the other hand, the reporter were favorably inclined toward Mr. Harding and impressed with the speech, he might see its reception as did the correspondent of the *New York Herald,* who quoted President Hardings's final sentence and then continued:

> There was a palpable moment of absolute silence. The president remained as if transfixed. The small group standing with him in the white-covered stand seemed stayed from speech or action by the deep and moving solemnity of the voluntary promise. Then a wave of applause started up from the fringe of the crowd nearest the portico, rolled backward and to the right and left, carried through the massed thousands and became a solid roar. The president waved a hand in happy acknowledgment and turned to meet the eager compliments of his friends.

Readers of the *Herald* on that March 5 must have thought the address an immense success; readers of the *Times* and the *World* undoubtedly gained quite a different opinion; and yet each correspondent may have described the event conscientiously as it appeared to him. In such cases it is almost impossible not to let personal feeling color one's report.

II

News may also be colored in the process of selection as well as in that of presentation. Let me take an example such as frequently occurs in my own experience. It is my duty to give to the press the news of a great university. I do not happen to be a newspaper reporter, but my problem is essentially the same as the reporter's. When the university's enrollment figures for the year are made up, the Freshman Class shows a gain in numbers. If, in my announcement to the press, I compare the 1921 figures to those of 1920, or with those of any other year since the war, the gain looks very large. On the other hand, if I compare them to those of 1911, when the Freshman Class happened to be unusually big, the gain looks less impressive. If I mention the fact that part of the gain is caused by a difference in the method of classifying undergraduates, which automatically adds to the Freshman Class a number of men who were formerly listed elsewhere, it looks still less significant. There are thus three or four ways of making the statement. Even though I am honestly anxious to give an accurate impression, it is hard to decide just what facts to select for presentation. And there is, of course, always a temptation to make the gain look more imposing than it actually is.

Or let us suppose that a reporter is sent to cover a dinner. Shall he devote his leading paragraph to the size and enthusiasm of the gathering, or to the consternation caused by the single untoward event of the evening—a violent and inappropriate statement made by one of the speakers? This again is a question of selection. Sometimes it is a toss-up in the reporter's mind between the two treatments of the event; and yet the opinion which thousands of readers form of the organization which held the dinner may depend on this apparently unimportant decision.

An added element of difficulty is caused by the speed with which newspapers have to work, and the circumstance that much of the color of a story is necessarily given it in the newspaper office by men who lack a firsthand acquaintance with the facts. There is no opportunity to wait a few hours for a chance to check facts; they are usually worthless unless given to the public instantly. City reporters telephone much of their news to the office, where their statements are taken down hurriedly in a telephone booth, and then thrown into shape by a member of the office staff. Always the headlines are written by the office staff; they have to be, because the reporter cannot tell what size and style of headline is needed, and because the writing of headlines requires a special training. The man who concocts them must read each news story rapidly and write his "head" promptly. He cannot waste time upon niceties of emphasis; the all-important thing for him is that the head shall have exactly the right number of letters to fill its space, and that it shall be original and dramatic enough to catch the reader's attention. Like the reporter, he finds that bias insists on creeping into his presentation of the gist of the news.

Most newspaper inaccuracy is not, however, the result so much of the inherent difficulty of properly collecting and presenting the facts, as of the ignorance, carelessness, and thoughtless indifference to truth of a considerable proportion of newspapermen.

By the very nature of newspaper organization, the men sent out on assignments usually know too little about the matter in hand. One day a man is instructed to get a story on the immigration problem; the next day, he had to write a breezy interview of a bootlegging case; the next day, he may have to report the visit of Dr. Einstein to a university. He has not the time, even if he had the inclination, to make a preliminary study of the immigration problem, the liquor laws, and the theory of relativity. Newspapers try to develop special abilities in their reporters and, so far as possible, to keep men assigned to the subjects which they know about; but the field of news is so immense that much of it has to be covered by inexpert men. Besides, many reporters have only a limited education; they know so little that they have no idea how their ignorance handicaps them. And they generally tend to be careless. Their immediate object is usually to get the most newsy and sensational story they can. If they are being paid at space-rates, a breezy story which pleases the jaded eye of the city editor will be printed and will put money in their pocket. If they are salaried reporters, such a story will at least give them prestige with the critics at the city desk. No reporter wants to get the reputation of returning empty-handed, or with a dull story. The temptation is to make a bluff at knowing the subject and slap the story together anyhow.

Here, for instance, are the headlines and the first two paragraphs of an item which appeared lately in a Boston paper:

DISCOVERS NEW NEBULAR MASS
Prof. Sliphe of Harvard Finds It Going at Record Speed

Prof. V. M. Sliphe of Harvard, stationed at the Flagstaff, Ariz., observatory, peered through his telescope a few nights ago, according to a dispatch received at the Cambridge observatory, and much to his surprise saw a faint, cloud-like, self-luminous mass of attenuated matter situated far outside the solar system, traveling at the rate of 2,000 kilometers per second. This rate of speed is twice as great as the fastest nebula yet discovered and 100 times greater than the average speed of the lowly star. In fact, it is the greatest velocity known to astronomy.

The telescope at Flagstaff is situated on San Francisco Peak at an altitude of 13,000 feet. Harvard astronomers are manifesting much interest in the matter because of its supposed great distance from the stars ordinarily seen in the heavens and because of the tremendous speed at which it is traveling.

Now, the facts of the case were that the discoverer's name was not Sliphe, but Slipher; that he was not connected with Harvard, but with the Lowell Observatory; that he did not discover the nebula, which had been known for a long time, but only ascertained its speed; that the telescope at Flagstaff is not at an altitude of thirteen thousand feet but of about seven thousand; and that it is not situated on San Francisco Peak but merely in the neighborhood. It would be difficult for ignorance and carelessness to bring about more errors in the space of two paragraphs. What happened was that the Lowell Observatory reported its discovery to the Harvard Observatory, which made a brief announcement to the press; and the news writer took this announcement, and tried, as he would put it, "to make a good story out of it."

"Make a good story." That is the cause of infinite newspaper inaccuracy. It is to the interest of each reporter and editor to make a small piece of news look like a big one. College officials soon become resigned to the fact that, to the press, any teacher at a college, no matter of how low a rank, is a "professor." An assistant in applied physiology at the Harvard Medical School, a man on one of the lowest rungs of the academic ladder, was arrested not long ago for having a still in his house; and the headline on the front page of a New York paper, the next morning, referred to him as a "noted Harvard professor." Ignorance of the significance of academic titles may have been partly responsible; but, pretty surely, the desire to make the story look as big as possible was a contributory cause.

The same desire often leads reporters at a public meeting to lay disproportionate emphasis on a sensational remark made by a speaker. The remark may have little real significance, and the reporters may misquote it because they happen to be half asleep when it is made, or are not even in the room and get it secondhand afterward from some neighbor of uncertain memory; but, if the remark seems striking enough to make a big story, that fact may outweigh in their minds every other consideration.

Akin to the temptation to make a small story look big is the temptation to make an otherwise dignified story look breezy. A Boston newspaper recently printed an interview with a Harvard physician on the importance of using the feet properly in standing and walking, as shown in the physical examinations of Harvard freshmen. It was an interesting interview, carefully prepared by an intelligent and well-equipped reporter. But the editor to whom the interview was submitted decided that it was too heavy: it needed to be brightened up. So he headed it—

WHY BE SAD? FEET ARE THE SOURCE OF ALL JOY
Harvard Expert Tells How to Drive Clouds Away in Six Short Weeks

And the illustration—a photograph of the physician—the editor surrounded with a border of "Joys" and "Glooms," after the fashion of the comic cartoons. In thus misrepresenting the nature of the interview, he succeeded in making ridiculous the man who had taken the trouble to give it; but to this particular editor nothing mattered except that he made it look like the sort of low-comedy stuff to which his mind was attuned.

The newspaper that goes in for entertainment at all costs is bound to distort the news, because it leaves out much that is important but not entertaining, and puts in much that is entertaining but not important. If General Dawes, at a congressional hearing, speaks his mind vigorously about critics of the A.E.F., that is important news; if, in doing so, he uses highly picturesque profanity, that makes for entertainment. To put in the profanity and leave out the argument might make the story more brisk, but it would be misrepresenting General Dawes and the significance of what he said.

Writing recently of the treatment of parliamentary news by the North-cliffe Press, Mr. A. G. Gardiner, formerly editor of the London *Daily News,* said, "Parliament was treated as a music-hall turn. If it was funny, it was reported; if it was serious, it was ignored.... The Midlothian Campaign of Gladstone, which used to fill pages of the newspapers, would today be dismissed in an ill-reported half-column summary, devoted not to the argument but to the amusing asides and the irrelevant interruptions." The same thing might be said of the Washington correspondence of all too many American newspapers. What makes so-called yellow journalism really dangerous is not so much its appetite for scandal as its continual distortion of the news in the interest of undiluted entertainment.

III

Sometimes, it must be admitted, misrepresentation is brought about not by the inherent difficulty of stating the facts without prejudice, not by ignorance, carelessness, or the desire to entertain, but by deliberate intention. The newspaper profession is made up of all sorts of people, some of whom eagerly seize opportunities to present the news so as to favor their friends and put in an unfavorable light their enemies—personal, political, and economic. It is this practice which that extraordinary diatribe, *The Brass Check,* by Mr. Upton Sinclair, is devoted to exposing. Mr. Sinclair cites case after case in which the press has falsified the news and comes to the conclusion that the newspapers are in a plot to twist the news to their own ends, and thus to serve the purposes of capital.

It is a pretty safe plan to take with several grains of salt most allegations regarding the existence of widespread conspiracies. We have been fed to repletion lately with supposed conspiracies of radicals, Bolsheviks, and Jews, and so forth, and we are happily beginning to acquire some common sense. To my mind the evidence of misrepresentation collected by Mr. Sinclair and by other critics of the press proves not that there is any conspiracy among newspaper men to withhold the truth from the public but merely that newspaper owners, editors, and reporters are fallible; actuated too often by self-interest; too often ready to take the "practical" view of things and to see on which side their bread is buttered; too often inclined to fight by illegitimate means what they dislike; and too often subject to those surges of mob-feeling that lead men to pillory those whom they detest.

Take, for example, that part of Mr. Sinclair's book in which he tells of his own unfortunate experiences with the press. It shows with what glee newspapermen—like other ordinary mortals—will sometimes join the pack to hunt those whom they dislike. Mr. Sinclair is unpopular with the press. When he founds Helicon Hall, a cooperative "home colony"; when he gets into difficulties with the Delaware authorities for playing Sunday tennis; when he disputes the amount of his bill for shredded wheat at a San Francisco hotel, the newspapers are after him like a gang of small boys after a stray dog.

Other examples of the same sort of hoodlumism on the part of newspapers come readily to mind. Recently the press howled similarly about the heels of Mr. Bouck White. When the inhabitants of the village where he was staying saw fit to tar and feather him because of charges his young French wife had made against him, the press joined in the fun, and in lengthy reports, satirically written, applied their own kind of tar and feathers. They did not like him or his economic views, and they leaped at the chance to make him an object of ridicule and scorn. Plots on the part of the capitalist press? Not a bit of it. Average men on the rampage, using the weapon of misrepresentation because it is nearest at hand.

There is no question that newspapers often give biased reports of strikes and other industrial conflicts. But, again, the charge of a conspiracy is too far-fetched. The reason these things happen is that the press is a human institution, and that much capital is required to run a newspaper. Owners of papers mostly have large financial interests and positive views on political, economic, and other matters. Many of them are excessively timid about offending financially influential people, which usually means conservative people. Newspaper owners are not all equally conscientious about the fairness of their news. Editors and reporters find out that what pays is to write the sort of news stories which pleases the man at the top. In rare cases, of course, there may be actual corruption; but more often what puts bias into the news is merely the permeation of the staff by a sense of expediency. They put their jobs first and the truth second.

Often, oddly enough, the motives that lead to such misrepresentation of the news are praiseworthy. A newspaper proprietor believes that the unions are a menace. He believes that every good citizen ought to understand and oppose their methods. He wants to stir up the public. He thinks of himself as crusading against radicalism. He would be ashamed to print in his paper a word of news which would seem to favor the unions. He does not go so far as to pass the word down that the news must be distorted, for he does not believe in distortion. He simply wants to keep his paper clean of pro-union propaganda, as he fancies it. An item in the paper meets his eye; to him it seems radical; he explodes, and soon the staff is on its guard against another explosion. And then, perhaps, actual misrepresentation takes place. It is so easy! If even honest reporters, trying their best, find it difficult to exclude prejudice from their reports, how simple it is, when you don't try too hard, to make a strikers' meeting look like a failure when it really was a success, or to make Mr. William Z. Foster look redder than he is, or to pick out just the proper incidents to show how local public opinion looks upon the issues of the strike! How easy to make Senator A's denunciation of Senator B appear the well-justified act of a man sorely tried and at least giving vent to righteous indignation! And all because the men on the staff of the paper are weak, like other human beings, and because the owner fails to realize that the triumph of any cause, no matter how excellent, should be to him secondary to the duty of telling the truth.

There is much less outright intimidation or domination of the newspapers by advertisers than is often supposed. Many a newspaper has defied department stores successfully. Domination of the press by the department stores was probably common thirty years ago; today it is comparatively infrequent. And the whole process of corrupting the news, where corruption today exists, is less often the deliberate work of men bent on falsehood than a process of drifting before the winds of circumstance, timidity, and self-interest.

The newspaper profession is steadily advancing, not only in the effectiveness of its news-gathering machinery but also in its standing in the community and in its ethical standards. Early in the last century there was so little recognition of the rights of the press that Henry Clay, making a political speech in Kentucky, ordered off the field a reporter who had the impertinence to report on him without first getting special permission. It was not until some time after the beginning of the Civil War that the Government at Washington made satisfactory arrangements for issuing its news to all newspapermen simultaneously, instead of giving it haphazardly to the first comer. Now the president and the members of his Cabinet confer with the press representatives once or twice a day; and, as a matter of course, reporters are given front seats at almost every kind of public occasion.

Two generations ago the leading New York editors called one another blackguards and scoundrels in their editorial columns—a practice which today would be considered disreputable. Some twenty years ago Mr. Henry Watterson declared that journalism was "without any code of ethics or system of self-restraint and self-respect." The standard of newspaper conduct and of impartiality has risen conspicuously since then. The papers of one political party cannot dismiss the deeds of their opponents with such brief notice as they could once. In the recent presidential campaign, a Republican paper in Boston gave more space than any of the Democratic papers to an appeal for Mr. Cox issued by a group of men in New York, while a Democratic paper in the same city ran a straw ballot and printed the results day by day on its front page, although they favored Mr. Harding. Despite all that I have said about the frequent tendency among newspaper owners to side with large financial interests, it must in fairness be acknowledged that most papers give front-page space to Mr. Gompers quite as readily as to Judge Gary. Editors now observe with the utmost care release dates on material furnished them in advance, and most newspapermen can be trusted with confidential information or with facts not yet ripe for publication.

Assiduous as Mr. Sinclair may be in picking out for display the black spots in the record of the Associated Press, I believe this great news-disseminating service to be about as thoroughly imbued with the spirit of impartiality as any organization of its size and extent could well be. Its reports from Washington are models of fairness as between Republicans and Democrats. When I wrote of the difficulty of preparing an unbiased report, perhaps I should have added, "But it can be done—witness the A.P. service from Washington." The conduct of the Associated Press in political campaigns is equally scrupulous. If sometimes, in some places, its correspondents reflect the economic prejudices of the owners of its member papers, no one should judge it for such transgressions without taking into account the tremendous influence that it wields elsewhere on behalf of accuracy.

IV

Yet, if the press is to carry successfully the increasing responsibility which results from the public's increasing reliance upon it, it must not be content with its present record of improvement. How can improvement be hastened?

I believe that the newspapers ought, first of all, to make a more deliberate effort to secure men of education and discrimination for reporters. Schools of journalism are valuable to this end, both on account of the preparation they give and of the added prestige they lend to the profession. One of the things which deter many men of ability and character from entering newspaper work is the prospect of low pay and difficult hours. A man on a morning paper has to be on his job when his friends are enjoying their hours of recreation and sleep. I once met an experienced newspaperman who breakfasted when his family took their dinner, at 7:00 PM, who worked all night, had his playtime in the early morning, dined while his family breakfasted, and then went to bed for the day: not a schedule that many people would look forward to as their lot in middle life! Most newspapermen do not get a Sunday holiday: their day of rest may come at any time in the week. Again, most newspaper offices are ugly, crowded, and grimy—far less agreeable places to work in than business offices.

The exceptions to this rule—such, for example, as the offices of the *New York Times* and the *Christian Science Monitor*—are conspicuous. All these circumstances tend to make journalism an unattractive calling.

In some cities reporters' unions are said to have proved useful in securing better conditions of work; but I cannot believe that this is the right solution to the problem. The reporter should be regarded and should regard himself not as a laborer but as a professional man. Whatever newspaper proprietors can do to enhance the dignity and prestige of his occupation, whether by increasing his pay, compensating him for his difficult hours by giving him more holidays—as Lord Northcliffe is already said to have done—or making his workplace more attractive, will bear dividends in the form of more intelligent and responsible work by a generally better type of reporter.

A deliberate attempt ought also to be made by the more conscientious newspaper publishers and editors, acting presumably through their various professional associations, to formulate in more definite terms a code of newspaper ethics. It would be useful if they would discuss and ventilate such ethical problems as that of the propriety of printing dispatches actually prepared in the newspaper office but purporting to come from a distance. Associations of publishers or editors might also advantageously offer prizes for accuracy in the treatment of critical events, the awards to be made after thorough investigation by an impartial jury. The Pulitzer prizes, now awarded annually, are cases in point; but these do not reward accuracy so much as reportorial brilliance and editorial initiative, which usually are financially profitable in any case. The important thing is to stimulate newspapers to present the unbiased truth.

Most of the suggestions usually made for the improvement of newspaper ethics seem to me to miss the mark. One idea constantly brought forward is that of the endowed newspaper, which would not depend on advertising for its revenue. The endowed paper might possibly be more accurate than its competitors; but again it might not, and it would all too surely be less interesting. To remove the necessity of making profits is to remove incentives to originality, as well as temptations. Municipal newspapers are often advocated, and Mr. Bryan would like to see an Official Bulletin, which would issue news of the federal government. But government control of any sort would bring about inevitably the sort of political bias least to be desired; and an Official Bulletin would almost certainly become an instrument of political propaganda by the party in power.

Another more fruitful suggestion is that of creating independent news agencies at important centers, such as Washington, to send out unprejudiced reports and thus to serve as a check upon the established press associations and the regular Washington correspondents. Such agencies would, I fear, only irritate newspapermen if they attempted direct competition with the press associations. They might serve a useful purpose, however, if they confined themselves to indirect competition, serving, not newspapers, but magazines, business houses, and the like, somewhat as several statistical agencies now furnish data on business conditions to banks and other subscribers. The trained Washington correspondents of various periodicals now do excellent service in giving the public a view of the workings of the government rather different from that gained through the eyes of the press. And a privately controlled Washington news agency, furnishing carefully prepared news from week to week, would be of use to individuals whose local newspapers have an inadequate Washington service, and yet who want to keep close track of government affairs, and also would tend to have a tonic effect upon the news-gathering organization of the press. It would challenge not any single press association or single newspaper but the whole profession. Nothing stimulates one to tell an accurate story so much as the knowledge that one's hearer has an independent means of getting his information, and will pick one up if one goes far wrong.

Yet even such agencies would have only a limited allure. They might be helpful in Washington or other critical points, but for the present we must remain dependent on the newspaper for our principal knowledge of what is going on all over the country and the world. And improvement of the newspaper profession must come about principally from within.

Criticism by the outside public there must be, however—constant, watchful, and constructive—accompanied by an increasing public appreciation of the dignity of journalism. In some quarters the obsolescent notion still prevails that reporters are impudent interlopers and busybodies. Thick-skinned reporters grow callous to such an attitude, but the thick-skinned are not always the most sensitive to accuracy. Ignorant and insolent as newspaper men sometimes are, their profession alone should be enough to command courteous treatment. It is useless to expect a high standard from men, unless the attitude of the community toward them contributes to their self-respect.

Meanwhile, it would be a good thing if all of us who read the newspapers—and that means pretty nearly everybody—knew enough about newspaper organization and methods to be better judges of the credibility of the news. I should like to see lectures on "How to Read the Newspapers" given in colleges and schools and elsewhere. It is as essential for the citizen of this day to be able to read the morning paper with a discriminating eye—to be able to distinguish the A.P. dispatch from the special correspondent's forecast of conditions, and the fact story from the rumor story, and to be able to take into account the probable bias of the paper and make allowance for it—as it is for a lawyer to learn to assess the value of evidence. Only as we are able to estimate the relative amount of credence to be given to conflicting reports, and to judge for ourselves the reliability of the sources of the news, do we come somewhere near seeing that true picture of the world about us which we must see if we are to play our part in it intelligently and independently.

The Legend on the License

JOHN HERSEY

The imminent death of the novel is announced from time to time, but the very repetitiousness of the bulletins testifies to stubborn vital signs. I bring other news from the hospital. Journalism is on a sickbed and is in a very bad way.

The trouble did not begin but came out into the open with the appallingly harmful phrase Truman Capote used in 1965 to categorize *In Cold Blood*. It was, he said, a "nonfiction novel." The blurring of fiction and journalism sanctioned by that phrase is now widely practiced and widely condoned. This has not been particularly good for fiction; it may be mortal to journalism.

In fiction that *is* fiction, no holds need be barred. Novelists may introduce or disguise real people and real events as they choose. Tolstoy disguised all but the generals. Dreiser's *An American Tragedy* was suggested by an actual crime, but he did not feel the need to call his creation "a true-life novel." Malraux, who had an enormous influence on some of the novelists of my generation (e.g., Ralph Ellison), often depicted originals—among others, Chiang Kai-shek in all the splendid irony of his left-wing youth. E. L. Doctorow has had harmless fun with Morgan, Ford, and others. And so on.

The only caution in all this is the one so acutely perceived by Flannery O'Conner (in *Mystery and Manners*): "It's always wrong of course to say that you can't do this or you can't do that in fiction. You can do anything you can get

From the *Yale Review*, Autumn 1980.

away with, but nobody has ever gotten away with much." In other words, there are tests. A test, for one thing, of quality, of art. Or, to put it more brutally for authors, a test of gifts. But the point is that always, in fiction, there is a saving notice on the license: THIS WAS MADE UP.

As to journalism, we may as well grant right away that there is no such thing as absolute objectivity. It is impossible to present in words "*the* truth" or "the whole story." The minute a writer offers nine hundred ninety-nine out of one thousand facts, the worm of bias has begun to wriggle. The vision of each witness is particular. Tolstoy pointed out that immediately after a battle there are as many remembered versions of it as there have been participants.

Still and all, I will assert that there is one sacred rule of journalism. The writer must not invent. The legend on the license must read: NONE OF THIS WAS MADE UP. The ethics of journalism, if we can be allowed such a boon, must be based on the simple truth that every journalist knows the difference between the distortion that comes from subtracting observed data and the distortion that comes from adding invented data.

The threat to journalism's life by the denial of this difference can be realized if we look at it from the reader's point of view. The reader assumes the subtraction as a given of journalism and instinctively hunts for the bias; the moment the reader suspects additions, the earth begins to skid underfoot, for the idea that there is no way of knowing what is real and what is not real is terrifying. Even more terrifying is the notion that lies are truths. Or at least these things used to be terrifying; the dulling of the terror that has come about through repeated exposure tells us how far this whole thing has gone.

Let me now drive my own stakes in the ground. I have always believed that the *devices* of fiction could serve journalism well and might even help it to aspire now and then to the level of art. But I have tried to honor the distinction between the two forms. To claim that a work is both fiction and journalism, or to assert, as Doctorow recently did, that "there is no longer any such thing as fiction or nonfiction; there is only narrative—these are, in my view, serious crimes against the public. In a backward look in *The New Journalism* Tom Wolfe, citing a piece of mine from 1944, remarked, "Here we start getting into the ancestry of the New Journalism." The word "ancestry" makes me feel a bit like the Peking Man, and in laying claim to authority in this field I prefer to think of myself as nothing more remote than a grandfather.

Now. After reading three recent publications—Tom Wolfe's *The Right Stuff,* an entertaining book, Wolfe's best so far; Norman Mailer's *The Executioner's Song,* a powerful work that unquestionably enhances Mailer's claim to the kind of literary top billing he has always so tiresomely whined after; and Truman Capote's "Handcarved Coffins," a gobbet of commercial trash by this once brilliant writer in his new collection, *Music for Chameleons*—I am one worried grandpa. These three hybrids clinch it. The time has come to redraw the line between journalism and fiction.

I

"Handcarved Coffins," which Capote calls both "nonfiction" and "a short novel," belongs here, in the company of the Wolfe and Mailer books, only because of Capote's place in the line of parentage of the hybrid form; it can be dealt with briefly. The story must represent to its author a nostalgic yearning for the remembered powers of *In Cold Blood,* the fine, shapely, hard-fibered novel (as novel) that appears to have been the model Norman Mailer wanted to knock off its pedestal, but couldn't quite, with *The Executioner's Song.* Vivid as *In Cold Blood* was as a novel, it had serious flaws on the nonfiction side, arising from the fact that its actions and dialogue had been reconstructed long after the described events, yet were presented in the book with all assurance as being exactly what had happened; the dialogue, rebuilt from a great distance, stood within the authenticating marks of direct quotation. Besides suffering from troubles like these, which are intrinsic to a genre that claims to be both fiction and not, "Handcarved Coffins" groans under others far more grievous.

For one thing, the tale does something that journalism simply must not do: It strains credulity well beyond the breaking point. There is a much-too-muchness about it, which convinces one that the fictionist has decidedly had the upper hand over the journalist. The story is told in interview form, through a series of dialogues between Capote and a number of characters, the most prominent being a detective from a certain State Bureau of Investigation, who is trying to solve a succession of ghastly murders that have been announced beforehand to the victims, in all cases but one, by the arrival in their hands of beautiful miniature coffins, carved from "light balsam wood" and containing candid photographs of the doomed persons. The murderer has dispatched two of his victims, an elderly pair, by insinuating into their parked car, to await their return to it, nine rattlesnakes that have been "injected with amphetamine." Perhaps we can swallow that one. But try this: A recipient of one of the little coffins, driving along a lonely road in "an eccentric vehicle of his own invention" with no top and no windshield, is cleanly decapitated by "a strong steel wire sharpened thin as a razor" and stretched across the road between a tree and a telephone pole at exactly the right height to catch him just under the chin; the wire "slice[s] off his head as easily as a girl picking petals off a daisy." And so on, murder after murder, until we have been taken far beyond the last shore of belief. (We will come back in due course to this crucial matter of belief.)

An even worse fault of this creaky tale is that it is told as if in a game of blindman's buff. It is the reader who is blindfolded. He has no idea where he is. The story takes place in an invisible place: a nameless town in an unspecified state. The characters are *there*, but they are unseeable as real people. Their names have been changed. Capote says he "had to omit a few identifying things" (*New York Times*, January 7, 1979)—which implies his having substituted other made-up ones. (The principal suspect "had long simian-like arms; the hands dangled at his knees, and the fingers were long, capable, oddly aristocratic.") Altogether, the ace among rules of reliable reporting—that the facts should be "hard"—is here repeatedly and fatally broken.

II

Tom Wolfe's *The Right Stuff* is a vivid book, a tainted book. It gives an account of the Mercury phase of the United States space program, and its thesis is that test pilots of rocket aircraft, genuinely, and the seven Mercury astronauts, more ambiguously, shared an ineffable quality compounded of spiffy courage, arrogant recklessness, dry-palmed sass, and super-jock male potency (on earth they indiscriminately balled "juicy little girls," and in the sky they whipped around in Pynchonesque flying phalluses), to all of which Wolfe gives the catchy tag "the right stuff." Wolfe's style-machine has never run more smoothly than in this book. The writing is at times wonderfully funny. Some of the passages on flying are classy. A quick and easy read.

Then why tainted? Because Wolfe is the paradigm of the would-be journalist who cannot resist the itch to improve on the material he digs up. The tricks of fiction he uses dissolve now and then into its very essence: fabrication. The notice on the license reads: THIS WAS NOT MADE UP (EXCEPT FOR THE PARTS THAT WERE MADE UP).

The source of the taint is the pair of pieces Wolfe wrote in 1965 for the *Herald-Tribune* Sunday magazine about the *New Yorker*. We must recall them at some length, because in them one finds in a gross form the fundamental defect that has persisted ever since in Wolfe's writing, and that is to be found in the work of many of the "new journalists," and also indeed in that of many "nonfiction novelists"—namely, the notion that mere facts don't matter.

In the introduction to *The New Journalism* Wolfe tried to laugh off his *New Yorker* pieces. He called them "some lighthearted fun.... A very droll *sportif* performance, you understand." They were nothing of the kind. They made up a vicious, slashing lampoon. Begging the question whether the *New Yorker* may at some point have deserved a serious critique, there seems to be no way to explain the stunningly irresponsible street cruelty of Wolfe's exercise except by guessing that he could not bear to face it that "his" New Journalism would have to be measured sooner or later against the meticulously accurate and vivid reporting of such *New Yorker* writers as the wonderful Joseph Mitchell or, let's say, Lillian Ross and Truman Capote; who in turn were writing in an honorable tradition, not New at all, reaching back to George Orwell, Henry Mayhew, James Boswell... .

Wolfe called his first piece "Tiny Mummies! The True Story of the Ruler of 43rd Street's Land of the Walking Dead." This "true" story was a collage of shameless inventions. Not satisfied with making up lots of little decorative details, such as imaginary colors and types of paper used at the *New Yorker* for memos and manuscripts, Wolfe reached farther into the territory of fiction to devise blunt weapons with which to assault William Shawn, the magazine's editor. He dreamed up a Shawn memorandum which was supposed to have warned the staff against talking to him; he gave a description of the magazine's editorial process which, according to an analysis of Wolfe's pieces by Renata Adler and Gerald Jonas, was erroneous "in every particular, large and small"; and he gave a picture of Shawn's role that "was not a little untrue, not half true, but totally, stupefyingly false."

Shawn's "retiring" nature, Wolfe asserted, could be accounted for by "what the records show, actually, in the Cook County (Chicago) Criminal Court"— that Leopold's and Loeb's original intended victim in their famous murder had been "a small and therefore manageable teen-age boy from the Harvard School," whose first name was William ("the court records do not give the last name"), and that the two had decided not to kill William Shawn "only because they had a personal grudge against him and somebody might remember that." Shawn's trauma is totally a Wolfe fantasy. The court records *do* give the last name of the intended victim, and the first as well. It was not a teen-aged William Shawn. It was a nine-and-a-half-year-old boy named John o. Levinson who testified at the trial.

The coda of the second piece, the climax of the whole charade, is a perfect example of a Wolfe fantasy flying out of control. Wolfe has been building a (false) picture of Shawn slavishly attached to the formulas of the founder of the magazine, Harold Ross. In this scene we see Shawn sitting alone at home, on the very evening when down at the St. Regis the staff is celebrating the magazine's fortieth anniversary. According to Wolfe, Shawn is listening to "that wonderful light zinc plumbing sound" of Bix Beiderbecke's recording of "I Can't Get Started": "(those other trumpet players, like Harry James, they never played the real 'I Can't Get Started')." At the end of the recording "Bix hits that incredible high one he died on, popping a vessel in his temporal fossa, bleeding into his squash, drowning on the bandstand.... *That* was the music of Harold Ross's lifetime.... Here, on that phonograph, those days are *preserved.* ..."

Adler and Jonas:

The facts are, of course, that *"That"* was not "the music of Harold Ross's life-time." Or anybody else's. The facts are that "Bix" did not die playing, nor did his death have anything to do with his "temporal fossa." He died in bed, of pneumonia. Nor did Beiderbecke make a recording of "the real 'I Can't Get Started.'" In fact, he never played it—with or without "that incredible high one." It would have been difficult for him to play it. "I Can't Get Started with You" was written in 1935, four years after Beiderbecke's death.

When Wolfe wrote his advertisements for himself in *The New Journalism,* nine years later, he still couldn't suppress his snickers at the reaction to his *New Yorker* caper, and to the subsequent new wave of nonfiction, on the part of "countless journalists and literary intellectuals," who, he said, were scream-ing, *"The bastards are making it up!* (I'm telling you, Ump, that's a spitball he's throwing ...)." But his laughter had an edge of nerves; altogether too many folks in the stands had seen and called attention to his applying a little greasy stuff to the pellet.

In the seven years since then, two things have happened: Wolfe has grown quite a bit more careful (and hard-working), and the public has become in-creasingly inured, or maybe the word is numb, to the blurring of fiction and journalism. *The Right Stuff* has been accepted as fairly accurate by people in the know. I talked with a number of journalists who had covered the space program, and while one complained of "outright lies" in the book, all the oth-ers seemed to think that Wolfe had "made an effort to be as accurate as he could be," that he had "done his homework," that he had made mistakes, but those had been errors of judgment and value that any conventional journal-ist might have made. Most of them thought he had been too kind to Scott Carpenter and too hard on John Glenn. The official National Aeronautics and Space Administration view was also favorable. Christopher Kraft, in charge of the Johnson Space Center in Houston, declined to talk about the book, but his public relations chief, John MacLeish, said after consultation with others that despite a number of technical errors there was "a high degree of accuracy" in the book. The two astronauts I talked with, John Glenn and Deke Slayton, said, respectively, that Wolfe was "accurate on the details of my flight" and "mostly pretty accurate."

Taint, then? Well, alas, yes. Some questions remain. Enough to add up. Enough so that, in the end, one cannot help wondering whether even these interested parties, in their numbed acceptance of the premise that there is no difference between fiction and nonfiction, between real life and a skillfully drawn mirror image of a dream of it, haven't been to some extent taken in. I give you the example of the way in which Senator Glenn, in speaking to me, paid tribute to the hypnotic ambiguity of Wolfe's prose. Glenn is pictured in the book as an insufferable prig, a prude, a killjoy, yet he said to me, "I came out pretty good in the book, so I can't complain." NASA seemed to think it had come out pretty well, too. Did it?

Wolfe's fiction-aping journalism, he wrote in 1973, "enjoys an advantage [over fiction] so obvious, so built in, one almost forgets what a power it has: the simple fact that the reader knows *all this actually happened*.... The writer is one step closer to the absolute involvement of the reader that Henry James and James Joyce dreamed of and never achieved. ..." Whew. That *is* a big advantage. But let's focus for a moment on much smaller things, such as that little word "all."

In defining the New Journalism, Wolfe wrote that a journalist need use just four devices of fiction to bring this amazing power to the page: scene-by-scene construction, dialogue, point of view, and what he called "status details." But the resources of fiction are by no means so barren as all that. One essential requisite and delight of fiction, for example, is the absolute particularity it can give to every individual, every character. Wolfe has apparently ruled this out; he is a generalizer. Let him find a vivid or funny trait in more than one member of a class, then without exception the whole class has it. Thirty-six military pilots show up at the Pentagon to apply for the space program; without exception they wear "Robert Hall clothes that cost about a fourth as much as their watches." "They had many names, these rockets, Atlas, Navajo, Little Joe, Jupiter, but they all blew up." All test pilots talked something he calls Army Creole. All seven astronauts went in for Flying and Drinking, Drinking and Driving, Driving and Balling. All Russian space vehicles were launched "by the Soviet's mighty and mysterious Integral"—though, as Wolfe knows, Integral was not a person or a state organ but a spaceship in Evgeny Zamyatin's novel, *We.* "Every wife ..." "Every young fighter jock ..." "Everyone ..." "Invariably ..." "All these people ..." "All ... (*"All this actually happened ..."*)

Another big advantage over other writers that Wolfe apparently feels he has is that since he is using fictional modes, he is, even though dealing with nonfictional matter, freed from the boring job of checking verifiable details. If something turns out to have been dead wrong—well, that was just the free play of fancy. Some of the many details Wolfe should have checked but obviously did not are: The kind of car John Glenn drove. Whether Slayton, pictured as an active partisan at the meeting Wolfe calls the Ko-nokai Seance, was even present. What operant conditioning means. The Latin name for the chimpanzee. What jodhpurs are. What cilia means. When the compass was invented ...

But there are disadvantages in the method, too, at least for the reader. One is the frequent juxtaposition of passages that are wholly made up with others that are only partly made up or, beyond the use of one of the four devices, not made up at all. Side by side, for example, are a long parody of an airline pilot's voice reassuring the passengers on the last leg of a flight from Phoenix to New York when the landing gear won't lock, and an account of how the test pilot Chuck Yaeger gets drunk, breaks two ribs falling off a horse on a moonlight gallop, doesn't tell the base doctor, and two days later goes up in an X-1 and buffets through the sound barrier, hurting so badly his right arm is useless. (Right stuff.) Both passages are funny, wildly hyperbolic, interchangeable in voice and tone. It is not hard to tell which of these is mostly made up (or is it wholly made up?). But what becomes not so easy, after many such oscillations, is to perceive exactly where the line between reporting and invention in any "real-life" episode actually lies.

This difficulty is immensely reinforced by the way Wolfe uses his third fictional device: point of view. At will, he enters the consciousness of his characters. We have the stream (or in Wolfe's case one has to say river) of consciousness of wives of astronauts, waiting out reentry. We find ourselves in each astronaut's mind as he barrels across the sky. For an awful moment we become Lyndon Johnson. We may be dismayed to find ourselves suddenly trapped in a chimpanzee's head. Finally (James and Joyce certainly never gave us *this* pleasure) we are right there in God's mind, out of patience with John Glenn and barking at him, "Try the automatic, you ninny." Beyond the dicey issue of freely inventive recreation of thoughts and dialogue, long after their transaction, a further trouble is that Wolfe never makes the slightest attempt, which any novelist would make as a matter of course, to vary the voice to fit each character. What we hear throughout, ringing in every mind, is the excited shout of Tom Wolfe. Each astronaut in turn *becomes* Tom Wolfe. Without even a little jiggle of lexical sex change each astronaut's wife becomes Tom Wolfe. Right Staffers who are alleged to speak nothing but Army Creole are garlanded with elegant tidbits like *esprit, joie de combat, mas allá!* The chimp talks pure Wolfe. God help us, God becomes Tom Wolfe and with His sweet ear chooses the Wolfeish "ninny."

"Class has always been Tom Wolfe's subject," John Gregory Dunne has written (*New York Review of Books*, November 8, 1979). Dunne sees Wolfe as exposing the unmentionable in a purportedly egalitarian society: the existence of class. Wolfe is always on the side of the outsider, the underdog. Low Rent is good. He declares himself a literary lumpenprole, one of "the Low Rent rabble at the door," one of "the Kentucky Colonels of Journalism and Literature." Placing such great emphasis on status seems to have affected Wolfe's decibel range. Whispering, as any outsider knows, is genteel. Understatement is upper class. A consequence of such understandings is the central disaster of this gifted writer's voice: He never abandons a resolute tone of screaming. The test of every sentence is: Will its sound waves shatter a wine glass at twenty feet? It is not surprising that he writes so beautifully about the rupture of the sound barrier.

While he has largely cooled his typographical excesses in this book (there are only three exclamation points, and no italicized words at all, on the first page), the aural and psychological overamplification is still very much there. The voice of every character, even that of a quiet woman like Glenn's wife, is Jovian. One can say that the charm in Wolfe is his enthusiasm. On nearly every page, though, this attractive quality sends him floating off the ground. When he is establishing the driving part of Flying and Drinking, Drinking and Driving, Driving and Balling, in which "all" astronauts indulged, his excitement over their recklessness at the wheel leads him to write, doubtless in a *sportif* spirit: "More fighter pilots died in automobiles than airplanes." No time period. According to navy statistics which Wolfe himself cites, there was a 23 percent probability that a navy career pilot would die in an aircraft accident. Did one in four die on the road? In 1952 sixty-two army air force pilots died in crashes in thirty-six weeks of flying at Edward Air Force Base, 1.7 per week. Did two a week die in cars? The point is not that this little example of possibly humorous overkill announces in itself the death of journalism. The point is that this one happened to be readily catchable. How many others are not? Are they on every page? How can we know? How can we ever know?

And so we come through many cumulative small doubts back to the issues of "accuracy." Let us grant that among Wolfe's works, this book is relatively "accurate" (perhaps because relatively much of it is based on written records, notably the NASA official history, *The New Ocean: A History of Project Mercury*). But "relatively 'accurate'" may not be good enough, when we look for the whole meaning of the work.

By now we are thoroughly skeptical, and, remembering John Glenn's having read the abuse he took at Wolfe's hand as praise, we begin to see abysses of ambiguity, of ambivalence, in the book. Wolfe loves what he loathes. The individual words mock and slash and ridicule; the sentences into which they are combined somehow ogle and stroke and admire. As Eric Korn put it *(Times Literary Supplement,* November 30, 1979), "If there's one thing more unlovable than the man of letters showing his contempt for physical valor, it's the man of letters fawning on physical valor. Wolfe contrives to do both at once." Glenn and NASA are both right and awfully wrong to think they come out "pretty good."

Looking back, we see that this double-think has been there, off and on, all through Wolfe's work. His class struggle seems to be in his own heart. The New Journalism was a product of the sixties, and like much of what hit the kids in that decade, Wolfe's struggle seems to have been a generational one. To adopt his voice: Young and new are good, old and old are bad; but o I love you Mummy and Daddy, you bitch and bastard. This lumpenprole affects beautifully tailored white suits and his prose often gives off a donnish perfume— *prima facie, beruf,* pick your language. If Tom Wolfe is at all interested in class, it is in a new elite of those few "outsiders" who, at any given moment, are "in." The quasi-fictional methods allowed Wolfe to be both out and in.

Precisely this ambiguity makes for real zippy entertainment—the dazzle of the magic show. Great fun. But. It leaves us with serious doubts about a mode of Journalism that straddles in its ambiguities the natural and obligatory substance of such a book: the horrendous issues of the space program, its cost, philosophy, technological priorities, and impact on national jingoism and machismo in a cold-war atmosphere which, as we saw in the winter of 1979–1980, could so easily be brought to dangerous warmth.

I believe that the double-think flaw is intrinsic to Wolfe's method. One who gets the habit of having it both ways in form slips into the habit of having it both ways in attitude and substance. The legend on the license really does matter.

As to deeper and subtler forms of social harm that this journalism also may cause, more later.

III

The case of Norman Mailer is much more complicated, because Mailer is so richly talented and so grossly perverse.

Readers know by now that the first half of *The Executioner's Song* is based on the horrifying story of two wanton murders in Utah by a bright, sick, witty, cowboyish paroled recidivist named Gary Gilmore, who, having been condemned to death for the crimes, staunchly insisted on being executed. The second half tells how the strong smell of money given off by this death-row drama drifted east with the weather systems and attracted New York's media vultures, the swiftest among them being one Lawrence Schiller, who had already picked the bones clean from other carrion: Jack Ruby, Marina Oswald, Susan Atkins, for examples. (Schiller had also—though Mailer finds it convenient to omit this from 1,056 pages which seem to leave absolutely nothing else out—arranged for Mailer to make bucks cleaning the dear flesh from the skeleton of poor Marilyn Monroe; and was, of course, to arrange the same for Mailer with Gilmore's remains.)

Besides nursing Gilmore along, making sure to keep the condemned man's death-resolve firm (else contracts might fly away), Schiller dug up a mass of background material, including the element that was eventually to attract the romantic fictionist in Mailer—the love story between Gilmore and a sad, dumb, compliant doxy named Nicole Baker, who had been married at thirteen, had been twice a mother and twice divorced by nineteen, had long been in and out of mental hospitals, and would do anything for her man, whoever he might happen to be, including "rubbing pee-pees" (for "Uncle Lee," at five), turning tricks (not exactly for a pimp, just for a nice guy who had some homey friends), ratting (to attractive cops), attempting suicide (at Gary's request through the mail), and spilling all the details of Gary's limp erections and requests to shave pubic hair and experiments in threesome (to Larry Schiller). Schiller's pumping out of this pathetic Nicole is a shocking tale of commercial sadism from which Mailer, who later used every jism-dripping morsel of the material, manages to remain somehow serenely detached. One of the conveniences of having a book be both fiction and journalism is that when the journalist's money-grubbing dirty tricks begin to stink, the novelist can soar away on wings of art, far above it all.

Mailer does want it both ways. Had he, like Orwell with *Down and Out in Paris and London,* for instance, or like Solzhenitsyn in his first three books, simply called his work a novel and let it go at that, we could perhaps have lived with the immediacy of the reality underlying the fiction—remembering that some reality underlies every fiction. But no. This had to be labeled "A True-Life Novel." (Mailer has played this doppelganger game before, of course. *Armies of the Night* was subtitled "The Novel as History, History as a Novel.") "I called [*The Executioner's Song*] a novel because it reads like one," Mailer has said in an interview *(New York Times,* October 26, 1979). And it does. He is right. A powerful and moving novel. But also: "This story does its best to be a factual account ... and the story is as accurate as one can make it." The book jacket praises the work as fiction and also calls it "a model of complete, precise, and accurate reporting." The legend on this license reads: THIS WAS MADE UP AND IT WAS SIMULTANEOUSLY NOT MADE UP.

It simply cannot have been both. What it cannot be, if we look closely, is "precise and accurate reporting." Asserting that it is can only mean sending journalism into the intensive-care unit.

There is a false syllogism at work here, having to do with a Wolfeish "all this actually happened." A: Gary Gilmore did kill, was condemned, did insist on being executed. B: Mailer has written an immensely detailed and artful novel about the Gary Gilmore case, in which he uses mostly real names. Therefore C: This must be reporting. Mailer puts it somewhat differently, though of course not diffidently. "God," he says *(New York Times,* January 27, 1980), "was at least as good a novelist as I am."

The novel is presented in terse, highly charged paragraphs, like tiny chapters, which allow Mailer both to keep the point of view rapidly shifting among a very large cast of vivid characters—Mormons, families in their cobwebs, druggies and deadbeats, a whirligig mother of a murderer, straight victims and their heart-breaking survivors, Nicole and her procession of men, jailbirds, jailers, civil libertarians, lawyers, television and movie con men, and, of course, the fascinating psychopath at the heart of the yarn, as well as many others; and also to build a grim, gripping suspense. Since we know the outcome from the very beginning, this latter is a brilliant feat. It is a deeply disturbing story, told by a bewitching minstrel of the dark side of the soul. But let us not say that it is accurate reporting.

Mailer reveals his method of work in three ways: by indirection through what we can infer from his picture of Schiller's researches; through his own direct account of his sources and routines in an afterword; and by what he has said about the book after its publication.

He freely admits that he has tinkered with dialogue. And here we go: Is a reporter entitled (was Capote, writing *In Cold Blood,* were Woodward and Bernstein, in *All the President's Men,* were Woodward and Armstrong, in *The Brethren,* entitled) to reconstruct extensive exchanges of direct speech from passages of action that had taken place long before the research—and claim that the published result is "precise and accurate"? Mailer evidently relied for bits of his dialogue on interviews of his own, many months after the events; but most of his raw material was at least secondhand, given to him by Schiller, who had extracted it, also mostly after the events, from the principals—so that the filtration leading to direct quotation is through three and (when the informant is repeating something another person has told him) even *four* sensibilities, to say nothing of a fallible memory or two or three. And then, on top of all that, for art's sake, Mailer has tinkered.

A more serious question is raised by what Mailer appears to have done with Gilmore's letters to Nicole. These are the stuff of old-fashioned melodrama—purloined letters. That is to say, a cub reporter for the *Deseret News* named Tamera Smith sweet-talked her way into Nicole's trust; Nicole asked Tamera to take the letters for safekeeping; Tamera promptly photocopies them without telling Nicole; and on Nicole's request returned the originals but not the copies. After Gilmore and Nicole had jointly attempted suicide, Tamera wrote a story partly based on the letters. Alerted by the story, the prosecutor's office then picked up the originals. And later "the carrion bird," as Mailer from his artistic distance calls Schiller, having clamped a money-lock on Gilmore's lawyers, bullied them into demanding the letters from the prosecutor under laws of discovery; and so got his hands (and eventually Mailer's) on them. Gilmore, the copyright owner, of course never gave his permission for the use of the letters. He never had a chance. He got four bullets in the heart.

The journalistic shadow on these letters, however, hasn't to do with this sordid history. The question is, rather, just how far Mailer moved them away from "precise and accurate" replication. What Mailer says about his editing of them in his afterword is wonderfully careful. He is frank to say he altered the interviews with Gilmore that Gary's lawyers taped, just as one would alter one's own remarks on a transcript: "The aim was not to improve his diction so much as to treat him decently." But watch the prestidigitator's hand very closely here:

> With Gilmore's letters, however, it seemed fair to show him at a level higher than his average. One wanted to demonstrate the impact of his mind on Nicole, and that might be best achieved by allowing his brain to have its impact on us. Besides, he wrote well at times. His good letters are virtually intact....

It is true that Gilmore had a weird and interesting mind, and there is no way of knowing exactly where and how much Mailer meddled. One clue is in "voice." Granting that one's spoken and written voices may differ markedly, there seems such a gulf between Gilmore's articulation on the tapes and in his letters that we can't help wondering exactly whose brain it is, in the latter, that is having its impact on us.

First, from the tapes (altered for decent treatment):

> I seen that she wasn't on the list until just, you know, yesterday. ...
>
> I guess perhaps they didn't quite take me literal.... .
>
> They act like they're really doing something by giving you a big meal, but it ain't like the menu in the paper. You don't get it good, you know.

And then this Mailerish voice in the letters:

> I'm so used to bullshit and hostility, deceit and pettiness, evil and hatred. Those things are my natural habitat. They have shaped me. I look at the

world through eyes that suspect, doubt, fear, hate, cheat, mock, are selfish and vain. All things unacceptable, I see them as natural.... There are dead cockroaches in the corners.... I can hear the tumbrel wheels creak.

What will I meet when I die? The Oldness? Vengeful ghosts? A dark gulf? Will my spirit be flung about the universe faster than thought? Will I be judged and sentenced, as so many churches would have us believe? Will I be called to and clutched at by lost spirits? Will there be nothing? ... Just an end?

Mailer may conceivably be able to produce photocopies of many letters like these with elevated language in Gilmore's longhand, but any reader who is the least bit interested in journalism will have grown suspicious long before reading them in print. For an interesting reason.

Almost without exception, reviewers of *The Executioner's Song* called attention to what they saw as the simple and direct language Mailer uses in the novel. "A meticulously limited vocabulary," Joan Didion wrote, "and a voice as flat as the horizon" *(New York Times,* October 7, 1979). Only one reviewer I have come across (Diane Johnson in the *New York Review of Books,* December 6, 1979) seemed even to notice what I quickly came to think of as Mailer's tag lines—touches of prose, nearly always final lines in the chapterettes, buffed to such hummingbird-feather iridescence as almost to hurt the eye with the lights of their beauty and intensity. Pure Mailer. From a journalistic standpoint, the significant thing about these tag lines is that each Mailerism is presented as if *within the point of view of a character.* This is not reporting; it is projection. And the cumulative force of the projections pushes the book right out of the country of journalism. To feel this cumulation, we must look at quite a few examples:

NICOLE *(on a visit to Gary in prison):* It was as if they stood on a ledge and sorrow was as light as all the air below the fall.

She felt modest in the middle of her own sorrow, as if some quiet person in heaven was crying with her too.

(On her druggy sister April): She was in touch with the heavy strings on the fiddle. (And): Most of the time she had a toothache in her expression.

BRENDA: Gary sat there like he was grinding bones in his mind.

SPENCE MCGRATH *(Gary's employer, watching Gary eat a brown-bag lunch):* [He] ate the food in all the presence of his own thoughts.

BESSIE GILMORE *(Gary's mother):* She thought it had to be the way a tomb would smell if a strong man was buried in it.

Pain was a boring conversationalist who never stopped, just found new topics.

The picture would flicker over her eyes like a moth in a closet.

"Oh Gary," whispered the child that never ceased to live in the remains of her oper-
ations and twisted joints.

MIKALL *(Gary's brother):* It was like a bigger dude squeezing your machismo to
see if it leaked.

LARRY SCHILLER: The memory burned into the skin right under the beard. At
times like that, fat felt comfortable—one more layer of asbestos against the
flames.

[Nicole was] like a waif in a house whose windows were wet with fog.

VERN DAMICO: Stranger's eyes were gleaming, like his hooves were flashing in
the air.

EARL DORIUS *(Assistant Attorney General):* >That hand moved around the clock
like anxiety circulating in one's chest.

DENNIS BOAZ *(Gary's first lawyer):* The mind could undulate like a jellyfish.

RIKKI BAKER: [Gary] got upset about it the way people can brood about bad
weather.

NOALL WOOTTON *(prosecutor, reaction to Gary's changes of mind during the trial):*
It was like dealing with a crazy pony who was off on a gallop at every wind.

JOHN WOODS *(psychiatrist):* [Gary] wished for some absolute dazzler of a lawyer who could handle the jury like a basketball and take them up and down
the court.

JERRY SCOTT *(state patrolman, taking Gary to prison after his sentencing):* Night
had come, and the ridge of the mountain came down to the Interstate like a
big dark animal laying out its paw.

Some scenes, if you rub them carefully between thumb and finger, turn out
to have a palpable nap of invention on them—not whole cloth, but finished
goods with miraculously tidy hems. For instance, some time after the execution, there is a scene in a drinking place near Provo called The Stirrup.

As Mailer tells it, three of the marksmen who had delivered bullets to Gilmore's chest were drinking and playing liars' dice in the bar one late afternoon.
A waitress named Willa Brant sat down with them. One of the men pulled out
of his pocket a bit of the webbing that had strapped Gilmore's arm to the death
chair and one of the slugs that, the guy said, had killed him, for her to touch.
After a while a young married woman whom Willa knew slightly, named Rene
Wales, came in and got talking with the executioners about the CBs in their
pickups. "Before you knew it" Mrs. Wales went out with one of them to check

out his radio. Forty-five minutes passed. Then the Mailer tag line: "Rene came in with the fellow, and both had a look on their faces like they'd been sopping up some of the gravy."

Now, the trouble with this as reporting is that it is told from the point of view of Willa Brant. But she is *not,* it turns out, one of the roughly 150 persons Mailer lists in his afterword as having been interviewed by Schiller, himself, or both. In telling of the scene she is said to be a friend of Toni Gurney, whose name we do find on the list. So Schiller or Mailer got the episode from someone who was not there, and *we* get it at third- or fourth-hand. But the anecdote is told in considerable fine detail. It bears all the marks of having been so promising to begin with, in this game of pass-the-whisper, that the fictionist in Mailer simply couldn't resist touching up the whisper he heard. He writes in his afterword: "The names ... of certain characters have been changed to protect their privacy"—and also, quite possibly, to ward off lawsuits. Of course we never know which names have been changed, so we can't tell whether Mrs. Wales's has been; we can only hope for her sake it has been. So the trouble with many scenes in the book is that we can never know where Mailer the reporter leaves off and Mailer the novelist takes over.

In fiction, the writer's voice matters; in reporting, the writer's authority matters. We read fiction to fortify our psyches, and in the pleasure that that fortification may give us, temperament holds sway. We read journalism—or most of us still do, anyway—to try to learn about the external world in which our psyches have to struggle along, and the quality we most need in our informant is some measure of trustworthiness. *The Executioner's Song* may satisfy us as fiction—it does me—precisely because the author's voice is so pungent, so active, so eloquent, so very alive. But there is deep trouble when we come to the journalistic pretensions of this novel, precisely because the temperament of the reporter is so intrusive, so vaunting, and, considering the specific story being told, so hard to trust.

When we read a novel of Mailer's, the wild shenanigans of his private life are none of our business, really; the art is there to speak for itself, and so is the strong voice of the weaver behind the arras. With good fiction, those are enough. But when we are told that a tale with the massive social implications of *The Executioner's Song* is "a model of complete, precise, and accurate reporting," we are entitled to know a bit more about the mind and temperament that have shaped our instruction. The facts about Mailer's life—and he himself has been the trumpeting source of most of our knowledge of them—raise some questions about the trustworthiness of the authority behind this book.

Like Hemingway before him, Norman Mailer has made himself at home in a fantasy of pugilism, and has challenged all champs and all pretenders in all weights to fifteen rounds in the ring of letters; he has scattered his macho boasts and seed among a block of wives, mistresses, and bare acquaintances; near dawn after a night of carousal and quarrels he made a pretty fair attempt on the life of one of these ladies with a cheap knife; he has romanticized marijuana, "the smoke of the assassins," and rewrote one novel "bombed and sapped and charged and stoned with lush, with pot, with benny, saggy, Miltown, coffee, and two packs a day"; in a rage while directing a pseudo-movie he tried to bite an earlobe off an actor with the right name for the scene, Rip Torn; considering a mayoral run in New York he advocated jousting in Central Park as a therapy for muggers.

Can we trust a reporter with such a bizarre history of brutality, insecurity, mischief, and voguishness when he gives us, thinly, just three implied reasons (do they seem to be *justifications?)* for Gary Gilmore's crimes: (1) the desperation of a young lover afraid of losing his beloved; (2) the damage done him by psychiatrists in, for instance, having transiently administered to him, long before the murders, a drug called Prolixin; and (3) a vague possibility, only glancingly hinted at, of a strain of infantilism in the killer?

Or can we trust this reporter when he devotes so much energy and space to rendering the sex and violence in the story—making of it not *Romeo and Juliet* but a mongrel, out of *Tristan and Isolde* by *Bonnie and Clyde*—and skimps the intricate, fascinating, and socially consequential questions of law and philosophy that hovered over the first execution in the country in many years?

Or when, in his eagerness to give us a dope-smoky, drive-in, stick-shift, gang-bang Western romance, he does not do anything like justice to the vision of the kindly people of the town of Provo, firmly (and perhaps, in the context of this drama, disastrously) fixed and drenched in Mormon ideas of the correctional effects of love and decency; or to their views of proper sexual conventions, and of the regions beyond death?

Am I saying that we can accept what Mailer says as a novelist and cannot accept what he says as a journalist? Baffled by the impossibility of knowing when he is which, I am. When we read a novel, we are asked to suspend disbelief, and as soon as we close the book we can be expected in normal circumstances to bring the suspension to an end along with the story, for in fiction, as Auden wrote is the case in poetry (in *The Dyer's Hand),* "all facts and beliefs cease to be true or false and become interesting possibilities." But when we read an ambitious journalistic work, we are asked to believe, and to carry belief away with the book. This is a crucial difference.

Why does Mailer claim so much? He has repeatedly said over the years that he would rather be known as a novelist than as a journalist. In a *Paris Review* interview some years ago, which he liked well enough to include in *Cannibals and Christians,* he said:

If what you write is a reflection of your own consciousness, then even journalism can become interesting. One wouldn't want to spend one's life at it and
I wouldn't want ever to be caught justifying journalism as a major activity (it's
obviously less interesting to write than a novel), but it's better, I think, to see
journalism as a venture of one's ability to keep in shape than to see it as an
essential betrayal of the chalice of your literary art. Temples are for women.

Disregard that last line. That was just Norman being a bad boy. But since the
publication of *The Executioner's Song,* he had insisted over and over, that, yes,
the book is both fiction and journalism. Asked how that could be, he said
on one occasion *(New York Times,* October 26, 1979): "A writer has certain
inalienable rights, and one is the right to create confusion."

At the risk of taking Mailer seriously at a moment when we can see his
tongue poking his cheek out, I would flatly assert that, for a reporter, that right
is distinctly and preeminently alienable. If there is any one "right" a journalist
never had to begin with, it is purely that one. This perversity of Mailer's brings
us straight home: The widespread acceptance of *The Executioner's Song* as a
"true-life story" is an ominous sign of journalism's ill health these days.

IV

Good writers care about what words mean. Francis Steegmuller said not long
ago *(New York Times,* March 26, 1980) that when Auden died his *Oxford
English Dictionary* was "all but clawed to pieces." The better the writer, it seems,
the more frequent the appeals to the lexicographer. Yet some very good writers have lately seemed to want to ignore what the dictionaries say about matters essential to their craft: That "fiction" means something; which something
is excluded from "nonfiction." Both the *OED* and *Webster's* point to original,
central, and rather copious meanings of "fiction": fashioning, imitating, or
inventing. Both dictionaries, in elaborating the active, current definition of
the word, lay stress on a fundamental antithesis. *OED:* "invention as opposed
to fact." *Webster:* "that which is invented, feigned, or imagined ...—opposed
to *fact* or *reality*" (emphasis *Webster's*).

Our grasp on *reality,* our relationship with the real world, is what is at stake
here. We have to grope our way through that world from day to day. To make
sense of our lives, we need to know what is going on around us. This need
plunges us at once into complicated philosophical issues, having to do with
trees falling in distant forests. Can we always rely on what others tell us about
what is "really" going on? A suspicion that we cannot has led to the great fal-

lacy, as I see it, of the New Journalism, and indirectly to the blurring in recent years of fiction and nonfiction.

That fallacy can be crudely stated as follows: Since perfect objectivity in reporting what the eyes have seen and the ears have heard is impossible, there is no choice but to go all the way over to absolute subjectivity. The trouble with this is that it soon makes the reporter the center of interest rather than the real world he is supposed to be picturing or interpreting. A filter of temperament discolors the visible universe. The report becomes a performance. What is, or may be, going on in "reality" recedes into a backdrop for the actor-writer; it dissolves out of focus and becomes, in the end, fuzzy, vague, unrecognizable, and false.

The serious writer of fiction hopes to achieve a poetic truth, a human truth, which transcends any apparent or illusory "reality." And, in good novels, the temperament of the author as expressed through the complex mix of elements that writers call "voice" subtly becomes part of the impression of human truth that the reader gets. The fictionist may at times use real people or real events, sometimes deliberately remaking and transforming them, in order to flesh out imitation or make invention seem like reality. This sleight of hand works beautifully if the novelist is gifted, artful, and inventive; it is a disaster (and an open invitation to libel suits) when the writing is bad, when the invention is weak or nonexistent—in short, when fiction is not fiction.

Two kinds of grave social harm, beyond those already suggested, come from works like Capote's and Wolfe's and Mailer's.

The first is that their great success, whether in kudos or cash or both, attracts imitators. The blurring of the crafts becomes respectable, fashionable, profitable, enviable. The infection spreads. If the great Mailer can do it, so can any tyro, and the only certainty is that the tyro will fuzz things up worse than Mailer does. Headlines tell us that Capote has sold "Handcarved Coffins" to the movies for "nearly $500,000." The blurring has long since made its way into investigative journalism, which, of all forms of reporting, bears the heaviest weight of social responsibility. In *The Brethren,* the Woodward and Armstrong book on the Supreme Court which recently spent some time at the top of the bestseller list, the processes of filtration we have seen in the Mailer novel are similarly at work. Clerks vouch for Justices' subjective states, moods, thoughts, and exact words—mostly recaptured in distant retrospect. Chief Justice Burger refused all contact with the authors, yet: "Burger vowed to himself that he would grasp the reins of power immediately. ..."

The second harm, related to the first, is far more serious. It is that these blurrings lead to, or at the very least help soften the way for, or confirm the reasonableness of, public lying. The message of Jules Feiffer's *Little Murders* is that tiny symbolic killings, done with the tongue, lead to big actual ones, done with guns. Habitual acceptance of little fibs leads to the swallowing whole of world-shaking lies. In the Dodge Aspen commercial, we are told we are watching two people in a following car through a hidden camera; what we watch (and overhear, as a hidden camera in a leading van could not possibly overhear) is a carefully rehearsed advertising routine. We write that off; it's just a formula; we're used to all that stuff. But have we also gotten used to writing off big lies? Did we write off—I am afraid the vast majority of Americans *did* write off—being told in official announcements that bombs were being dropped on North Vietnam, when in fact they were being dropped on Cambodia?

It would be preposterous, of course, to hold Mailer's and Wolfe's recent inventions responsible, retroactively, for lies told a decade ago. But the point is that the two phenomena—the blurring of fiction and journalism, as Mailer and Wolfe and many others have practiced it (for quite a bit more than a decade), and public lying, as Kissinger and Nixon and many others have practiced it (and some still do)—the two have had something like a symbiotic relationship with each other. Each has nourished and needed the other. Each in its way has contributed to the befogging of the public vision, to subtle failures of discrimination, and to the collapse of important sorts of trust.

But how could the blurring possibly be corrected at this late date? Hasn't the process gone too far? Isn't all this much too complicated? Aren't the shadings too subtle?

Not at all. It is very simple. To redraw the line we need merely think clearly about the legends on the licenses. All we need do is insist upon two rules:

The writer of fiction must invent. The journalist must not invent.

Part 5
Making the Press Professional

Within the field of journalism, an anti-intellectual strain runs deep. In the 1860s, for instance, Horace Greeley, the powerful New York editor, had dismissed a university education—of any sort—with the quip that he would "not hire a college graduate who did not show he could overcome the handicap of a college education." A. J. Liebling, one of the early graduates of Columbia's undergraduate journalism program, derided his education there. In a chapter in his memoir, "How to Learn Nothing," he wrote of his alma mater: "It had all the intellectual status of a training school of future employees of the A&P."

The journalism school at Columbia had been endowed early in the last century by Joseph Pulitzer, who had written a long, sometimes rambling essay to rebut critics of the then potential school and to reassure the trustees of Columbia. He had an abiding belief that journalists need not be "born" to the field. They could also be trained. It was Pulitzer's hope that a school devoted to journalism would upgrade the standards of reporters. At first rebuffed by Columbia, his offer of an endowment was accepted in 1903, but by the time Columbia's journalism school opened its doors in 1912, five other journalism programs had begun, including one at the University of Missouri in 1908, now generally recognized as the nation's first journalism school. In his essay, Pulitzer predicted with confidence that "before the century closes schools of journalism will be generally accepted as a feature of specialized higher education, like schools of law or of medicine." That prediction had not come to pass.

Pulitzer wrote at a time when barriers to enter the field of journalism were very modest. Journalism remains a quasi-profession, which does not *require* advance training or any type of credential. Over the century since Pulitzer wrote, journalists became better educated, often breaking into the establishment by virtue of their influence. The journalism school at Columbia began as an undergraduate program. In the mid-1930s it became a graduate school.

In compiling data for his study of Washington correspondents, Leo Rosten did not even bother to tabulate the percentage with graduate degrees. Rosten studied the Washington press corps for a dissertation at the University of Chicago. Originally published in the *Journalism Quarterly* and later turned into a book, *The Washington Correspondents* (it sold poorly), Rosten's research remains a model of its type in trying to understand journalists. Implicitly, his study dealt with the question of whether who covers Washington makes any difference. His study is full of surprising nuggets. For instance, he observes that Indiana was the state that contributed an extraordinarily high proportion of journalists to the nation.

For most of the last century, journalists have operated under a special assumption: they were generalists who could absorb any new material quickly and efficiently. It did not matter if they were untrained in a specialty such as science, economics, law, or Chinese, so long as they could grasp quickly the essence of a story. This journalistic conceit has often been challenged. It was dealt a severe jolt by the President's 1968 Commission on Civil Disorders, which investigated the cause of ghetto riots a year earlier. (The commission was popularly known as the Kerner Commission after its chairman, Otto Kerner, the governor of Illinois, whose later career was a checkered one. He was appointed a federal judge, and then he served time in the federal penitentiary for tax-related crimes.) The commission found that too often journalists were reporting solely "from the standpoint of a white man's world" and that more black journalists were needed to report on issues relating to race.

The underlying message of this chapter went against the grain of what so many journalists held sacred: the notion that reporters leave their beliefs at home and can cover any story. In the years since the report, specialists have become increasingly visible in American newsrooms, but the number of minority reporters has grown slowly, and newsrooms are far from representative of the country's minority population.

Selections from the College of Journalism

JOSEPH PULITZER

The man who writes, the man who month in and month out, week in and week out, day in and day out, furnishes the material which is to shape the thoughts of our people, is essentially the man who more than any other determines the character of the people and the kind of government this people shall possess.
—*President Theodore Roosevelt*

The editor of the *North American Review* has asked me to reply to an article recently printed in its pages criticizing the College of Journalism which it has been my pleasure to found and permanently to endow in Columbia University. In complying with his request I have enlarged the scope of the reply to include all other criticisms and misgivings, many honest, some shallow, some based on misunderstanding, but most representing only prejudice and ignorance. If my comment upon these criticisms shall seem to be diffuse and perhaps repetitious, my apology is that—alas!—I am compelled to write by voice, not by pen, and to revise the proofs by ear, not by eye—a somewhat difficult task.

Some of my critics have called my scheme "visionary." If it be so I can at least plead that it is a vision I have cherished long, thought upon deeply, and followed persistently. Twelve years ago I submitted the idea to President Low of Columbia, when it was declined. I have ever since continued to perfect and organize the scheme in my mind, until it is now accepted. In examining the criticisms and misgivings I have endeavored to do so without prejudice, anxious only to find the truth. I admit that the difficulties are many, but after weighing them all impartially I am more firmly convinced than ever of the

From the *North American Review,* May 1904.

ultimate success of the idea. Before the century closes schools of journalism will be generally accepted as a feature of specialized higher education, like schools of law or of medicine.

And now for our critics and objectors.

MUST A JOURNALIST BE "BORN"?

They object, the critics and cavilers, that a "newspaperman" must depend solely upon natural aptitude, or, in the common phrase, that he must be "born, not made."

Perhaps the critics can name some great editor, born full-winged like Mercury, the messenger of the gods? I know of none. The only position that occurs to me which a man in our Republic can successfully fill by the simple fact of birth is that of an idiot. Is there any other position for which a man does not demand and receive training—training at home, training in schools and colleges, training by master craftsmen, or training through bitter experience—through the burns that make the child dread the fire, through blunders costly to the aspirant?

This last is the process by which the profession of journalism at present obtains its recruits. It works by natural selection and the survival of the fittest, and its failures are strewn along the wayside.

The "born editor" who has succeeded greatly without special preparation is simply a man with unusual ability and aptitude for his chosen profession, with great power of concentration and sustained effort. He is one who loves his work and puts his whole heart and mind into it. He is in the strictest sense an educated man, but he has merely substituted self-education for education by others, making up for any deficiencies in his training by the unreserved sacrifice of strength, energy, and pleasure. Even in his case might it not be an advantage to have a system of instruction that would give him the same results at a saving of much time and labor?

Education begins in the cradle, at home, with a mother's teaching, and is continued by other influences through life. A college is one of those influences—useful, but with no magical power. A fool trailing an alphabet of degrees after his name is still a fool, and a genius, if necessary, will make his own college, although with a painful waste of effort which might be better reserved for productive work. I seem to remember that Lincoln, whose academy was a borrowed book read by the light of a pine-knot on the hearth, studied Euclid in Congress when nearly forty. But would it not have been better if that work had been done at fourteen?

All intelligence requires development. The highest profits by it; the lowest is helpless without it. Shakespeare's best play, *Hamlet,* was not his first, but his nineteenth, written after growth and maturity—after the hard work, the experience, the exercise of faculties and the accumulation of knowledge gained by writing eighteen plays. As Shakespeare was a "born" genius, why did he not write *Hamlet* first?

John Stuart Mill had natural talents, but they were strained to the last possible limit of accomplishment by a course of early training that was not only thorough but inhuman. His father was his college—a great college, better than any in England. Like Mill, Herbert Spencer, Buckle, Huxley, Tyndall, and Lewes were without college education, but their mental discipline was most severe. Cobden was undoubtedly a genius born, but if we compare his original style—turgid, clumsy—with the masterly clearness and force of his trained maturity, can we doubt that his brain was developed by the hardest work, just as Sandow's muscles were developed?

Of course in every field natural aptitude is the key to success. When the experiment was tired of turning Whistler into a disciplined soldier, even West Point had to lay down its arms. Your saw mill may have all the modern improvements, but it will not make a pine board out of a basswood log. No college can create a good lawyer without a legal mind to work on, nor make a successful doctor of a young man whom nature designed to sell tape. Talleyrand took holy orders, but they did not turn him into a holy man.

The great general, even more than the great editor, is supposed to be born, not made. The picturesque historian tells us that he "fell like a thunderbolt upon the enemy," and we imagine a miracle-working magician. But the truth is that the brilliant general is simply a man who has learned how to apply skillfully the natural laws of force, and who has the nerve to act on his knowledge. Hannibal, the greatest of all in my opinion, is called a typical example of native military genius. But can we forget that he was the son and pupil of Hamilcar, the ablest soldier of his generation, born in the camp, never outside the military atmosphere, sworn in earliest boyhood to war and hatred of Rome, and endowed by his father with all the military knowledge that the experience of antiquity could give? He was educated. In his father he had a military college to himself. Can we think of Napoleon without remembering that he had the best military education of his time at the college of Brienne, and that he was always an eager student of the great campaigns of history? Frederick the Great lost his head in his first battle. It took him years to learn his trade and finally to surpass his instructors. There is not a cadet at any military school who is not expected as a necessary part of his professional preparation to study every important battle on record—to learn how it was fought, what mistakes were committed on each side, and how it was won.

Every issue of a newspaper represents a battle—a battle for excellence. When the editor reads it and compares it to its rivals he knows that he has scored a victory or suffered a defeat. Might not the study of the most notable of these battles of the press be as useful to the student of journalism as is the study of military battles to the student of war?

WHAT SHOULD NOT BE TAUGHT?

What is a College of Journalism? It is an institution to train journalists. What is a journalist? Not any business manager or publisher, or even proprietor. A journalist is the lookout on the bridge of the ship of state. He notes the passing sail, the little things of interest that dot the horizon in fine weather. He reports the drifting castaway whom the ship can save. He peers through fog and storm to give warning of dangers ahead. He is not thinking of his wages, or of the profits of his owners. He is there to watch over the safety and the welfare of the people who trust him.

Few men in the business office of a newspaper know anything about the principles of journalism. The proprietor himself is not necessarily a journalist. He may be, if he is capable of understanding public questions, of weighing public interests, of carrying out public tasks; if he is in touch with public feeling, realizes public duties, is in sympathy with the public welfare, and is capable of presenting his ideas to the people, either by his own pen or by the pens of others. But it is quite conceivable that some proprietors are deficient in these points.

My hope is that this College of Journalism will raise the standard of the editorial profession. But to do this it must mark the distinction between real journalists and men who do a kind of newspaper work that requires neither culture nor conviction, but merely business training. I wish to begin a movement that will raise journalism to the rank of a learned profession, growing in the respect of the community as other professions far less important to the public interests have grown.

There is an obvious difference between a business and a profession. An editor, an editorial writer, or a correspondent is not in business. Nor even a capable reporter. These men are already in a profession, though they may not admit it, or even realize it, as many of them unhappily do not. Ill or well, they represent authorship, and authorship is a profession.

The man in the counting room of a newspaper is in the newspaper business. He concentrates his brain (quite legitimately) upon the commercial aspects of things, upon the margin of profit, upon the reduction of expenses, upon buying white paper and selling it printed—and that is business. But a man who has the advantage, honor, and pleasure of addressing the public every day as a writer or thinker is a professional man. So, of course, is he who directs these writers and reporters, who tells them what to say and how to say it, who shows them how to think—who inspires them, though he may never write a line himself, and decides what the principles of the paper shall be. For example, the greatest editor in the whole history of European journalism, John Delane, never wrote any articles of his own, although for thirty-six years he was the head, the heart, the brain, of the London *Times,* But he directed every writer, he furnished the thought, the policy, the initiative; he bore the responsibility, and he corrected both manuscript and proofs.

In this relation perhaps it may be interesting to note that Delane studied law and was admitted to the bar before he became [the *Times*] editor at the age of twenty-four. But it was without any intention of practicing. His father, who was a lawyer for the *Times,* destined him for its service from his boyhood, and he joined its staff as a reporter soon after passing his legal examinations. Delane, with his editorial revision, elimination, and substitution, was like some of the great old painters, who seem to have much of their work, measured by mere bulk, done for them by pupils. Rubens, or Van Dyck, or Raphael furnished the idea, the design, the composition, in an original drawing; the pupils did the drudgery of execution. Then the artist added the finishing touches that lifted the picture to the rank of masterpiece. Only in that way could the enormous output ascribed to those masters have been produced. So it was with Delane, and so it is with every editor who knows how to make the most of his powers.

That a newspaper, however great as a public institution and as a public teacher, must also be a business is not to be denied, but there is nothing exceptional in this. Elements of business, of economy, of income and outgo, are in the government of the city, the state, the nation, in art, in every school, in every college, in every university, indeed, in every church. But a bishop, even though he receives pay for his work, is not regarded as a businessman; nor is a great artist, though he charge the highest possible price for his paintings and die as rich as Meissonier or Rubens. Many distinguished lawyers, such as Mr. Tilden—one of the greatest—were shrewd businessmen, able probably to outwit the majority of publishers, yet they were rightly considered members of a learned profession.

George Washington had extraordinary business capacity. By intelligent economy, method, sound judgment, and the closest attention to details he accumulated the greatest American fortune of his time. Yet when he was called to serve the country in the field he did it without a salary. At Mount Vernon he was a businessman; in history he is a soldier, a statesman, and the father of his country.

To sum up, the banker or broker, the baker or the candlestick maker is in business—in trade. But the artist, the statesman, the thinker, the writer—all who are in touch with the public taste and mind, whose thoughts reach beyond their own livelihood to some common interest—are in professions.

DANGERS OF PLUTOCRACY AND DEMAGOGY

Our improvement is in proportion to our purpose.

—Marcus Aurelius

Nothing less than the highest ideals, the most scrupulous anxiety to do right, the most accurate knowledge of the problems it has to meet, and a sincere sense of its moral responsibility will save journalism from subservience to business interests, seeking selfish ends, antagonistic to the public welfare. For instance, Jay Gould once owned the principal Democratic newspaper of America. He had obtained it from Col. "Tom" Scott in a trade for the Texas Pacific Railroad, and I was fortunate enough to be able to relieve him of his unprofitable burden. C. P. Huntington bought a New York newspaper and turned it into a Democratic organ, he himself, like Gould, being an ardent Republican. He hoped in this way to influence Mr. Cleveland's administration and the Democrats in Congress against making the Pacific railroads pay their debts of about $120,000,000 to the government. Incidentally he testified under oath that his journalistic experiment cost him over a million dollars, although his newspaper was so obscure that its utterances were hardly more than soliloquies. Mr. Huntington did somehow succeed in delaying for a number of years the enforcement of the Treasury's claims. More dangerous, however, than the plutocratic control of newspapers for sordid private ends is their control by demagogues for ambitious, selfish ends. The people know, with unerring instinct, when a newspaper is devoted to private rather than to public interests; and their refusal to buy it limits its capacity for harm. But when a demagogic agitator appeals to "the masses" against "the classes" and poses as the ardent friend of the people against their "oppressors," assailing law and order and property as a means of gaining followers among the discontented and unthinking, the newspaper becomes a dangerous power for evil. Especially is this true when money is freely used to mislead the people.

Commercialism has a legitimate place in a newspaper, namely, in the business office. The more successful a newspaper is commercially, the better for its moral side. The more prosperous it is, the more independent it can afford to be, the higher salaries it can pay to editors and reporters, the less subject it will be to temptation, the better it can stand losses for the sake of principle and conviction. But commercialism, which is proper and necessary in the business office, becomes a degradation and danger when it invades the editorial rooms. Once let the public come to regard the press as exclusively a commercial business and there is an end of its moral power. Influence cannot exist without public confidence. And that confidence must have a human basis. It must rest in the end on the character of the journalist. The editor, the real "journalist" of the future, must be a man of such known integrity that he will be above the suspicion of writing or editing against his convictions. He must be known as one who would resign rather than sacrifice his principles to any business interest. It would be well if the editor of every newspaper were also its proprietor, but every editor can be at least the proprietor of himself. If he cannot keep the paper from degrading itself, he can refuse to be a party to the degradation.

By far the larger part of the American press is honest, although partisan. It means to do right; it would like to know how. To strengthen its resolution and give to its wisdom the indispensable basis of knowledge and independence is the object of training in journalism.

THE MARCH OF PROGRESS

I know but two ways by which society can be governed: the one is by Public Opinion, the other by the Sword.

—*Macaulay*

We are embarked, whether we like it or not, upon a revolution in thought and life. Progress is sweeping forward with accelerating force, outstripping in decades the advance of former centuries and millenia. All professions, all occupations but one, are keeping step with that majestic march. Its inspiration has fired all ranks of the marching army, or must we except the standard-bearers? The self-constituted leaders and enlighteners of the people—what are they doing? Standing still, lost in self-admiration, while the hosts march by? Are they even doing as well as that? Is it not a fact that the editors of seventy years ago were, as a rule, better informed in law, politics, government, and history than those of today? The statesmen and lawyers and political students who used to do editorial work for ambition or intellectual pleasure have ceased to frequent the newspaper offices. There is no trade so humble that it is not developing a standard of competence based on thorough training. For the more intellectual professions—law, medicine, art, architecture, music, engineering in all its varied branches—the years of preparation are stretching over ever-lengthening periods.

Is the most exacting profession of all—the one that requires the widest and the deepest knowledge and the firmest foundations of character—to be left entirely to the chances of self-education? Is the man who is everybody's critic and teacher the only one who does not need to be taught himself? ...

PUBLIC SERVICE THE SUPREME END

What are great gifts but the correlative of great work? We are not born for ourselves but for our kind, for our neighbors, for our country.

—*Cardinal Newman*

It has been said by some that my object in founding the College of Journalism was to help young men who wish to make this their vocation. Others have commended it as an effort to raise journalism to its real rank as one of the learned professions. This is true. But while it is a great pleasure to feel that a large number of young men will be helped to a better start in life by means of this college, this is not my primary object. Neither is the elevation of the profession which I love so much and regard so highly. In all my planning the chief end I had in view was the welfare of the Republic. It will be the object of the college to make better journalists, who will make better newspapers, which will better serve the public. It will impart knowledge—not for its own sake, but to be used for the public service. It will try to develop character, but even that will be only a means to the one supreme end—the public good. We are facing that hitherto-unheard-of portent—an innumerable, worldwide, educated, and self-conscious democracy. The little revolutions of the past have been effected by a few leaders working upon an ignorant populace, conscious only of vague feelings of discontent. Now the masses read. They know their grievances and their power. They discuss in New York the position of labor in Berlin and in Sydney. Capital, too, is developing a worldwide class feeling. It likewise has learned the power of cooperation.

What will be the state of society and of politics in this Republic seventy years hence, when some of the children now in school will be still living? Shall we preserve the government of the Constitution, the equality of all citizens before the law and the purity of justice—or shall we have the government of either money or the mob?

The answers to these questions will depend largely upon the kind of instruction the people of that day draw from their newspapers—the textbooks, the orators, the preachers of the masses.

I have said so much of the need for improvement in journalism that to avoid misconception I must put on record my appreciation of the really admirable work so many newspapermen are doing already. The competent editorial writer, for instance—how much sound information he furnishes every day! How generally just his judgments are, and how prompt his decisions! Unknown to the people he serves, he is in close sympathy with their feelings and aspirations, and, when left to himself and unhampered by party prejudices, he generally interprets their thought as they would wish to express it themselves.

It is not too much to say that the press is the only great organized force which is actively and as a body upholding the standard of civic righteousness. There are many political reformers among the clergy, but the pulpit as an institution is concerned with the Kingdom of Heaven, not with the Republic of America. There are many public-spirited lawyers, but the bar as a profession works for its retainers, and no law-defying trust ever came to grief from a dearth of legal talent to serve it. Physicians work for their patients and architects for their patrons. The press alone makes the public interest its own. "What is everybody's business is nobody's business"—except the journalist's; it is his by adoption. But for his care almost every reform would fall stillborn. He holds officials to their duty. He exposes secret schemes of plunder. He promotes every hopeful plan of progress. Without him public opinion would be shapeless and dumb. He brings all classes, all professions together, and teaches them to act in concert on the basis of their common citizenship.

The Greeks thought that no republic could be successfully governed if it were too large for all the citizens to come together in one place. The Athenian democracy could all meet in the popular assembly. There public opinion was made, and accordingly as the people listened to a Pericles or to a Cleon the state flourished or declined. The orator that reaches the American democracy is the newspaper. It alone makes it possible to keep the political blood in healthful circulation in the veins of a continental republic. We have—it is unfortunately true—a few newspapers which advocate dangerous fallacies and falsehoods, appealing to ignorance, to partisanship, to passion, to popular prejudice, to poverty, to hatred of the rich, to socialism, sowing the seeds of discontent— eventually sure, if unchecked, to produce lawlessness and bloodshed. Virtue, said Montesquieu, is the principle of a republic, and therefore a republic, which in its purity is the most desirable of all forms of government, is the hardest of all to preserve. For there is nothing more subject to decay than virtue.

Our Republic and its press will rise or fall together. An able, disinterested, public-spirited press, with trained intelligence to know the right and courage to do it, can preserve that public virtue without which popular government is a sham and a mockery. A cynical, mercenary, demagogic press will produce in time a people as base as itself. The power to mold the future of the Republic will be in the hands of journalists of future generations. This is why I urge my colleagues to aid the important experiment which I have ventured to endow. Upon their generous aid and cooperation the ultimate success of the project must depend.

The Social Composition of Washington Correspondents

LEO C. ROSTEN

The newspaperman is a man sensitized to the observation of aspects of the real world, with a talent for translating segments of reality into the grammar of "stories." In the inflections which creep into his recording of events, there are embedded, however obscurely, a personality and an autobiography. Under the arid mobilization of facts in a news dispatch on the budget, there is a construct of individual temperament. The dominant impulse of the scientist is to know; the driving motivation of the journalist is to tell. What he tells, what he considers worth telling, and how he tells it are the products of a social-psychological structure of desire, calculation and inhibition.

The material which follows presents selected data on 127 newspaper correspondents in Washington (representing 180 leading daily newspapers, all the press associations and all syndicates, and including the leading columnists), which they supplied by answering two lengthy questionnaires I submitted to them in 1936. This is a sample more than large enough to permit generalization about the press corps in the capital.

These data afford new insight into the sociology of the press corps, and suggest verifiable analytic statements about what is loosely called the "psychology of journalists" and the "character of journalism."

From the *Journalism Quarterly,* June 1937.

Words are the journalist's tools, and it would seem a defensible hypothesis that newspapermen are drawn from a psychological environment which placed a premium upon articulacy. One would thus expect many reporters to be the children of parents who handled ideas rather than things: teachers, clergymen, lawyers, editors rather than farmers or industrial workers. One would expect newspapermen to have been exposed to the attraction of talk, particularly talk about social and political affairs, in homes with literate preoccupations. And one would expect them to have middle-class origins, rather than stemming from the ranks of manual labor: deference for verbalization and a drive to achieve facility in it would be more pronounced in the former than the latter.

In the light of this approach it is not wholly fortuitous that out of 123 Washington correspondents, 97 (76.3 percent) are the children of professional, proprietary or clerical groups, according to the occupational categories of Professor William F. Ogburn, the so-called white-collar class. Fifty-five (44.7 percent) correspondents' fathers were members of a profession. Of the professional group, 14 (11.3 percent) were editors or newspapermen, 13 (10.5 percent) were lawyers. The labor population, including skilled, semi-skilled, and unskilled workers, contributed only 14 men to the corps, exactly the number contributed by newspapermen alone. The farmers of the country produced but 9.7 percent of the group.

These figures gain significance from the fact that in 1900, the date closest to the average year of birth of the newspapermen studied, the professions formed only 4.3 percent of the country's population, whereas the farm population was 35.6 percent and the labor population totaled 48.4 percent. If we tabulate these figures side by side, as in Table I, the emphases become sharper.

Compare these figures to those of Robert F. Harrel, who conducted a study of 505 American editors, editorial writers, department managers, managing editors, special writers and others. Out of his 505 cases 32.0 percent had fathers of a professional status, as compared to our 43.3 percent. Fathers of 8.3 percent were journalists, as compared to 11 percent among the Washington correspondents. By this comparison about 11.3 percent more of the fathers of the Washington press corps were in the professions than was true of a sample of other journalists in the country, and about 2.7 percent more were newspapermen themselves. Both studies demonstrate the high percentage of journalists whose fathers were members of a profession or a "white-collar group."

The economic strata from which the press corps came are equally interesting. Families of 57.5 percent of the correspondents had incomes of $2,500 or more while the newspapermen were in grammar school; 62.1 percent while they were in high school; 64.4 percent while they were in college or of college

TABLE 1

Occupational Group	Percentage of Corps Contributed	Percentage of Population in 1900
Professions	44.7	4.3
Labor (skilled, semi-skilled, unskilled)	11.3	48.4
Farmers	9.7	35.6

age. For the same three periods the family incomes of less than $2,500 accounted for 42.3 percent, 37.7 percent, and 35.4 percent, respectively.

The significance of these figures may be suggested by the fact that, according to the earliest analysis of income stratifications, the 1918 estimates of the National Bureau of Economic Research, upon which economists still depend, 9 percent of the gainfully employed earned less than $2,500 a year. Only 2 percent percent earned $5,000 or more. The average annual earning figures for employed wage earners, as compiled by Paul H. Douglas and F. T. Jenison, show that in 1910 the *average* annual earning per wage earner was $573; in 1918 it was $997; and in 1920 it was $1,337. As late as 1928 it was only $1,405 per year. It is safe to conclude that the correspondents came from families which had incomes considerably above those of the averages for the country's wage earners as a whole.

The size of the communities in which the correspondents were born and reared, and in which they received their elementary education, is of relevance. More than a third—38.5 percent—of the corps was born in towns which had a population of less than 2,500 in 1900. Almost exactly one-half (49.6 percent) come from communities of less than 10,000; 62.2 percent from those of less than 25,000. The number born and reared in cities of 100,000 or more totaled only 16.6 percent of the group.

It has often been remarked that Indiana contributes an extraordinarily high proportion of journalists to the nation. An analysis of the Washington correspondents supports this. Indiana ranked first, when the states were listed according to the number of correspondents born in each, with 10.2 percent of the corps (distributed evenly between the ages of 28 and 63). Illinois was second with 9.4 percent. The preeminence of Indiana is increased by the facts that (a) only seven Indiana papers were included in the study (3.8 percent of the 180); and (b) in 1930 Indiana had only 2.6 percent of the population of the nation (in 1900 her population was approximately 3 percent).

The reasons for Indiana's curious position as an incubator of literary and journalistic figures have never been fully explained. Professor Harold D. Lasswell suggests one possible explanation: Indiana has long been a "balance of power" state, a strategic lever in national elections. As Louise Overacker and Merriam and Gosnell have shown in their studies of national political parties and elections, campaign funds out of proportion to the size of the state, or to its votes in the Electoral College, have traditionally been poured into Indiana. This fact may account for the political consciousness and talents of Indianans, and the prominence of politics as an attractive career. It seems possible that the intelligences of the middle class, rather than go into law, finance or business, as would be the case in metropolitan centers, are drawn to those occupations which confer prestige upon the felicitous use of words: politics or writing.

Reporting is, at bottom, a career compact of an essentially antagonistic attitude to the inertia, log-rolling and ineptitude of the two major parties. Scratch a journalist and you find a reformer. To what type of political consciousness were the Washington correspondents exposed in their impressionable years? The political identification of the fathers of the press corps shows that 72.7 percent were either Democrats or Republicans (44 were Republicans, 41 Democrats) , 13.6 percent were independent, and the rest were distributed in categories described as liberal, socialist, progressive, radical, labor or "no party." Since the combined Republican-Democratic vote from 1896 to 1912 was approximately 98 percent of the total vote cast (1890–1912 may be taken to encompass the most impressionable years of the majority of the correspondents), the 30 percent of the correspondents' fathers who were not affiliated with one of the two orthodox political parties represents a marked divergence from the general political pattern of the country. The large proportion of teachers, lawyers, doctors and journalists among the fathers of the correspondents makes this plausible.

The future will probably see a larger percentage of journalists drawn from the ranks of liberals, independents, socialists and third-party sympathizers. The intensification of crises precipitates discontent with the circumlocutions of "respectable" political parties in the intellectuals of the middle class, caught between the hammer of hard-pressed industrial capitalism and the anvil of proletarian violence. Dissatisfaction is communicated to the sons of intellectuals in the atmosphere of homes characterized by the rising insecurity of middle-class men who handle symbols for a living. The sons of lawyers, clergymen, journalists and teachers may well be possessed of heightened reformist energies impelling them to embark upon a career which throws them into vital contact with the organs of the body politic, and which opens the possibility of "tearing away the veils of pretense and hypocrisy," exposing politics and politicians in the disenchanted light of "hard-boiled" journalism.

Journalism is often called a "game" in the argot of its practitioners. But many newspapermen like to embellish their status by insisting upon the designation of their trade as a "profession." Since the first requisite of a profession is the exclusion of the unfit, "the profession of journalism" is chiefly a convenient term of reference. The professional aspect of newspaper work may be defended by the recognition that it requires a congeries of skills and techniques. But it is a profession with no professional standards, no professional discipline, no examining or accrediting bodies, and no agreement upon norms for testing competence. From this point of view the educational background of the Washington correspondents is particularly relevant.

Of 127 members of the press corps, 60 (47.2 percent) are college graduates in possession of a four-year degree from an accredited institution of higher learning. Thirty-six (28.3 percent) attended college but received no degree. Twenty-two of these 36 (17.3 percent) went to college for only one or two years. Twenty-three correspondents (18.1 percent) had no college work at all (eight attended high school for less than four years). Two did not have any high school education.

The academic record of the Washington correspondents cannot, obviously, be compared to that of other professional groups, since all lawyers, doctors, teachers or engineers are, *ipso facto,* college graduates and usually have earned higher degrees. But their record is more impressive than that shown by Mr. Harrel's sample group of American editors, managing editors, feature writers and other such workers. The analysis shows that in 1931 only 40.8 percent of 505 successful journalists in editorial positions were college graduates (as compared to the 47.2 of the press corps), and that 67.4 percent attended college (92 Washington correspondents would fall in this category—72.4 percent of the entire group). Whereas 8.4 percent of Mr. Harrel's cases did not attend high school, only 1.5 percent of our group was spared secondary school education.

The record of the Washington correspondents who finished their academic work is auspicious. Sixteen were awarded the Phi Beta Kappa honor. Ten won scholarships. Two were graduated *magna cum laude.* Eight members of the press corps received Master of Arts degrees. Of these, four were Rhodes scholars, completing their university careers at Oxford. Four Washington correspondents included in this study were awarded the honorary LL.D.

Much more suggestive for our purposes is the *kind* of education which was chosen by the Washington correspondents. The newspaperman in the capital is today faced by the necessity of reporting news which is a compound of economics, political science, monetary problems, constitutional and international law, public administration, and social service. The activity of the New Deal ranges from the field of public works to the esoteric art of encouraging piscatorial copulation. Such responsibilities require intellectual poise, if not specialized competence, in the face of intricate events. A *systematic* approach to the hectic cosmos of Washington would necessitate sophistication in the fields of political economy, in all its ramifications; an *impressionistic* approach, which is the approach of journalism, would profit by at least a limited experience in the disciplines of the social sciences.

The curricular specialization of those correspondents who received a university education shows a pronounced liberal arts and humanities emphasis, with a corresponding lack of contact with the formal areas of economics, political science or sociology. Of the college men and women of the press corps, 19.0 percent wrote "liberal arts" as their field of major application; 10.2 percent were chiefly concerned with journalism; and 9.4 percent had most of their work in English and in pre-legal arts and humanities. Only four correspondents majored in political science; only three in economics. Thus only seven of the newspapermen, 5.4 percent of the total, may be credited with more than a cursory academic contact with the social sciences.

Now the meaning of these figures is enhanced by remembering that men who are burdened with the duty of recording the events of the contemporary scene would seem to be in need of a disciplined frame of reference within which to orient themselves, and by which to appraise the significance of men, measures and goals. Without some framework within which competing plans and theories (whether of prices, slum clearance or industrial unionization) can be related to an inclusive system, or without some analytic point of view with which to place social phenomena in a perspective of time and a configuration of totality, the observer is left with little but an unsystematized bundle of preferences and an incoherent mélange of impressions. He can do little more than interpret acts and issues according to emotional impulses and affective hopes. His insights may be keen and his sensitivity high, but his ability to understand is limited to the one-dimensional sphere of distilled facts. This is not merely an academic gauge, the validity of which newspapermen challenge. In an anonymous questionnaire submitted to the same 127 Washington correspondents who had supplied data on their educational background, the following statement was contained, to be checked "yes," "no," or "uncertain": I often feel the need of knowing more economics for my job.

A heavy majority, 86.6 percent, of those who answered said "yes" (a higher degree of agreement than on all but one other question asked); 10.6 percent "no"; 2.6 percent were uncertain. Extensive interviews and personal contacts with more than 150 members of the press corps in the capital over a fourteen-month period led me to the conclusion that a pronounced majority of the correspondents often feel inadequate to cope with the bewildering complexity of the news they are assigned to cover.

It may be objected that the newspaperman is not required to be an economist or a social scientist, that his job is to report facts, that his talents should be those of getting news, that his energies should be devoted to accurate and interesting writing. The well-known aphorism of Richard Probert, former head of the Associated Press bureau in Washington, may be cited to challenge the argument: "The Washington correspondent has got to write news for the milkman in Omaha." The objections are not relevant. What concerns us at this point of analysis is the attitude of the newspapermen themselves to their own adequacy for their tasks. It is the degree of intellectual security with which they can regard the multitude of matters which they are supposed to describe and, in however small measure, clarify to their readers. For men without "a frame of reference" and with an uncontrolled impressionistic (rather than analytic) approach to issues are driven to a surface interpretation of events. They are oriented with reference to normative words of ambiguous content: "liberty," "Americanism," "justice," "democracy," "socialism," "communism." And words are unstable points of anchor in a world of changing words. Newspapermen evidence a marked insecurity in the presence of social theories or political conceptualization. In this light the caustic reportorial reaction to "New Deal professors," "crack-pot theories," "the Brain Trust," "Frankfurter's bright young men" soon suggests the projection of doubts of personal adequacy upon men who have unwittingly increased personal and professional insecurities. The newspaperman compensates for his inner uncertainty (or his inner conviction of incompetence) by lusty deprecations of those whose intellectual equipment he vaguely fears. He soothes his injured sense of self-esteem by the oblique device of irony about those whose respect he would in actuality prefer to enjoy.

These comments are germane to an understanding of the thinking and the non-conscious drives of the newspapermen in the capital. They are especially applicable to the corps since 1933, when the character of Washington news changed, for better or for worse, from news of political personalities and party intrigues to news charged with a high degree of socioeconomic content. There were not many professors in the capital ante-1933, nor a deluge of governmental activity which invaded fields where academic competence was imperative.

There is a supporting insight into the attitude of the Washington correspondent in the following excerpts from conversations with various members of the press corps:

"I used to get into a cold sweat when I had to write up Roosevelt's money policy."

"Going off the gold standard was a story that gave me a headache I never want to have again."

"The news has taken a crazy turn. We're used to giving the dope about how Joe Robinson cracks the whip, or why the Chamber of Commerce fought the Zilch bill. Now we've got to write about hogs, unemployment, the price of copper and the interstate commerce clause in the Constitution."

One correspondent sheepishly confessed to me that when Professor Warren's theories of prices had the ear in the White House, he dutifully read through the treatise of Warren and Pearson on gold. "I got more confused than ever, so I dropped it. I write the stuff up as I understand it. That's more than 9(!) percent of my readers will understand anyway."

During the period when monetary problems were the hottest news in the capital many correspondents consulted E. A. Goldenweiser of the Federal Reserve Board, or members of the staff of the Brookings Institution. To these reporters there was a compensation of the kind found in the remark of one veteran newspaper man: "To do the job, what you know or understand isn't important. You've got to know whom to ask. I didn't understand most of what Goldenweiser told me, but I took careful notes and wrote it up verbatim. Let my readers figure it out. I'm their reporter, not their teacher."

And there is a triumphant prop for self-reassurance in this last comment: I'd like to see the Tugwells or the Frankfurters try to write the stories they're breaking for the girls and boys who read Little Orphan Annie. That would be a laugh. No matter how low I get to feeling, I always know I'm doing a better job than they could.

The Role of the Mass Media in Reporting of News About Minorities

COMMISSION ON CIVIL DISORDERS

INTRODUCTION

The president's charge to the Commission asked specifically: "What effect do the mass media have on the riots."

The question is far-reaching, and a sure answer is beyond the range of presently available scientific techniques. Our conclusions and recommendations are based upon subjective as well as objective factors; interviews as well as statistics; isolated examples as well as general trends.

Freedom of the press is not the issue. A free press is indispensable to the preservation of the other freedoms this Nation cherishes. The recommendations in this chapter have thus been developed under the strong conviction that only a press unhindered by government can contribute to freedom.... .

The Commission also determined, very early, that the answer to the president's question did not lie solely in the performance of the press and broadcasters in reporting the riots proper. Our analysis had to consider also the overall treatment by the media of the Negro ghettos, community relations, racial attitudes, urban and rural poverty—day by day and month by month, year in and year out.

On this basis, we have reached three conclusions:

This report was written in 1968.

First, that despite instances of sensationalism, inaccuracies, and distortions, newspapers, radio, and television, on the whole, made a real effort to give a balanced, factual account of the 1967 disorders.

Second, that despite this effort, the portrayal of the violence that occurred last summer failed to reflect accurately its scale and character. The overall effect was, we believe, an exaggeration of both mood and event.

Third, and ultimately most important, we believe that the media have thus far failed to report adequately on the causes and consequences of civil disorders and the underlying problems of race relations.

With these comments as a perspective, we discuss first the coverage of last summer's disturbances. We will then summarize our concerns with overall coverage of race relations.

COVERAGE OF THE 1967 DISTURBANCES

We have found a significant imbalance between what actually happened in our cities and what the newspaper, radio, and television coverage of the riots told us happened. The Commission, in studying last summer's disturbances, visited many of the cities and interviewed participants and observers. We found that the disorders, as serious as they were, were less destructive, less widespread, and less of a black-white confrontation than most people believed.

Lacking other sources of information, we formed our original impressions and beliefs from what we saw on television, heard on the radio, and read in newspapers and magazines. We are deeply concerned that millions of other Americans, who must rely on the mass media, likewise formed incorrect impressions and judgments about what went on in many American cities last summer.

As we started to probe the reasons for this imbalance between reality and impression, we first believed that the media had sensationalized the disturbances, consistently overplaying violence and giving disproportionate amounts of time to emotional events and militant leaders. To test this theory, we commissioned a systematic, quantitative analysis, covering the content of newspaper and television reporting in 15 cities where disorders occurred. The results of this analysis do not support our early belief. Of 955 television sequences of riot and racial news examined, 837 could be classified for predominant atmosphere as either "emotional," "calm," or "normal." Of these, 494 were classified as calm, 262 as emotional, and 81 as normal. Only a small proportion of all scenes analyzed showed actual mob action, people looting, sniping, setting fires, or being injured or killed. Moderate Negro leaders were shown more frequently than militant leaders on television news broadcasts.

Of 3,779 newspaper articles analyzed, more focused on legislation which should be sought and planning which should be done to control ongoing riots and prevent future riots than on any other topic. The findings of this analysis are explained in detail later in this chapter. They make it clear that the imbalance between actual events and the portrayal of those events in the press and on the air cannot be attributed solely to sensationalism in reporting and presentation.

We have, however, identified several factors which, it seems to us, did work to create incorrect and exaggerated impressions about the scope and intensity of the disorders.

First, despite the overall statistical picture, there were instances of gross flaws in presenting news of the 1967 riots. Some newspapers printed scare headlines unsupported by the mild stories that followed. All media reported rumors that had no basis in fact. Some newsmen staged riot events for the cameras. Examples are included in the next section.

Second, the press obtained much factual information about the scale of the disorders—property damage, personal injury, and deaths—from local officials who often were inexperienced in dealing with civil disorders and not always able to sort out fact from rumor in the confusion. At the height of the Detroit riot, some news reports of property damage put the figure in excess of $500 million. Subsequent investigation shows it to be $40 to $45 million. The initial estimates were not the independent judgment of reporters or editors. They came from beleaguered government officials. But the news media gave currency to these errors. Reporters uncritically accepted, and editors uncritically published, the inflated figures, leaving an indelible impression of damage up to more than 10 times greater than actually occurred.

Third, the coverage of the disorders—particularly on television—tended to define the events as black-white confrontations. In fact, almost all of the deaths, injuries, and property damage occurred in all-Negro neighborhoods, and thus the disorders were not "race riots" as that term is generally understood.

Closely linked to these problems is the phenomenon of cumulative effect. As the summer of 1967 progressed, we think Americans often began to associate more or less neutral sights and sounds (like a squad car with flashing red lights, a burning building, a suspect in police custody) with racial disorders, so that the appearance of any particular item, itself hardly inflammatory, set off a whole sequence of association with riot events. Moreover, the summer's news was not seen and heard in isolation. Events of these past few years—the Watts riot, other disorders, and the growing momentum of the civil rights movement—conditioned the responses of readers and viewers and heightened their reactions. What the public saw and read last summer thus produced emotional reactions and left vivid impressions not wholly attributable to the material itself.

Fear and apprehension of racial unrest and violence are deeply rooted in American society. They color and intensify reactions to news of racial trouble and threats of racial conflict. Those who report and disseminate news must be conscious of the background of anxieties and apprehension against which their stories are projected. This does not mean that the media should manage the news or tell less than the truth. Indeed, we believe that it would be imprudent and even dangerous to downplay coverage in the hope that censored reporting of inflammatory incidents somehow will diminish violence. Once a disturbance occurs, the word will spread independently of newspapers and television. To attempt to ignore these events or portray them as something other than what they are can only diminish confidence in the media and increase the effectiveness of those who monger rumors and the fears of those who listen.

But to be complete, the coverage must be representative. We suggest that the main failure of the media last summer was that the totality of its coverage was not as representative as it should have been to be accurate. We believe that to live up to their own professed standards, the media simply must exercise a higher degree of care and a greater level of sophistication than they have yet shown in this area—higher, perhaps, than the level ordinarily acceptable with other stories.

This is not "just another story." It should not be treated like one. Admittedly, some of what disturbs us about riot coverage last summer stems from circumstances beyond media control. But many of the inaccuracies of fact, tone, and mood were due to the failure of reporters and editors to ask tough enough questions about official reports and to apply the most rigorous standards possible in evaluating and presenting the news. Reporters and editors must be sure that descriptions and pictures of violence, and emotional or inflammatory sequences or articles, even though "true" in isolation, are really representative and do not convey an impression at odds with the overall reality of events. The media too often did not achieve this level of sophisticated, skeptical, careful news judgment during last summer's riots.

THE MEDIA AND RACE RELATIONS

Our second and fundamental criticism is that the news media have failed to analyze and report adequately on racial problems in the United States and, as a related matter, to meet the Negro's legitimate expectations in journalism. By and large, news organizations have failed to communicate to both their black and white audiences a sense of the problems America faces and the sources of potential solutions. The media report and write from the standpoint of a white man's world. The ills of the ghetto, the difficulties of life there, the Negro's burning sense of grievance are seldom conveyed. Slights and indignities are part of the Negro's daily life, and many of them come from what he now calls the "white press"—a press that repeatedly, if unconsciously, reflects the biases, the paternalism, the indifference of white America. This may be understandable, but it is not excusable in an institution that has the mission to inform and educate the whole of our society.

Our criticisms, important as they are, do not lead us to conclude that the media are a cause of riots, any more than they are the cause of other phenomena which they report. It is true that newspaper and television reporting helped shape people's attitudes toward riots. In some cities, people who watched television reports and read newspaper accounts of riots in other cities later rioted themselves. But the causal chain weakens when we recall that, in other cities, people in very much the same circumstances watched the same programs and read the same newspaper stories but did not riot themselves.

The news media are not the sole source of information and certainly not the only influence on public attitudes. People obtained their information and formed their opinions about the 1967 disorders from the multiplicity of sources that condition the public's thinking on all events. Personal experience, conversations with others, the local and long distance telephone are all important as sources of information and ideas and contribute to the totality of attitudes about riots.

No doubt, in some cases, the knowledge or the sight on a television screen of what had gone on elsewhere lowered inhibitions, kindled outrage or awakened desires for excitement or loot—or simply passed the word. Many ghetto residents we interviewed thought so themselves. By the same token, the news reports of riots must have conditioned the response of officials and police to disturbances in their own cities. The reaction of the authorities in Detroit was almost certainly affected in some part by what they saw or read of Newark a week earlier. The Commission believes that none of these private or official reactions was decisive in determining the course of the disorders. Even if they had been more significant than we think, however, we cannot envision a system of governmental restraints that could successfully eliminate these effects. And an effort to formulate and impose such restraints would be inconsistent with fundamental traditions in our society.

These failings of the media must be corrected and the improvement must come from within the media. A society that values and relies on a free press as intensely as ours is entitled to demand in return responsibility from the press and conscientious attention by the press to its own deficiencies. The Commission has seen evidence that many of those who supervise, edit, and report for the news media are becoming increasingly aware of and concerned about their performance in this field. With that concern, and with more experience, will come more sophisticated and responsible coverage. But much more must be done, and it must be done soon.

The Commission has a number of recommendations designed to stimulate and accelerate efforts toward self-improvement. And we propose a privately organized, privately funded Institute of Urban Communications as a means for drawing these recommendations together and promoting their implementation.

NEWS COVERAGE OF CIVIL DISORDERS—SUMMER 1967

THE METHOD OF ANALYSIS

As noted, the Commission has been surveying both the reporting of disorders last summer and the broader field of race relations coverage. With respect to the reporting of disorders, we were trying to get a sense of content, accuracy, tone, and bias. We sought to find out how people reacted to it and how reporters conducted themselves while carrying out their assignments. The Commission used a number of techniques to probe these matters and to provide cross-checks on data and impressions.

To obtain an objective source of data, the Commission arranged for a systematic, quantitative analysis of the content of newspapers, local television, and network coverage in 15 cities for a period from 3 days before to 3 days after the disorder in each city. The cities were chosen to provide a cross-section in terms of the location and scale of the disorders and the dates of their occurrence.

Within each city, for the period specified, the study was comprehensive. Every daily newspaper and all network and local television news films were analyzed, and scripts and logs were examined. In all, 955 network and local television sequences and 3,779 newspaper articles dealing with riot and race relations news were analyzed. Each separate analysis was coded and the cards were cross-tabulated by computer to provide results and comparisons for use by the Commission. The material was measured to determine the amount of space devoted to news of riot activity; the nature of the display given compared with other news coverage; and the types of stories, articles, and television programming presented. We sought specific statistical information on such matters as the amount of space or time devoted to different kinds of riot stories, the types and identities of persons most often depicted or interviewed, and the frequency with which race relations problems were mentioned in riot stories or identified as the cause of riot activity.

The survey was designed to be objective and statistical. Within its terms of reference, the Commission was looking for broad characterizations of media tone and content.

The Commission is aware of the inherent limitations of content analysis techniques. They cannot measure the emotional impact of a particular story or television sequence. By themselves, they provide no basis for conclusions as to the accuracy of what was reported. Particular examples of good or bad journalistic conduct, which may be important in themselves, are submerged in a statistical average. The Commission therefore sought through staff interviews and personal contact with members of the press and the public to obtain direct evidence of the effects of riot coverage and the performance of the media during last summer's disturbances.

CONCLUSIONS ABOUT CONTENT

Television

1. Content analysis of television film footage shows that the tone of the coverage studied was more "calm" and "factual" than "emotional" and "rumor-laden." Researchers viewed every one of the 955 television sequences and found that twice as many "calm" sequences as "emotional" ones were shown. The amount and location of coverage were relatively limited, considering the magnitude of the events. The analysis reveals a dominant, positive emphasis on control of the riot and on activities in the aftermath of the riot (53.8 percent of all scenes broadcast), rather than on scenes of actual mob action, or people looting, sniping, setting fires, or being injured or killed (4.8 percent of scenes shown). According to participants in our Poughkeepsie conference, coverage frequently was of the post-riot or interview variety because newsmen arrived at the scene after the actual violence had subsided. Overall, both network and local television coverage was cautious and restrained.

2. Television newscasts during the periods of actual disorder in 1967 tended to emphasize law enforcement activities, thereby overshadowing underlying grievances and tensions. This conclusion is based on the relatively high frequency with which television showed and described law enforcement agents, police, National Guardsmen, and army troops performing control functions.

Television coverage tended to give the impression that the riots were confrontations between Negroes and whites rather than responses by Negroes to underlying slum problems. The control agents were predominantly white. The ratio of white male adults to Negro male adults shown on television is high (1:2) considering that the riots took place in predominantly Negro neighborhoods. And some interviews with whites involved landlords or proprietors who lost property or suffered business losses because of the disturbances and thus held strongly antagonistic attitudes.

The content analysis shows that by far the most frequent "actor" appearances on television were Negro male adults, white male adults, law enforcement agents, and public officials. We cannot tell from a content analysis whether there was any preconceived editorial policy of portraying the riots as racial confrontations requiring the intervention of enforcement agents. But the content analysis does present a visual three-way alignment of Negroes, white bystanders, and public officials or enforcement agents. This alignment tended to create an impression that the riots were predominantly racial confrontations involving clashes between black and white citizens.

3. About one-third of all riot-related sequences for network and local television appeared on the first day following the outbreak of rioting, regardless of the course of development of the riot itself. After the first day there was, except in Detroit, a very sharp decline in the amount of television time devoted to the disturbance. In Detroit, where the riot started slowly and did not flare out of control until the evening of July 24, 48 hours after it started, the number of riot-related sequences shown increased until July 26 and then showed the same sharp drop-off as noted after the first day of rioting in the other cities. These findings tend to controvert the impression that the riot intensifies television coverage, thus in turn intensifying the riot. The content analysis indicates that whether or not the riot was getting worse, television coverage of the riot decreased sharply after the first day.

4. The Commission made a special effort to analyze television coverage of Negro leaders. To do this, Negro leaders were divided into three categories: (a) celebrities or public figures, who did not claim any organizational following (e.g., social scientist Dr. Kenneth B. Clark, comedian Dick Gregory); (b) "moderate" Negro leaders, who claim a political or organizational following; and (c) "militant" Negro leaders who claim a political or organizational following. During the riot periods surveyed, Negro leaders appeared infrequently on network news broadcasts and were about equally divided among celebrity or public figures, moderate leaders, and militant leaders. On local television, Negro leaders appeared more often. Of the three categories, "moderate" Negro leaders were shown on local stations more than twice as often as Negro leaders identified primarily as celebrities or public figures and three times more frequently than militant leaders.

Newspapers

1. Like television coverage, newspaper coverage of civil disturbances in the summer of 1967 was calmer, more factual, and more restrained than outwardly emotional or inflammatory. During the period of the riot there were many sto-

ries dealing exclusively with non-riot racial news. Considering the magnitude of the events, the amount of coverage was limited. Most stories were played down or put on inside pages. Researchers found that almost all the articles analyzed (3,045 of 3,770) tended to focus on one of 16 identifiable subjects. Of this group, 502 articles (16.5 percent) focused primarily on legislation which should be sought and planning which could be done to control ongoing riots and prevent future riots. The second largest category consisted of 471 articles (15.5 percent) focusing on containment or control of riot action. Newspaper coverage of the disorders reflects efforts at caution and restraint.

2. Newspapers tended to characterize and portray last summer's riots in national terms rather than as local phenomena and problems, especially when rioting was taking place in the newspaper's own city. During the actual disorders, the newspapers in each city studied tended to print many stories dealing with disorders or racial troubles in other cities. About 40 percent of the riot or racial stories in each local newspaper during the period of rioting in that city came from the wire services. Furthermore, most newspaper editors appear to have given more headline attention to riots occurring elsewhere than to those at home during the time of trouble in their own cities.

ACCURACY OF THE COVERAGE

We have tested the accuracy of coverage by means of interviews with local media representatives, city and police officials, and residents of the ghettos. To provide a broad base, we used three separate sources for interview data: The Commission's field survey teams, special field teams, and the findings of a special research study.

As is to be expected, almost everyone had his own version of "the truth," but it is noteworthy that some editors and reporters themselves, in retrospect, have expressed concern about the accuracy of their own coverage. For example, one newspaper editor said at the Commission's Poughkeepsie conference:

We used things in our leads and headlines during the riot I wish we could have back now, because they were wrong and they were bad mistakes. ...

We used the words "sniper kings" and "nests of snipers." We found out when we were able to get our people into those areas and get them out from under the cars that these sniper kings and these nests of snipers were the constituted authorities shooting at each other, most of them. There was just one confirmed sniper in the entire eight-day riot, and he was drunk and had a pistol and was firing from a window.

Television industry representatives at the conference stressed their concern about "live" coverage of disorders and said they try, whenever possible, to view and edit taped or filmed sequences before broadcasting them. Conference participants admitted that live television coverage via helicopter of the 1965 Watts riot had been inflammatory, and network news executives expressed doubts that television would ever again present live coverage of a civil disorder.

Most errors involved mistakes of fact, exaggeration of events, overplaying of particular stories, or prominently displayed speculation about unfounded rumors of potential trouble. This is not only a local problem; because of the wire services and networks, it is a national one. An experienced riot reporter told the Commission that initial wire service reports of a disturbance tend to be inflated. The reason, he said, is that they are written by local bureau men who in most cases have not seen a civil disorder before. When out-of-town reporters with knowledge in the field or the wire services' own riot specialists arrive on the scene, the situation is put into a more accurate context.

Some examples of exaggeration and mistakes about facts are cataloged here. These examples are by no means exhaustive. They represent only a few of the incidents discovered by the Commission and, no doubt, are but a small part of the total number of such inaccuracies. But the Commission believes that they are representative of the kinds of errors likely to occur when, in addition to the confusion inherent in civil disorder situations, reporters are rushed and harried or editors are superficial and careless. We present these as examples of mistakes that we hope will be avoided in the future.

In particular, we believe newsmen should be wary of how they play rumors of impending trouble. Whether a rumor is reliable and significant enough to deserve coverage is an editorial decision. But the failure of many headlined rumors to be borne out last summer suggests that these editorial decisions often are not as carefully made as the sensitivity of the subject requires.

- In Detroit, a radio station broadcast a rumor based on a telephone tip that Negroes planned to invade suburbia one night later; if plans existed, they never materialized.
- In Cincinnati, several outlets ran a story about white youths arrested for possessing a bazooka; only a few reports mentioned that the weapon was inoperable.
- In Tampa, a newspaper repeatedly indulged in speculation about impending trouble. When the state attorney ruled the fatal shooting of a Negro youth justifiable homicide, the paper's news columns reported: "There were fears today that the ruling would stir new race problems for Tampa tonight." The day before, the paper quoted one "top lawman" as telling reporters "he now fears that Negro residents in the Central Avenue Project and in the West Tampa trouble spots feel they are in competition and are

trying to see which can cause the most unrest—which area can become the center of attraction."

- A West Coast newspaper put out an edition headlined: "Rioting Erupts in Washington, D.C./Negroes Hurl Bottles, Rocks at Police Near White House." The story did not support the headline. It reported what was actually the fact: that a number of teenage Negroes broke store windows and threw bottles and stones at police and firemen near downtown Washington, a mile or more from the White House. On the other hand, the same paper did not report unfounded local rumors of sniping when other news media did.

Television presents a different problem with respect to accuracy. In contrast to what some of its critics have charged, television sometimes may have leaned over too far backward in seeking balance and restraint. By stressing interviews, many with whites in predominantly Negro neighborhoods, and by emphasizing control scenes rather than riotous action, television news broadcasts may have given a distorted picture of what the disorders were all about.

The media—especially television—also have failed to present and analyze to a sufficient extent the basic reasons for the disorders. There have, after the disorders, been some brilliant exceptions. As the content analysis findings suggest, however, coverage during the riot period itself gives far more emphasis to control of rioters and black-white confrontation than to the underlying causes of the disturbances.

GHETTO REACTIONS TO THE MEDIA COVERAGE

The Commission was particularly interested in public reaction to media coverage; specifically, what people in the ghetto look at and read and how it affects them. The Commission has drawn upon reports from special teams of researchers who visited various cities where outbreaks occurred last summer. Members of these teams interviewed ghetto dwellers and middle-class Negroes on their responses to news media. In addition, we have used information from a statistical study of the mass media in the Negro ghetto in Pittsburgh.

These interviews and surveys, though by no means a complete study of the subject, lead to four broad conclusions about ghetto reactions and, to a lesser degree, middle-class Negro reactions to the media.

Most Negroes distrust what they refer to as the "white press." As one interviewer reported:

The average black person couldn't give less of a damn about what the media say. The intelligent black person is resentful at what he considers to be a totally false portrayal of what goes on in the ghetto. Most black people see the newspapers as mouthpieces of the "power structure."

These comments are echoed in most interview reports the Commission has read. Distrust and dislike of the media among ghetto Negroes encompass all the media, though, in general, the newspapers are mistrusted more than television. This is not because television is thought to be more sensitive or responsive to Negro needs and aspirations but because ghetto residents believe that television at least lets them see the actual events for themselves. Even so, many Negroes, particularly teenagers, told researchers that they noted a pronounced discrepancy between what they saw in the riots and what television broadcast.

Persons interviewed offered three chief reasons for their attitude. First, they believe, as suggested in the quotation above, that the media are instruments of the white power structure. They think that these white interests guide the entire white community, from the journalists' friends and neighbors to city officials, police officers, and department store owners. Publishers and editors, if not white reporters, they feel, support and defend these interests with enthusiasm and dedication.

Second, many people in the ghettos apparently believe that newsmen rely on the police for most of their information about what is happening during a disorder and tend to report much more of what the officials are doing and saying than what Negro citizens or leaders in the city are doing and saying. Editors and reporters at the Poughkeepsie Conference acknowledged that the police and city officials are their main—and sometimes their only—source of information. It was also noted that most reporters who cover civil disturbances tend to arrive with the police and stay close to them—often for safety and often because they learn where the action is at the same time as the authorities—and thus buttress the ghetto impression that police and press work together and toward the same ends (an impression that may come as a surprise to many within the ranks of police and press).

Third, Negro residents in several cities surveyed cited as specific examples of media unfairness what they considered the failure of the media:

- To report the many examples of Negroes helping law enforcement officers and assisting in the treatment of the wounded during disorders.
- To report adequately about false arrests.
- To report instances of excessive force by the National Guard.
- To explore and interpret the background conditions leading to disturbances.
- To expose, except in Detroit, what they regarded as instances of police brutality.

- To report on white vigilante groups which allegedly came into some disorder areas and molested innocent Negro residents.

Some of these problems are insoluble. But more firsthand reporting in the diffuse and fragmented riot area should temper easy reliance on police information and announcements. There is a special need for news media to cover "positive" news stories in the ghetto before and after riots with concern and enthusiasm.

A multitude of news and information sources other than the established news media are relied upon in the ghetto. One of our studies found that 79 percent of a total of 567 ghetto residents interviewed in seven cities first heard about the outbreak in their own city by word of mouth. Telephone and word-of-mouth exchanges on the streets, in churches, stores, pool halls, and bars provide more information—and rumors—about events of direct concern to ghetto residents than the more conventional news media.

Among the established media, television and radio are far more popular in the ghetto than newspapers. Radios there, apparently, are ordinarily listened to less for news than for music and other programs. One survey showed that an overwhelmingly large number of Negro children and teenagers (like their white counterparts) listen to the radio for music alone, interspersed by disc jockey chatter. In other age groups, the response of most people about what they listen to on the radio was "anything," leading to the conclusion that radio in the ghetto is basically a background accompaniment.

But the fact that radio is such a constant background accompaniment can make it an important influence on people's attitudes and perhaps on their actions once trouble develops. This is true for several reasons. News presented on local "rock" stations seldom constitutes much more than terse headline items which may startle or frighten but seldom inform. Radio disc jockeys and those who preside over the popular "talk shows" keep a steady patter of information going over the air. When a city is beset by civil strife, this patter can both inform transistor radio-carrying young people where the action is, and terrify their elders and much of the white community. "Burn, baby, burn," the slogan of the Watts riot, was inadvertently originated by a radio disc jockey.

Thus, radio can be an instrument of trouble and tension in a community threatened or inundated with civil disorder. It can also do much to minimize fear by putting fast-paced events into proper perspective. We have found commendable instances, for example, in Detroit, Milwaukee, and New Brunswick, of radio stations and personalities using their air time and influence to try to calm potential rioters. In the next section, we recommend procedures for meetings and consultations for advance planning among those who will cover civil disorders. It is important that radio personnel, and especially disc jockeys and talk show hosts, be included in such preplanning.

Television is the formal news source most relied upon in the ghetto. According to one report, more than 75 percent of the sample turned to television for national and international news, and a larger percentage of the sample (86 percent) regularly watched television from 5:00 to 7:00 PM, the dinner hours when the evening news programs are broadcast.

The significance of broadcasting in news dissemination is seen in Census Bureau estimates that, in June 1967, 87.7 percent of nonwhite households and 94.8 percent of white households had television sets.

When ghetto residents do turn to newspapers, most read tabloids, if available, far more frequently than standard-size newspapers and rely on the tabloids primarily for light features, racing charts, comic strips, fashion news, and display advertising.

CONDUCT OF PRESS REPRESENTATIVES

Most newsmen appear to be aware and concerned that their very physical presence can exacerbate a small disturbance, but some have conducted themselves with a startling lack of common sense. News organizations, particularly television networks, have taken substantial steps to minimize the effect of the physical presence of their employees at a news event. Networks have issued internal instructions calling for use of unmarked cars and small cameras and tape recorders, and most stations instruct their cameramen to film without artificial light whenever possible. Still, some newsmen have done things "for the sake of the story" that could have contributed to tension.

Reports have come to the Commission's attention of individual newsmen staging events, coaxing youths to throw rocks and interrupt traffic, and otherwise acting irresponsibly at the incipient stages of a disturbance. Such acts are the responsibility of the news organization as well as of its individual reporter.

Two examples occurred in Newark. Television cameramen, according to officials, crowded into and in front of police headquarters, interfering with law enforcement operations and "making a general nuisance of themselves." In a separate incident, a New York newspaper photographer covering the Newark riot repeatedly urged and finally convinced a Negro boy to throw a rock for the camera. Crowding may occasionally be unavoidable; staging of events is not.

We believe every effort should be made to eliminate this sort of conduct. This requires the implementation of thoughtful, stringent staff guidelines for reporters and editors. Such guidelines, carefully formulated, widely disseminated, and strictly enforced, underlie the self-policing activities of some news organizations already, but they must be universally adopted if they are to be effective in curbing journalistic irresponsibility.

The Commission has studied the internal guidelines in use last summer at the Associated Press, United Press International, the *Washington Post*, and the Columbia Broadcasting System. Many other news organizations, large and small, have similar guidelines. In general, the guidelines urge extreme care to ensure that reporting is thorough and balanced and that words and statistics used are appropriate and accurate. The AP guidelines call for broad investigation into the immediate and underlying causes of an incident. The CBS guidelines demand as much caution as possible to avoid the danger of camera equipment and lights exacerbating the disturbance.

Internal guidelines can, and all those studied do, go beyond problems of physical presence at a disturbance to the substantive aspects of searching out, reporting, and writing the story. But the content of the guidelines is probably less important than the fact that the subject has been thoughtfully considered and hammered out within the organization, and an approach developed that is designed to meet the organization's particular needs and solve its particular problems.

We recommend that every news organization that does not now have some form of guidelines—or suspects that those it has are not working effectively— designate top editors to (a) meet with its reporters who have covered or might be assigned to riots, (b) discuss in detail the problems and procedures which exist or are expected, and (c) formulate and disseminate directives based on the discussions. Regardless of the specific provisions, the vital step is for every news-gathering organization to adopt and implement at least some minimal form of internal control.

RECOMMENDATIONS TO IMPROVE RIOT COVERAGE

A NEED FOR BETTER COMMUNICATION

A recurrent problem in the coverage of last summer's disorders was friction and lack of cooperation between police officers and working reporters. Many experienced and capable journalists complained that policemen and their commanding officers were at best apathetic and at worst overtly hostile toward reporters attempting to cover a disturbance. Policemen, on the other hand, charged that many reporters seemed to forget that the task of the police is to restore order.

After considering available evidence on the subject, the Commission is convinced that these conditions reflect an absence of advanced communication and planning among the people involved. We do not suggest that familiarity with the other's problems will beget total amity and cooperation. The interests of the media and the police are sometimes necessarily at variance. But we do believe that communication is a vital step toward removing the obstacles produced by ignorance, confusion, and misunderstanding of what each group is actually trying to do.

MUTUAL ORIENTATION

What is needed first is a series of discussions, perhaps a combination of informal gatherings and seminar-type workshops. They should encompass all ranks of the police, all levels of media employees, and a cross-section of city officials. At first these would be get-acquainted sessions—to air complaints and discuss common problems. Working reporters should get to know the police who would be likely to draw duty in a disorder. Police and city officials should use the sessions for frank and candid briefings on the problems the city might face and official plans for dealing with disturbances.

Later sessions might consider procedures to facilitate the physical movement of personnel and speed the flow of accurate and complete news. Such arrangements might involve nothing more than a procedure for designating specific locations at which police officers would be available to escort a reporter into a dangerous area. In addition, policemen and reporters working together might devise better methods of identification, communication, and training.

Such procedures are infinitely variable and depend on the initiative, needs, and desires of those involved. If there is no existing institution or procedure for convening such meetings, we urge the mayor or city manager to do so in every city where experience suggests the possibility of future trouble. To allay any apprehension that discussions with officials might lead to restraints on the freedom to seek out and report the news, participants in these meetings should stipulate beforehand that freedom of access to all areas for reporters will be preserved.

DESIGNATION OF INFORMATION OFFICERS

It is desirable to designate and prepare a number of police officers to act as media information officers. There should be enough of these so that, in the event of a disturbance, a reporter will not have to seek far to find a policeman ready and able to give him information and answer questions. Officers should be of high enough rank within the police department to have ready access to information.

CREATION OF AN INFORMATION CENTER

A nerve center for reliable police and official government information should be planned and ready for activation when a disturbance reaches a predetermined point of intensity. Such a center might be located at police headquarters or city hall. It should be directed by an experienced, high-ranking information specialist with close ties to police officials. It is imperative, of course, that all officials keep a steady flow of accurate information coming into the center. Ideally, rooms would be set aside for taping and filming interviews with public officials. Local television stations might cut costs and relieve congestion by pooling some equipment at this central facility. An information center should not be thought of as replacing other news sources inside and outside the disturbance area. If anything, our studies suggest that reporters are already too closely tied to police and officials as news sources in a disorder. An information center should not be permitted to intensify this dependence. Properly conceived, however, a center can supplement on-the-spot reporting and supply news about official action.

OUT-OF-TOWN REPORTERS

Much of the difficulty last summer apparently revolved around relations between local law enforcement officials and out-of-town reporters. These reporters are likely to be less sensitive about preserving the "image" of the local community.

Still, local officials serve their city badly when they ignore or impede national media representatives instead of informing them about the city, and cooperating with their attempts to cover the story. City and police officials should designate liaison officers and distribute names and telephone numbers of police and other relevant officials, the place they can be found if trouble develops, and other information likely to be useful.

National and other news organizations, in turn, could help matters by selecting a responsible home office official to act as liaison in these cases and to be accessible by phone to local officials who encounter difficulty with on-the-spot representatives of an organization.

GENERAL GUIDELINES AND CODES

In some cases, if all parties involved were willing, planning sessions might lead to consideration of more formal undertakings. These might include (a) agreements on specific procedures to expedite the physical movement of men and equipment around disorder areas and back and forth through police lines;

(b) general guidelines on the behavior of both media and police personnel; and (c) arrangements for a brief moratorium on reporting news of an incipient disturbance. The Commission stresses once again its belief that, though each of these possibilities merits consideration, none should be formulated or imposed by unilateral government action. Any procedure finally adopted should be negotiated between police and media representatives and should assure both sides the flexibility needed to do their respective jobs. Acceptance of such arrangements should be frankly based on grounds of self-interest, for negotiated methods of procedure can often yield substantial benefits to each side—and to the public which both serve.

At the request of the Commission, the Community Relations Service of the Department of Justice surveyed recent experiences with formal codes. Most of the codes studied (a) set forth in general terms common-sense standards of good journalistic conduct, and (b) established procedures for a brief moratorium (seldom more than 30 minutes to an hour) on reporting an incipient disturbance.

In its survey, the Community Relations Service [CRS] described and analyzed experiences with codes in 11 major cities where they are currently in force. Members of the CRS staff conducted interviews with key citizens (newsmen, city officials, and community leaders) in each of the 11 cities, seeking comments on the effectiveness and practicality of the codes and guidelines used. CRS's major findings and conclusions are:

- All codes and guidelines now in operation are basically voluntary arrangements usually put forward by local authorities and accepted by the news media after consultation. Nowhere has an arrangement or agreement been effected that binds the news media without their assent.
- No one interviewed in this survey considered the code or guidelines in effect in his city as useless or harmful. CRS thought that, where they were in effect, the codes had a constructive impact on the local news media. Observers in some cities, however, thought the increased sense of responsibility manifested by press and television was due more to experience with riot coverage than to the existence of the codes.
- The more controversial and often least understood aspect of guidelines has been provision for a brief voluntary moratorium on the reporting of news. Some kind of moratorium is specified in the codes of six cities surveyed (Chicago, Omaha, Buffalo, Indianapolis, Kansas City, and Toledo), and the moratorium was invoked last summer in Chicago and Indianapolis. In each case, an effort to prevent quite minor racial incidents from escalating into more serious trouble was successful, and many thought the moratorium contributed.

- The confusion about a moratorium, and the resulting aversion to it, is unfortunate. The specific period of delay is seldom more than 30 minutes. In practice, under today's conditions of reporting and broadcasting, this often will mean little if any delay before the full story gets into the paper or on the air. The time can be used to repair and edit the story and to verify and assess the reports of trouble. The only loss is the banner headline or the broadcast news bulletin that is released prematurely to avoid being beaten by "the competition." It is just such reflexive responses that can lead to sensationalism and inaccuracy. In cities where a moratorium is part of the code, CRS interviewers detected no discontent over its presence.
- The most frequent complaint about shortcomings in existing codes is that many of them do not reach the underpinnings of crisis situations. Ghetto spokesmen, in particular, said that the emphasis in the codes on conduct during the crisis itself tended to lead the media to neglect reporting the underlying causes of racial tension.

At the Poughkeepsie conference with media representatives, there was considerable criticism of the Chicago code on grounds that the moratorium is open-ended. Once put into effect it is supposed to be maintained until "the situation is under control." There were doubts about how effective this code had been in practice. The voluntary news blackout in Detroit for part of the first day of the riot—apparently at the request of officials and civil rights groups—was cited as evidence that suppression of news of violence does not necessarily defuse a riot situation.

On the basis of the CRS survey and other evidence, the Commission concludes that codes are seldom harmful, often useful, but no panacea. To be of any use, they must address themselves to the substance of the problems that plague relations between the press and officialdom during a disorder, but they are only one of several methods of improving those relations. Ultimately, no matter how sensitive and comprehensive a code or set of guidelines may be, efficient, accurate reporting must depend on the intelligence, judgment, and training of newsmen, police, and city officials together.

REPORTING RACIAL PROBLEMS IN THE UNITED STATES

A FAILURE TO COMMUNICATE

The Commission's major concern with the news media is not in riot reporting as such, but in the failure to report adequately on race relations and ghetto problems and to bring more Negroes into journalism. Concern about this was expressed by a number of participants in our Poughkeepsie conference. Disorders are only one aspect of the dilemmas and difficulties of race relations in America. In defining, explaining, and reporting this broader, more complex, and ultimately far more fundamental subject, the communications media, ironically, have failed to communicate.

They have not communicated to the majority of their audience—which is white—a sense of the degradation, misery, and hopelessness of living in the ghetto. They have not communicated to whites a feeling for the difficulties and frustrations of being a Negro in the United States. They have not shown understanding or appreciation of—and thus have not communicated—a sense of Negro culture, thought, or history.

Equally important, most newspaper articles and most television programming ignore the fact that an appreciable part of their audience is black. The world that television and newspapers offer to their black audience is almost totally white, in both appearance and attitude. As we have said, our evidence shows that the so-called white press is at best mistrusted and at worst held in contempt by many black Americans. Far too often, the press acts and talks about Negroes as if Negroes do not read the newspapers or watch television, give birth, marry, die, and go to PTA meetings. Some newspapers and stations are beginning to make efforts to fill this void, but they have still a long way to go.

The absence of Negro faces and activities from the media has an effect on white audiences as well as black. If what the white American reads in the newspapers or sees on television conditions his expectation of what is ordinary and normal in the larger society, he will neither understand nor accept the black American. By failing to portray the Negro as a matter of routine and in the context of the total society, the news media have, we believe, contributed to the black-white schism in this country.

When the white press does refer to Negroes and Negro problems it frequently does so as if Negroes were not a part of the audience. This is perhaps understandable in a system where whites edit and, to a large extent, write news. But such attitudes, in an area as sensitive and inflammatory as this, feed Negro alienation and intensify white prejudices.

We suggest that a top editor or news director monitor his news production for a period of several weeks, taking note of how certain stories and language will affect black readers or viewers. A Negro staff member could do this easily. Then the staff should be informed about the problems involved.

The problems of race relations coverage go beyond incidents of white bias. Many editors and news directors, plagued by shortages of staff and lack of reliable contacts and sources of information in the city, have failed to recognize the significance of the urban story and to develop resources to cover it adequately.

We believe that most news organizations do not have direct access to diversified news sources in the ghetto. Seldom do they have a total sense of what is going on there. Some of the blame rests on Negro leaders who do not trust the media and will not deal candidly with representatives of the white press. But the real failure rests with the news organizations themselves. They—like other elements of the white community—have ignored the ghettos for decades. Now they seek instant acceptance and cooperation,

The development of good contacts, reliable information, and understanding requires more effort and time than an occasional visit by a team of reporters to do a feature on a newly discovered ghetto problem. It requires reporters permanently assigned to this beat. They must be adequately trained and supported to dig out and tell the story of a major social upheaval—among the most complicated, portentous, and explosive our society has known. We believe, also, that the Negro press—manned largely by people who live and work in the ghetto—could be a particularly useful source of information and guidance about activities in the black community. Reporters and editors from Negro newspapers and radio stations should be included in any conference between media and police-city representatives, and we suggest that large news organizations would do well to establish better lines of communication to their counterparts in the Negro press.

In short, the news media must find ways of exploring the problems of the Negro and the ghetto more deeply and more meaningfully. To editors who say "we have run thousands of inches on the ghetto which nobody reads" and to television executives who bemoan scores of under-watched documentaries, we say: find more ways of telling this story, for it is a story you, as journalists, must tell—honestly, realistically, and imaginatively. It is the responsibility of the news media to tell the story of race relations in America, and, with notable exceptions, the media have not yet turned to the task with the wisdom, sensitivity, and expertise it demands.

NEGROES IN JOURNALISM

The journalistic profession has been shockingly backward in seeking out, hiring, training, and promoting Negroes. Fewer than 5 percent of the people employed by the news business in editorial jobs in the United States today are Negroes. Less than 1 percent of editors and supervisors are Negroes, and most of them work for Negro-owned organizations. The lines of various news organizations to the militant blacks are, by admission of the newsmen themselves, almost nonexistent. The plaint is, "we can't find qualified Negroes." But this rings hollow from an industry where, only yesterday, jobs were scarce and promotion unthinkable for a man whose skin was black. Even today, there are virtually no Negroes in positions of editorial or executive responsibility and there is only one Negro newsman with a nationally syndicated column.

News organizations must employ enough Negroes in positions of significant responsibility to establish an effective link to Negro actions and ideas, and to meet legitimate employment expectations. Tokenism—the hiring of one Negro reporter, or even two or three—is no longer enough. Negro reporters are essential, but so are Negro editors, writers, and commentators. Newspaper and television policies are, generally speaking, not set by reporters. Editorial decisions about which stories to cover and which to use are made by editors. Yet, very few Negroes in this country are involved in making these decisions, because very few, if any, supervisory editorial jobs are held by Negroes. We urge the news media to do everything possible to train and promote their Negro reporters to positions where those who are qualified can contribute to and have an effect on policy decisions.

It is not enough, though, as many editors have pointed out to the Commission, to search for Negro journalists. Journalism is not very popular as a career for aspiring young Negroes. The starting pay is comparatively low and it is a business which has, until recently, discouraged and rejected them. The recruitment of Negro reporters must extend beyond established journalists, or those who have already formed ambitions along these lines. It must become a commitment to seek out young Negro men and women, inspire them to become—and then train them as—journalists. Training programs should be started at high schools and intensified at colleges. Summer vacation and part-time editorial jobs, coupled with offers of permanent employment, can awaken career plans.

We believe that the news media themselves, their audiences, and the country will profit from these undertakings. For if the media are to comprehend and then to project the Negro community, they must have the help of Negroes. If the media are to report with understanding, wisdom, and sympathy on the problems of the cities and the problems of the black man—for the two are increasingly intertwined—they must employ, promote, and listen to Negro journalists.

THE NEGRO IN THE MEDIA

Finally, the news media must publish newspapers and produce programs that recognize the existence and activities of the Negro, both as a Negro and as part of the community. It would be a contribution of inestimable importance to race relations in the United States simply to treat ordinary news about Negroes as news of other groups is now treated.

Specifically, newspapers should integrate Negroes and Negro activities into all parts of the paper, from the news, society, and club pages to the comic strips. Television should develop programming which integrates Negroes into all aspects of televised presentations. Television is such a visible medium that some constructive steps are easy and obvious. While some of these steps are being taken, they are still largely neglected. For example, Negro reporters and performers should appear more frequently—and at prime time—in news broadcasts, on weather shows, in documentaries, and in advertisements. Some effort already has been made to use Negroes in television commercials. Any initial surprise at seeing a Negro selling a sponsor's product will eventually fade into routine acceptance, an attitude that white society must ultimately develop toward all Negroes.

In addition to news-related programming, we think that Negroes should appear more frequently in dramatic and comedy series. Moreover, networks and local stations should present plays and other programs whose subjects are rooted in the ghetto and its problems.

INSTITUTE OF URBAN COMMUNICATIONS

The Commission is aware that in this area, as in all other aspects of race relations, the problems are great and it is much easier to state them than to solve them. Various pressures—competitive, financial, advertising—may impede progress toward more balanced, in-depth coverage and toward the hiring and training of more Negro personnel. Most newspapers and local television and radio stations do not have the resources or time to keep abreast of all the technical advances, academic theories, and government programs affecting the cities and the lives of their black inhabitants.

During the course of this study, the Commission members and the staff have had many conversations with publishers, editors, broadcasters, and reporters throughout the country. The consensus appears to be that most of them would like to do much more but simply do not have the resources for independent efforts in either training or coverage.

The Commission believes that some of these problems could be resolved if there were a central organization to develop, gather, and distribute talent, resources, and information and to keep the work of the press in this field under review. For this reason, the Commission proposes the establishment of an Institute of Urban Communications on a private, nonprofit basis. The Institute would have neither governmental ties nor governmental authority. Its board would consist in substantial part of professional journalists and, for the rest, of distinguished public figures. The staff would be made up of journalists and students of the profession. Funding would be sought initially from private foundations. Ultimately, it may be hoped, financial support would be forthcoming from within the profession.

The Institute would be charged, in the first instance, with general responsibility for carrying out the media recommendations of the Commission, though as it developed a momentum and life of its own it would also gain its own view of the problems and possibilities. Initial tasks would include:

1. *Training and Education for Journalists in the Field of Urban Affairs.* The Institute should organize and sponsor, on its own and in cooperation with universities and other institutions, a comprehensive range of courses, seminars, and workshops designed to give reporters, editors, and publishers the background they need to cover the urban scene. Offerings would vary in duration and intensity from weekend conferences to grants for year-long individual study on the order of the Nieman fellowships.

All levels and all kinds of news outlets should be served. A most important activity might be to assist disc jockeys and commentators on stations that address themselves especially to the Negro community. Particularly important would be sessions of a month or more for seasoned reporters and editors, comparable to middle-management seminars or mid-career training in other callings. The press must have all the intellectual resources and background to give adequate coverage to the city and the ghetto. It should be the first duty of the Institute to see that this is provided.

2. *Recruitment, Training, and Placement of Negro Journalists.* The scarcity of Negroes in responsible news jobs intensifies the difficulties of communicating the reality of the contemporary American city to white newspaper and television audiences. The special viewpoint of the Negro who has lived through these problems and bears their marks upon him is, as we have seen, notably absent from what is, on the whole, a white press. But full integration of Negroes into the journalistic profession is imperative in its own right. It is unacceptable that the press, itself the special beneficiary of fundamental constitutional protections, should lag so far behind other fields in giving effect to the fundamental human right to equality of opportunity.

To help correct this situation, the Institute will have to undertake far-ranging activities. Providing educational opportunities for would-be Negro journalists is not enough. There will have to be changes in career outlooks for Negro students and their counselors back to the secondary-school level. And changes in these attitudes will come slowly unless there is a change in the reality of employment and advancement opportunities for Negroes in journalism. This requires an aggressive placement program, seeking out newspapers, television, and radio stations that discriminate, whether consciously or unconsciously, and mobilizing the pressures, public, private, and legal, necessary to break the pattern. The Institute might also provide assistance to Negro newspapers, which now recruit and train many young journalists.

3. *Police-Press Relations.* The Commission has stressed the failures in this area and has laid out a set of remedial measures for action at the local level. But if reliance is placed exclusively on local initiative we can predict that in many places—often those that need it most—our recommended steps will not be taken. Pressure from the federal government for action along the lines proposed would be suspect, probably, by both press and local officials. But the Institute could undertake the task of stimulating community action in line with the Commission's recommendations without arousing local hostility and suspicion. Moreover, the Institute could serve as a clearinghouse for exchange of experience in this field.

4. *Review of Media Performance on Riots and Racial Issues.* The Institute should review press and television coverage of riot and racial news and publicly award praise and blame. The Commission recognizes that government restraints or guidelines in this field are both unworkable and incompatible with our Constitution and traditions. Internal guidelines or voluntary advance arrangements may be useful, but they tend to be rather general and the standards they prescribe are neither self-applying nor self-enforcing. We believe it would be healthy for reporters and editors who work in this sensitive field to know that others will be viewing their work and will hold them publicly accountable for lapses from accepted standards of good journalism. The Institute should publicize its findings by means of regular and special reports. It might also set a series of awards for especially meritorious work of individuals or news organizations in race relations reporting.

5. *An Urban Affairs Service.* Whatever may be done to improve the quality of reporting on urban affairs, there always will be a great many outlets that are too small to support the specialized investigation, reporting, and interpreting needed in this field. To fill this gap, the Institute could organize a comprehensive urban news service, available at a modest fee to any news organization that wanted it. The Institute would have its own specially trained reporters, and it would also cull the national press for news and feature stories of broader interest that could be reprinted or broadcast by subscribers.

6. *Continuing Research.* Our own investigations have shown us that academic work on the impact of the media on race relations, its role in shaping

attitudes, and the effects of the choices it makes on people's behavior is in a rudimentary stage. The Commission's content analysis is the first study of its type of contemporary riot coverage, and it is extremely limited in scope. A whole range of questions needs intensive, scholarly exploration, and indeed the development of new modes of research and analysis. The Institute should undertake many of these important projects under its own auspices and could stimulate others in the academic community to further research.

Along with the country as a whole, the press has too long basked in a white world, looking out of it, if at all, with white men's eyes and a white perspective. That is no longer good enough. The painful process of readjustment that is required of the American news media must begin now. They must make a reality of integration—in both their product and personnel. They must insist on the highest standards of accuracy—not only reporting single events with care and skepticism but placing each event into meaningful perspective. They must report the travail of our cities with compassion and in depth.

In all this, the Commission asks for fair and courageous journalism—commitment and coverage that are worthy of one of the crucial domestic stories in America's history.

Index

Abernethy v. Hutchinson (1825), 10
accuracy: and 1967 riots, 253–67; of
    The Executioner's Song, 223–29;
    and honesty, 18–20, 83, 108–10; and
    lying, 24, 28, 40, 71, 73–75, 83, 90,
    91, 106, 132–33, 140, 231–32; and
    misrepresentation, 83, 90, 91, 127–28,
    153, 206–9; in news media, 24, 56,
    90–91, 175–76, 199, 209–11; and *New
    York Times*, 103, 142–50, 152–53; of *The
    Right Stuff*, 218–19, 221–22; and truth,
    25, 55–57, 78, 106–8, 155, 198–212. *See
    also* bias; point of view
Adams, Llewellyn Sherman, 99
Adler, Renata, 217–18
advertising: and business, 32, 43–44, 78,
    87, 91, 198, 210; and circulation, 23,
    94, 98
Agnew, Spiro, x, xii, 133, 153; at Des
    Moines, 102, 112–19; at Middlesex
    Club, 123–30; at Montgomery
    Chamber of Commerce, 119–23

Alien Registration Act (1940), 83
Allen, Frederick Lewis, ix, xi, 173, 198–
    212
All the President's Men (Woodward &
    Bernstein), 224
American Broadcasting Corporation
    (ABC), 114
"The American Newspaper" (Irwin),
    43–61
American Newspapers Publishers'
    Association, 24, 93, 95, 99
American Society of Newspaper Editors,
    29, 41
An American Tragedy (Dreiser), 213
antitrust laws, 81–82
Appeal to Reason (journal), 71
Armies of the Night (Mailer), 223
Armstrong, Scott, 224, 231
Associated Press, 95, 251, 267; and
    Kerensky, 166; and La Follette, 34–36;
    and Lindbergh, 30–31; and Nixon
    coverage, 145; and Russian revolution

coverage, 166, 167; and Sinclair, 37–38, 209
Astor, Vincent, 37
astronauts, Mercury, 216, 218–22
Atkins, Susan, 223
Atlantic Monthly, 68
Auden, W. H., 229–30

Bacon, Robert L., 32
Bailey, Herbert, 162, 166
Baker, Alfred L., 32
Baker, Nicole, 223–26
Ballyhoo (Bent), 23
Baltimore Sun, 121
Banking and Currency (Lindbergh), 26
Beiderbecke, Bix, 217–18
Benchley, Robert, xi
Bennett, James Gordon, 22, 38
Benson, Allan, 74
Bent, Silas, 23, 31
Berger, Mike, 189–90
Berger, Peter, 140
Bernstein, Carl, 224
Bernstein, Theodore, 181
The Best American Essays, 1987 (Talese), 173
Beyond the Melting Pot (Glazer), 141
bias: in journalism, 101–3, 125, 171, 181, 186, 200, 214; of network commentators, 112–20, 123; in press, 47–48, 91, 154, 186, 207–12, 257, 272; in selection by media, x–xi, 71, 114–16, 152, 162, 165, 200–206
Bigart, Homer, 177, 189
Black Panthers, 141
Blake, Tiffany, 54
Bolshevism, 41; and Lindbergh, 24, 26–27; and Russian Revolution, 156–58, 163–64, 170
Boston Globe, 52
Boston Post, 55
Boston Transcript, 59
Boswell, James, 217

Bradlee, Ben, 142
Brandeis, Louis, x, 1, 3–17
Branson, Herman R., 147–48
The Brass Check (Sinclair), xi, 2, 37–38, 41, 43–44, 62–78, 206
The Brethren (Woodward & Armstrong), 224, 231
Brinkley, David, 115
Brooker, Charles F., 32
Brookings Institution, 252
Brooklyn Daily Eagle, 34
Broun, Heywood, 39, 40
Brown, Robert J., 146–47
Brown, Sam, 141
Bruce, Knight, 8
Bryan, William Jennings, 57, 68
Buchanan, Patrick, 102
Bunyan, John, x, 101
Burger, Warren, 231
business, big: influence of, xi, 2, 39, 43, 66, 207; Lindbergh on, 26–29; and newspapers, 24, 32–35, 75–78, 136. *See also* capitalism; corporations

Camus, Albert, 193
Cannibals and Christians (Mailer), 229
capitalism, 43, 71–78, 109–11, 136, 206–7. *See also* business, big; corporations
Capone, Al, 41
Capote, Truman: *In Cold Blood*, 213, 224; "Handcarved Coffins," 214–15, 231
Carmichael, Stokely, 115
Carpenter, Scott, 218
censorship, 81, 102, 116, 120, 133, 158, 198, 256
Chafee, Zechariah, Jr., 44, 92
Cheek, James, 147
Chiang Kai-shek, 213
Chicago moratorium, 270–71
Chicago Post, 59
Chicago Tribune, 27, 32, 34, 47, 52, 73
Christian Science Monitor, 210
Churchill, Winston, 23, 114, 122, 196

circulation, 23, 94, 116, 185
Civil Rights movement, 255
Civil Service Commission, 145
Clark, John M., 92
Clark, Kenneth B., 260
Clay, Henry, 208
Cleaver, Eldridge, 118
Cold War, 133–34, 222
Collier's Magazine, 43, 45, 46, 105
Columbia Broadcasting System (CBS),
    114, 126–30, 267
Columbia Spectator, 135
Columbia University School of
    Journalism, x, 233–35
Commentary, xii, 131
commentators, 112–20, 123
Commission on Civil Disorders (1968),
    x, 234, 253–78
common law, 3, 4, 6–8, 17
communications industry:
    government regulation of, 79–84,
    120; and monopoly, 70, 82, 84, 90,
    91, 93–98, 116–17, 120–21; as public
    service, 73–75, 81–82, 85, 88, 95,
    242–44; theory of, 174–76; and urban
    affairs, 267–78
Congressional Record, 34
Coolidge, Calvin, 201
copyright law, 7, 11
corporations: government regulation
    of, 109–11; and media concentration,
    x–xi, 43–44, 81–82, 91, 93–98, 115–17,
    120–21, 240; and social responsibility,
    109–10, 172, 207. *See also* business, big;
    capitalism
corruption, 2, 107–10, 134–36
Cotton, "Ham," 39
Crane, Charles R., 32
credibility gap, 125
The Crimes of the Times (Sinclair), 36
Cronin, Thomas E., 135–36
Cronkite, Walter, 125
Cuban Missile Crisis, 114

Daedalus, 174, 175, 198
Daily Chronicle (London), 162
Daily Herald (London), 93
Daily Mail (London), 93
Daily News (London), 206
Dana, Charles A., 63, 75
Darnton, Robert: and cultural milieu, x,
    xii, 174, 196, 197; "Writing News and
    Telling Stories," 175–97
Darrow, Clarence, 23
Dawson, Mitchell, 31
Dearborn Independent, 67, 72
defamation, 5, 16–17. *See also* libel
Defoe, Daniel, 173
Delane, John, 239
democracy: and educated readers, 242–
    43; and freedom of the press, 80, 86,
    92, 151, 253; role of press in, 103, 117–
    18, 123, 127, 133–34, 153, 158–59
Democratic National Convention (1968),
    117, 120
Deseret News, 224
Des Moines Register, 119
Des Moines speech (Agnew), 102, 112–19
Detroit News, 96
Detroit riots (1967), 255, 257, 260, 262,
    264, 271
Detroit Times, 96
Dickinson, John, 92
Didion, Joan, 226
Doctorow, E. L., 213–14
documentaries, 80, 114, 126–30
Douglas, Paul H., 247
Down and Out in Paris and London
    (Orwell), 223
Dreiser, Theodore, 213
Dunne, John Gregory, 220
The Dyer's Hand (Auden), 229

Ecclesiastical Polity (Hooker), 108
Editor & Publisher (journal), 94
editors: and editorial page, 56, 71, 87,
    119, 141, 199, 208; education of, 236,

241, 243, 246, 249; *and Emporia*
editorials, x, 18–21; and judgment,
50, 53–54, 57–60; Kerner commission
on, 255–58, 261–64, 266–67, 272–74;
and Lindbergh, 26, 28, 30–31; at the
New York Times, 37, 40, 151–52, 158,
162, 172; role of, 74, 140, 142, 176–97,
204–5, 207, 210; and self-criticism,
149, 152
Eisenhower, Dwight D., 122
Eldon, Lord, 9–11, 13
Ellison, Ralph, 213
Emporia Gazette editorials, x, 2, 18–21
Encyclopedia Britannica, 44
"The End of Free Lunch" (Liebling),
93–100
EPIC News, 39
Epstein, Edward Jay, 141
Ernst, Margaret, 27
ethics: code of, 22–24, 29, 58–59, 73,
172, 208, 210; in journalism, 44, 139,
198–200, 214. *See also* standards
L'Étranger (Camus), 193
Evans, Arthur M., 27
Evening News (London), 93
Everybody's (magazine), 101
*The Executioner's Song (*Mailer), 214–15,
222–30

fairness, 24, 71, 115, 117, 207–9
Fargo Courier-News, 70
Federal bureaucracies, 137–38
Federal Communications Commission
(FCC), 81–82, 91, 115, 126–27
Federal Interagency Committee on
Education (FICE), 146–47
Feiffer, Jules, 231
fiction: devices of, 214, 219–20; and new
journalism, xii, 173–74, 213–32
Figaro, 166
Finch, Robert, 147
First Amendment, 80, 83, 87, 116
Ford, Henry, 72, 213

foreign correspondents, 95, 97–98, 178,
186, 196
Foster, William Z., 208
Frankel, Max, 137
Frankfurter, Felix, 251–52
Franklin, Benjamin, 197
freedom of the press: and democracy,
80, 86, 92, 151, 253; and Hutchins
Commission report, 79–92; and
Kerner report, 253, 257; role of public
in, 79, 87–90, 116; Seldes on, 2, 22–41
Freedom of the Press (Seldes), 2, 22–41
Freeman, Orville, 128
Friendly, Fred, 117
The Front Page (Hecht and MacArthur),
xi

Gardiner, A. G., 206
Garrison, William Lloyd, 123
Gary, E. H., 32
Gavin, James M., 99
Gavit, John P., 38
Gay, Peter, 151
Gilmore, Gary, 222–26, 229
Glazer, Nathan, 140, 141, 150
Glenn, John, 218–22
Godkin, E. L., 64
Goldenweiser, E. A., 252
Gompers, Samuel, 209
Gould, Jay, 240
government regulation: of
communications industry, 79–84, 120;
of corporations, 109–11; of the press,
89, 90, 98, 132, 151, 153, 198, 210
Graphic (London), 22, 23, 170
Grasty, Charles H., 168
Greeley, Horace, 233
Gregory, Dick, 260
Gridiron Club (Washington, D.C.), 133

Haines, Dora, 25
Haines, Lynn, 25
Halberstam, David, 152, 189

Hall, Chapin, 39
Hamlin, Hannibal, 124
"Handcarved Coffins" (Capote), 214–15, 231
Hand, Learned, 116
Harding, Warren G., 201–2, 209
Harper's Magazine, 173
Harrel, Robert F., 246, 249
Harriman, E. H., 32
Harriman, W. Averell, 102, 113
Harris polls, 114
Hartford Courant, 132
Harvard Crimson, 135
Harvard Law Review, x, 1, 3
Harwood, Richard, 152
headlines, 200, 203–5, 255, 261–63, 271
Heard, Alexander, 147
Hearst newspapers, 31, 53–54
Hearst, William Randolph, 40–41, 94, 96
Helicon Home Colony, 38, 207
Hemingway, Ernest, 228
Henderson, Vivian, 145, 148, 152
Henry, Patrick, 57
Hentoff, Nat, 2
Hersey, John, x; and new journalism, xii, 174, 213–32
Hiroshima (Hersey), 174
Ho Chi Minh, 113
Hocking, William E., 92
Hofstadter, Richard, 153
Hooker, Bishop, 108
"How to Learn Nothing" (Liebling), 233
Hughes, Helen MacGill, 193
Humphrey, Hubert, 117, 119–20
Hunger in America (documentary), 127–28
Huntington, C. P., 240
Hutchins Commission, x, xi, 44, 79–92, 151
Hutchins, Robert Maynard, 44, 79–92, 151

In Cold Blood (Capote), 213, 215, 224
in fact (newsletter; Seldes), xi, 2

Institute of Urban Communication, 258, 275–78
Irwin, Will, 43–61
Isaacs, Norman E., 151

James, Edwin L., 189
James, Harry, 217–18
James, Henry, 219–20
Jenison, F. T., 247
Jerome, William Travers, 64
Johnson, Diane, 226
Johnson, Lyndon, 113, 136, 138–39, 220
Jonas, Gerald, 217–18
journalism: and adherence to fact, xii, 128, 158, 198–212, 214–16, 230–32; canons of, 24, 29; as entertainment, 142, 205–6; responsibilty of, 36, 44, 153, 172, 209, 231; schools of, x, 37, 89–92, 135, 188, 209, 233–44; sociological research on, 245–52
journalism, new. *See* new journalism
Journalism Quarterly, 234, 245
journalism, yellow. *See* yellow journalism
Journal of the Plague Year (Defoe), 173
Joyce, James, 219–20
The Joys of Yiddish (Rosten), xi
Jung, Carl, 193
The Jungle (Sinclair), xi, 37–38, 43

Kansas City Star, 52, 59
Kelman, Steven, 140
Kennedy administration, 136, 185
Kennedy, John F., 99, 114, 123, 133, 152, 189
Kent, William, 32
Kerensky government, 155, 163–69
Kerner Commission Report (1968), x, 234, 253–78
Kerner, Otto, 234
Khaldun, Ibn, 98, 100
Kihss, Peter, 177
King, Cecil, 93
Kissinger, Henry, 232
Kolbert, Elizabeth, 174

Korn, Eric, 221
Kornilov rebellion, 156, 163–69
Kraft, Christopher, 218
Kristol, Irving, 134, 141, 142–43

La Follette, Robert M., 2, 32–36, 39
Lancet (journal), 10
Laqueur, Walter, 151
Lardner, Ring, 22
Lasswell, Harold D., 92, 247–48
Law, Bonar, 160, 162
Lawrence, Andrew, 54
The Law (Vailland), 133
Leaks, 103, 139, 187
Lee, James Melvin, 37, 40–41, 199
"The Legend on the License" (Hersey),
    213–32
Legislative Correspondents Association
    (Albany, New York), 133
Levinson, John O., 217
Levi-Strauss, Claude, 193
Lewis, Sinclair, 22
libel: laws of, 4–6, 14–17; and press, 26,
    38; retraction for, 35, 83, 85, 91
liberalism, xii, 38–40, 136–37, 186
Liberator (magazine), 71
Liebling, A. J., xi, 44, 93–100, 233
Life (magazine), 174
Lincoln, Abraham, 124, 236
Lindbergh, Charles A., 2, 24–29
Lindbergh, Charles A., Jr., 2, 23–24,
    27–31
Lindbergh, Eva, 24
Lippmann, Walter, ix, x–xi, 103, 116–17,
    199; "A Test of the News," 154–72
Lipset, Seymour Martin, 140
Literary Digest, 67
Little Murders (Feiffer), 231–32
Los Angeles Municipal News, 68–69
Los Angeles Times, 38–40, 73, 102
Luce, Clare Booth, 189
Luce, Henry R., 44
Lynes, Russell, 173

Macaulay, Thomas, 241
MacDonald, Jamie, 189
MacLeish, Archibald, 44, 92
MacLeish, John, 218
MacNamara, Robert, 185
Mailer, Norman, 214–15, 222–30
Le Malentendu (Camus), 193
Malraux, André, 213
Manchester Guardian, 132, 186
"The Man with the Muckrake"
    (Roosevelt), x, 105–11
the *Masses*, 37
Matthews, T. S., 142
Mayhew, Henry, 217
McArthur, Douglas, 122
McCarthy, Joseph, 103, 138, 140–41, 151–52
McClure's Magazine, x, 43, 101
McCormick, Robert Rutherford, 96
media. *See* communications industry;
    news media
Mercury astronauts, 216, 218–22
Merriam, Charles E., 92, 248
Merz, Charles, ix, 103, 154–72
Middlesex Club (Boston), 123–30
Middleton, Drew, 190
Mill, John Stuart, 237
Minneapolis Journal and Tribune, 27–30
minorities, 90, 234, 253–78
Mitchell, Joseph, 217
monopolies, 70, 82, 84, 90, 91, 93–98,
    116–17, 120–21
Monroe, Marilyn, 223
Montgomery speech (Agnew), 119–23
Morgan, J. P., 213
Morris, Oliver S., 70–71
motion picture industry, 40, 71, 73–75,
    79–81, 86, 88
Moynihan, Daniel Patrick, x, xii, 102–3,
    131–53
muckrakers, x–xi, 2, 101–2, 105–7, 134–36,
    149. *See also* reform
Munsey, Frank, 98
Munsterberg, Hugo, 200

Music for Chameleons (Capote), 215

Mystery and Manners (O'Conner), 213–14

NASA (National Aeronautics and Space Administration), 218–19, 221–22

Nation, 71

National Association for Equal Opportunity in Higher Education, 146–48

National Broadcasting Corporation (NBC), 114, 116

Newark riots (1967), 257, 266

Newark Star Ledger, 174, 176, 191

New Deal, 249–52. *See also* Roosevelt, Franklin

Newhouse, Samuel I., 96

new journalism, xii, 22, 173–74, 213–32

New Journalism (Wolfe), 214, 216, 218

The New Ocean: A History of Project Mercury, 221

New Republic (magazine), ix, 40, 154

News-Chronicle (London), 93

news media: competition among, 81–82, 94–98, 121, 131, 187, 210–11; concentration of, x–xi, 43–44, 80–82, 91, 93–98, 115–17, 120–21, 240; conspiracies among, 206–7; corrections in, 83, 91, 103, 142–43, 149, 151–52; government regulation of, 89, 90, 98, 132, 151, 153, 198, 210; and one-ownership towns, 94–96, 187; and the presidency, 113–19, 131–53, 185, 208–9; public's role in, 43, 79, 87–90, 119, 184–91, 211–12; and self-criticism, 79, 82, 84–87, 120, 174, 211, 266; state ownership of, 68–69; tabloid, 29, 38, 196, 266; and Washington press corps, 132–33, 185, 245–52; and "white press," 256–57, 263–65, 271–78

"Newsmen's Fantasies, Audiences, and Newswriting" (Pool and Shulman), 175

newspapers: 1967 riot coverage of, 253–54, 257–58, 260–61, 266; as capitalistic, 72–78, 136, 206–7; commercial interests of, 44, 51–52, 60, 238–41

"Newspapers and the Truth" (Allen), 198–212

newsroom: reference groups of, 177, 184–91, 197; status system of, 177–80, 182–83, 188

Newsweek (magazine), 149

New York American, 30, 66–67

New York Call, 71

New York Daily Mirror, 97–98, 121, 191

New York Daily News, 30–31, 40, 97–98

New Yorker (magazine), xi, 44, 141, 174, 216–18

New York Evening Post, 35–36, 38, 63–65, 68

New York Evening Sun, 98

New York Herald, 33, 37, 38, 202

New York Herald-Tribune, 97–98, 121, 216

New York Journal-American, 121

New York Mirror, 30

New York Post, 59, 132

New York Sun, 32, 38, 52, 59, 63, 75, 121

New York Times, 73, 97–98, 102, 116, 121, 201–2; and accuracy, 103, 142–50, 152–53; and Agnew, 124; Darnton at, 174, 176–97; institutional structure of, 177–84; and La Follette, 34, 36; and Lindbergh, 26–27; and Lippmann, ix, xii, 154–72; Nixon coverage of, 122–23, 148; and presidency, 134, 136–39; reputation of, 132, 210; and Russian Revolution coverage, ix, 103, 154–72; and Sinclair, 36–37, 39–41, 44, 66–67

New York Tribune, 34, 37

New York University School of Journalism, 37

New York Worker, 71

New York World, 32, 73, 121, 201–2

New York World-Telegram, 39–40, 121

Niebuhr, Reinhold, 44, 92

Nieman fellowships, 87, 276

Nixon administration: and press, 119, 143, 145–48; Vietnam policy of, 112–13, 121–22, 133–34, 232

Nixon, Richard M., xii, 99, 102, 133, 136, 138

Nonpartisan Leader, 28, 70

Nonpartisan League, 25, 26–29, 70–71

nonprofit institutions, 86, 88, 91

North American Review, 235

Northcliffe Press, 199, 206

Noyes, Newbold, Jr., 97

objectivity: difficulty of, 115–16, 139–40, 143, 173, 201–2, 214, 231; goal of, 119, 125, 129, 141–42, 155–56, 158, 171

Ochs newspapers, 53

O'Connor, Flannery, 213–14

Odhams Press, 93

Ogburn, William F., 246

Old Homestead (Thompson), 51

Only Yesterday (Allen), xi

On the Witness Stand (Munsterberg), 200

Orwell, George, 217, 223

Oswald, Marina, 223

Paris Review, 229

Patterson, Joseph Medill, 96

Pearson's (magazine), 71

peer group, 180–83, 187–88, 197

Pennsylvania Gazette, 197

People (London), 93

Peoples Speaking to Peoples, 84, 91

Periodical Publishers' Associaiton, 32

Perkins, George W., 32

Perry, Bliss, 68

Petit Journal, 167

Pew, Marlen, 29, 31

Phillips, McCandlish, 177

Pilgrim's Progress (Bunyan), x, 101, 105–6

piping, 181

point of view: in *The Executioner's Song*, 224, 226, 228; and journalism, 53, 55–56, 117, 156–57, 174, 186, 220

police relations, 186–87, 191–97, 264–65, 267–71, 277

political campaigns, 32–36, 99

politics: and news media, 120–23, 153, 248; and newspapers, 38–40, 55, 69, 98, 240, 243

Pool, Ithiel de Sola, 175

Pool-Shulman study, 175–76, 188

Populist Party, 63

Pravda, 73, 98

Prelude to Bolshevism (Kerensky), 167

"The Presidency and the Press" (Moynihan), 131–53

the press. *See* news media

"The Press and the Individual" (Seldes), 22–41

Prince Albert v. Strange (1849), 7–8, 11

privacy rights: Brandeis and Warren on, x, 1, 3–17; and Lindbergh, 22–23, 29–31; redress for, 5, 13, 15–17, 22

Probert, Richard, 251

professionalism: and journalism schools, x, 37, 89–92, 135, 188, 209, 233–44; and news media, 85, 142–43, 210–11, 273–77; standards of, 73, 151, 171–72, 208, 211, 249

Progressive Party, 2, 32, 35

Project Nassau, 128–30

Propaganda, 78, 126–27, 157, 158, 175, 198, 210

property rights, literary and artistic, 6–10, 11, 13–17

public opinion: and Harris polls, 114; media influence on, 38, 112, 114–16, 119–21; sources of, 60, 154, 158, 241–43

Public Opinion (Lippman), x–xi

Public Opinion Quarterly, 175

publishers: obligations of, 43, 59, 83, 94–95, 140, 210; power of, 30, 33–34, 181–82, 264

Pulitzer, Joseph, x, 233–44

Pulitzer prizes, 210

Quigley, Walter, 25

radio industry, 79–80; and 1967 riots,
    254, 258, 265–66; and FCC, 81–82;
    standards for, 87–91, 277
Raskin, A. H., 143, 152
readership: images of, 175–77, 184–85, 188,
    197; and journalism, 36, 132, 136–37,
    142, 172, 211–12, 214
Redfield, Robert, 92
reform: news media role in, 71, 109–11,
    242, 248; of press, 44, 172, 209–12. *See
    also* muckrakers
reporters: and assignments, 177–80, 183–
    85, 193, 203; and Lindbergh, 29–30;
    minorities among, 234, 272–75; and
    peer group, 180–83, 187–88, 197; role
    of, 56–59, 73–74, 142; specialization
    among, 184–85, 197, 203, 234, 249–50;
    standards for, 73, 181–82, 190, 233;
    training of, x, 151, 172, 176–91, 233–
    44, 276; union for, 74, 210
Report of the Commission on
    Freedom of the Press. *See* Hutchins
    Commission
Reston, James, 115, 142, 186
Reuters, 162
Richardson, Elliot L., 145
Ridder, Herman, 24–25, 39
The Right Stuff (Wolfe), 214, 216–22
"The Right to Privacy" (Warren and
    Brandeis), 1, 3–17
Rockefeller, John D., 61
Rockwell, George Lincoln, 115
Roe, Gilbert E., 36
Rogers, Will, 114
Roosevelt, Franklin, 135–36, 139, 251.
    See also New Deal
Roosevelt, Theodore, xii, 32, 37, 235; and
    the press, 36, 58, 101–3; "The Man
    with the Muckrake," x, 105–11
Rosenthal, A.M., 142, 183–84, 189–90
Ross, Harold, 217–18

Ross, Lillian, 217
Rosten, Leo, x, xi, 234, 245–52
Rovere, Richard, 133
Ruby, Jack, 223
Ruml, Beardsley, 44, 92
rumors, 255–56, 262–63, 265; and gossip,
    4–5, 9, 30, 54
Russell, Isaac, 37, 74
Russian Revolution coverage, ix, 103,
    154–72

Safire, William, 102
San Francisco Bulletin, 47
San Francisco Call, 48, 60
San Francisco News, 39
Schiller, Lawrence, 222–25, 227–28
Schlesinger, Arthur M., 44, 92
Scott, Col. "Tom," 240
Scripps-Howard papers, 40, 50, 53, 94
Seibold, Louis, 201
Seldes, George, ix, xi, 2, 22–41
The Selling of the Pentagon
    (documentary), 126–30
sensationalism, 23, 29, 43, 91, 107–8, 129,
    204–5, 254–56
Sevareid, Eric, 124
The Shame of the Cities (Steffens), 134
Shawn, William, 217
Shulman, Irwin, 175
Shuster, George N., 92
Sinclair, Upton, ix, 24, 173, 206, 209; *The
    Brass Check*, xi, 2, 43–44, 62–78; and
    newspapers, 36–41
Sinclair vs. the New York Times, 36
Slander, 4–6, 14–17, 106, 116
Slayton, Deke, 218, 220
Smith, Tamera, 224–25
"The Social Composition of Washington
    Correspondents" (Rosten), 245–52
socialism, 26, 40, 68–70, 78
social responsibility theory, 44
Solzhenitsyn, Alexander, 223
Spock, Benjamin, 133

squeal sheets, 192–94
staging events, 128–29, 255, 266
Stalin, Joseph, 122
standards: and guidelines, 266, 269–71,
    277; of journalism, 44, 90–91, 256,
    277–78; of professionalism, 73,
    151, 171–72, 208, 211, 249; for radio
    industry, 87–91, 277; for reporters, 73,
    181–82, 190, 233; for television, 139–40.
    See also ethics
Stanton, Frank, 126, 128
Star (London), 93
Starr, Roger, 134
Steegmuller, Francis, 230
Steffens, Lincoln, 101, 134
stereotyping, 118, 193–94, 196–97
Stevenson, Robert Louis, 45
Stillman, James, 32
"The Stolen Story" (Williams), 49
St. Paul Pioneer Press and Dispatch,
    27–29
Students for a Democratic Society (SDS),
    140–41
Style Book of the New York Times, 177, 181

tabloid press, 29, 38, 196, 266
Talese, Gay, 173, 190
television, xi, 187; Agnew's criticism of,
    112–30; and coverage of 1967 riots,
    254–67; and Kerner Commission,
    253–78; minorities in, 274–75; as
    monopoly, 116–17, 120–21; and Nixon/
    Kennedy debates, 99; standards for,
    139–40
"A Test of the News" (Lippmann and
    Merz), 154–72
textbook presidency, 135–37
Thomson, Roy, 93
Time, Inc., 44
Time-Life, 124
Time (magazine), 30, 124, 142, 149, 174
Times (London), 132, 162, 166, 239
Times Talk, 189

Times v. Sullivan (1964), xii
"Tiny Mummies" (Wolfe), 217
Today, 39
Tolstoy, Leo, 213–14
Torn, Rip, 229
Townley, A. C., 27–28
Trilling, Lionel, 102, 135
Trotsky, Leon, 160, 162
Truman, Harry S., 131
Tuck v. Priester (1887), 11
Tugwell, Rexford, 252
Twelfth Amendment (1804), 123

United Nations, 84
United Press International, 38, 267
University of Missouri School of
    Journalism, 233
urban affairs, 267–78

Vailland, Roger, 133
Victoria, Queen, 8
Vietnam War: and Nixon administration,
    112–13, 121–22, 133–34, 232; press
    coverage of, 140–41, 189, 232

Wald, George, 135
Warren, Samuel, x, 1, 3–17
The Washington Correspondents (Rosten),
    234
Washington Evening Star, 132, 136, 143
Washington, George, 239
Washington Post, 34, 124, 143, 169;
    as national press, 149, 267; and
    presidency, 121, 136–39; reputation of,
    132, 152
Washington Post Company, 121
Washington press, 150, 185, 208, 234,
    245–52
Washington Star, 97
Washington Times-Herald, 121
Watterson, Henry, 59, 60, 208
Watts riots (1967), 255, 262, 265
The Wayward Pressman (Liebling), 44

White, Byron, 117
White, Theodore H., 117
White, William Allen, 2, 22–23; *and Emporia* editorials, x, 18–21
Whitney, John Hay, 98
Wicker, Tom, 185, 189
Wilkins, Roy, 118
Williams, Harold, 162, 164, 166, 168, 171
Wilson, James Q, 137
Wilson, Woodrow, 24, 37
wire services, 187, 261–62. *See also* Associated Press; United Press International
Wolfe, Frank E., 68

Wolfe, Tom: and new journalism, 214–22, 231–32; and *New Yorker* article, 216–18; *and The Right Stuff,* 214, 216–22
Woodward, Bob, 224, 231
"Writing News and Telling Stories" (Darnton), 175–97
Wyatt v. Wilson (1820), 9

Yaeger, Chuck, 220
Yale Review, 174, 213
yellow journalism, 38, 50–51, 57, 59, 66, 72, 197, 206
Your Country at War (Lindbergh), 25–26